"If you have the gift, this book will show you how to use it."
—Victoria Wisdom, Literary Agent, Becsey, Wisdom & Kalajian

"Contains chapter and verse on all aspects of screenwriting, and addresses every key and fundamental principle from how far to indent dialogue to how to speak to the agent's assistant."
—Script

"Offers all the essential information in one neat, script-sized volume.... New screenwriters will find The Screenwriter's Bible *invaluable; experienced screenwriters will find it an excellent addition to their reference shelf."*
—Hollywood Scriptwriter

"Delivers more in 314 pages than can be found in several screenwriting books. A true gem that measures up to its title."
—Writer's Connection

"The best screenwriting book available, and the book to buy if you're buying just one."
—Dov S-S Simens, Founder, Hollywood Film Institute

"...Easy to read and surprisingly broad in its coverage."
—New York Screenwriter

"The formatter alone is worth the price of the book."
—Melissa Jones, Hollywood Story Analyst

"Good, common sense. Sets up practical guidelines without encroaching on the writer's creativity. Easy to follow—feels like a workbook that will be used and not just read. The author is encouraging, but reminds the writer of the realities of the business."
—Candace Monteiro, Co-owner, Monteiro Rose Agency

"Just what the script doctor ordered . . . a 'must have' reference tool for new and experienced screenwriters. Straightforward, to the point, and accurate."
—Wisconsin Screenwriter's Forum

The Bible provides clear answers to crucial questions:

- How do I find an agent in today's difficult marketplace?

- How do I sell my script if I don't have an agent?

- How do I break into Hollywood when I live in Peoria?

- How do I summon my Muse and increase my creative energy?

- What is the Character/Action Grid and what makes it so fast and effective in evaluating and revising my work?

- What common formatting mistakes turn off agents and readers?

- What are the tricks to effective scene construction and transition?

- How do I write a query letter that will get my script read?

- How do I build a winning, compelling pitch? What are the unwritten rules?

- Where is Hollywood's *back door* and how do I get through it?

- How do I break into television and the cable markets?

- What are the ten keys to creating captivating characters?

- What basic plot paradigms do virtually all stories conform to?

- What writing opportunities are often overlooked by screenwriters?

- What is *high concept* and how can I use it to sell my screenplay?

- Where can I find a clear writing process that will motivate me to finish my script?

- How can I add dimension, depth, and emotion to virtually any story?

- What are the ten tools every writer needs (and few have) before approaching the market?

- Where can I find a list of contests, software, help lines, and other resources?

- What is the single most important key to writing great dialogue?

- Where can a new writer find an inexpensive critique of his or her script?

- How does Hollywood really work?

- How do you write a spec script?

It's all in *The Bible*

Here's what the third edition contains that the previous edition did not:

- Nearly 120 pages of new information.

- 12 pages of worksheets with detailed instructions to guide you in creating a strategic marketing plan for your script.

- Dozens of new examples and written illustrations of key writing principles.

- A total of 44 new pages devoted solely to marketing your script.

- A sample spec treatment, a sample coverage, a sample release, and another sample query letter.

- Nearly 40 pages of scenes written in the new spec writing style and a complete analysis of each. You must write a spec script to break in; now, at last, you have guidance with clear examples.

- Character/Action Grid worksheets for convenience in developing your story.

- Recent changes in format and marketing strategy that can make a difference.

- More information on formatting TV scripts.

- More than 100 new resource listings and more than 50 contests, including all the majors.

- Expanded index.

Completely up-to-date and completely reliable
EVERYTHING YOU NEED UNDER ONE COVER

THE SCREENWRITER'S bible

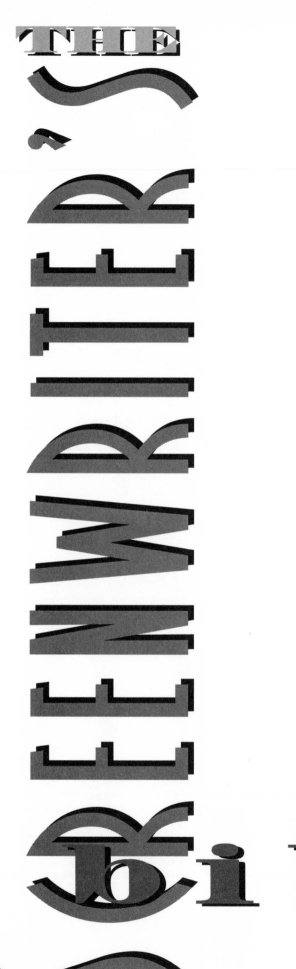

THE SCREENWRITER'S BIBLE

A COMPLETE GUIDE TO WRITING, FORMATTING, AND SELLING YOUR SCRIPT

3RD EDITION
EXPANDED
& UPDATED

BY DAVID TROTTIER

SILMAN-JAMES PRESS
Los Angeles

Martin Carbonella, Excerpt from *Knife in My Heart,* © 1998 Martin Carbonella.

Debi Tuccio, Excerpt from *Oh What a Night,* © 1998 Debi Tuccio. Reprinted courtesy of *Script Magazine*, 5638 Sweet Air Road, Baldwin, MD 21013.

Leslie Paonessa, coverage of *The Secret of Question Mark Cave,* © 1996 Leslie Paonessa, All Rights Reserved. Reprinted courtesy of Leslie Paonessa, 2231 Montana Avenue #3, Santa Monica, CA 90403.

Daniel Stuenzi, Excerpt from *The Helpers,* © 1998 Daniel Stuenzi

Jose Barranca, *A Cuban Cigar* query letter, © 1997 Jose Barranca

Kerry Cox, *Bed of Lies* query letter, © 1993 *The Hollywood Scriptwriter*, All Rights Reserved. Reprinted courtesy *The Hollywood Scriptwriter.*

Joni Sensel, Excerpts from "More Queries From Hell" and *The Wizard of Oz* query letter, © 1993 Northwest Screenwriter, All Rights Reserved. Reprinted courtesy Joni Sensel and Northwest Screenwriter.

Karen Mitura, *Heart of Silence* query letter, © 1993 Forum Publishing. Reprinted courtesy Karen Mitura and the *Screenwriter's Forum.*

Jeff Warshaw, *The Silk Maze* query letter, © Jeff Warshaw. Reprinted courtesy the author.

First Silman-James Press Edition
10 9 8 7 6 5 4 3 2 1

Library of Congress Cataloging-in-Publication Data

Trottier, David.
The screenwriter's bible : a complete guide to writing, formatting, and selling your script / by David Trottier. -- 3rd ed., expanded and updated
p. cm.
Includes bibliographical references and index.
1. Motion picture authorship. 2. Television authorship.
I. Title.
PN1996.T6 1998   808.2'3--dc21   98-8671

ISBN: 1-879505-44-4

Cover design by Heidi Frieder

Printed in the United States of America.

Silman-James Press
1181 Angelo Drive
Beverly Hills, CA 90210

*Dedicated to the developing screenwriter
and to students and clients
who have inspired me with their dedication and creative vision.*

*A special thanks to three writers
who years ago encouraged me to write:
Greg Alt, Don Moriarty, and Stephen J. Stirling*

Contents

How to use the third edition of *The Bible*

I have spent more than a decade working with aspiring writers in southern California and around the world. Throughout this period, I have realized that there are core principles and techniques that help writers get off to a fast start. In this volume, I help you begin the journey and guide you along the way. Not that you won't need help and encouragement from others—you will—but every aspect of screenwriting is covered in this work. That's why I call it *The Screenwriter's Bible*.

There are six guidebooks or sections in *The Bible*. Each book is self-contained and can be read independently of the others. In addition, each can be used as a handy reference. You will find yourself turning to *The Bible* again and again. Most writers, regardless of experience, will benefit from a thorough reading of all six books. Here's a helpful insight into each book or section.

- *Book I: How to Write a Screenplay* is based on my award-winning cassette series and national seminar. My hope is that you'll find it a concise and clear presentation of screenwriting essentials. Use it as a textbook, or as a refresher when you're stuck. Books I and II can be used concurrently as you write your script. In fact, Book I will occasionally refer you to Book II (actually a *work*book) at appropriate junctures.

- *Book II: 7 Steps to a Stunning Script* is a workbook that takes you step by step through the writing process. The first step deals with creativity, "summoning your Muse," and overcoming blocks. The other six steps include the pre-writing, writing, and revision phases.

- *Book III: Correct Format for Screenplays & TV Scripts* not only provides the crucial formatting standards by which your script will be judged, but teaches something of screenwriting itself. Even if you have a complete knowledge of formatting, reading this book will improve your writing style. In addition to a complete formatting index at the end (pages 156-158), this useful book is cross-referenced throughout.

- *Book IV: Writing Your Breakthrough Spec Script* is an annotated guide to spec writing. Since samples of spec scripts are so rare, this section will prove valuable to you because you must write a spec script to break into the business. Try your hand at revising the poorly written sample scenes and then compare your version with mine. Also review the first ten pages of an actual spec script with my line-by-line analysis.

- *Book V: How to Sell Your Script* presents a detailed marketing plan with useful worksheets that takes the mystery out of selling to Hollywood and to the many other screenwriting markets. The plan is comprehensive as well as specific. With it, you'll be able to target your market with effective sales strategies.

- Finally, *Book VI: Resources and Index* lists more than 200 screenwriting resources that you can use from the moment your idea is born to the consummation of a deal. The expanded general index at the end will help you find the topics you want in an instant.

The Screenwriter's Bible is sold with the understanding that neither the publisher nor the author are engaged in rendering legal advice. If legal assistance is required, the services of an entertainment attorney or other professional should be sought.

I invite you to share with me your reactions to *The Bible* and hope it becomes a help and a guide to your personal writing success. I wish you the best.

David Trottier
Summer, 1998

Note: For book updates, visit www.clearstream.com and search for "Bible Updates."

HOW TO WRITE A SCREENPLAY

BOOK I

A Primer

How stories work

THE NEXT GREAT SCREENWRITER

You may have heard that breaking into the movie business is tough. It is.

However, if you write a script that features a character who has a clear and specific goal, where there is strong opposition to that goal leading to a crisis and an emotionally satisfying ending, your script will automatically find itself in the upper five percent. Few would-be writers have mastered even the basics of screenwriting. And most screenplays fail on the above criteria alone.

Now if your script also presents a well-crafted story with a strong story concept and an original character people can sympathize with, there are agents and producers awaiting the advent of the next great screenwriter.

You can be that next great screenwriter. You'll have to work, learn your craft, and develop discipline. You'll need to apply the fine art of pleasant persistence. And there are going to be disappointments. But you can do it! Now stop for just a moment, buck up, and say that to yourself.

Everyone begins the same. Everyone writes one or more feature-length scripts of about 110 pages. Even if you want to write for television, your best entrance is with a feature script that you can use as a sample. Book I is designed to help you write that one spec script that's going to get you noticed.

What is a spec script? It's the script you're writing now on the speculation that someone will buy it later. (Book II gives you specific direction in the actual writing of the script. Books III and IV will help you with formatting and style. Book V helps you sell it. And Book VI provides support.)

THE STRENGTH OF THE SCREENPLAY FORM

As the next great screenwriter, you're obviously going to write a screenplay. A screenplay differs from a stageplay or novel.

A novel may describe a character's thoughts and feelings page after page. It's a great medium for internal conflict. A stageplay is almost exclusively verbal. Soap operas and sitcoms fit into this category. A movie is primarily visual. Yes, it will contain dialogue. It may even deal with internal things. But it is primarily a visual medium that requires visual writing. I have never read a "first screenplay" that did not have too much dialogue and too little action. You may have that same common tendency to tell rather than show.

For example, picture a **stageplay** where a babysitter cuts paper dolls with her scissors. The children are upstairs playing. From the other side of the room, a robber enters. He approaches her with a knife. Just in time, she turns and stabs him with the scissors. Not particularly exciting. In an actual stageplay, these people would probably talk to each other for ten minutes before the physical confrontation, because the conflict in a stageplay comes out in dialogue. That's the strength of the stageplay form.

A **novel** may focus on the thoughts and feelings of each character. That's the strength of the novel form—inner conflict. The babysitter is contemplating suicide. And this is the robber's first job. He's not sure he can go through with it.

However, a **screenplay** will focus on the visual aspects of the scene. The scissors penetrate one of the paper dolls. The doorknob slowly turns. The babysitter doesn't notice. Outside, the dog barks, but the kids upstairs are so noisy that she doesn't hear the dog. A figure slides in through the shadows. His knife fills the screen. He moves toward her. The dog barks louder. The intruder inches closer. But she is completely absorbed in cutting paper dolls. He looms over her. His knife goes up. The dog barks louder still. She suddenly becomes aware, turns, and impales the man with the scissors. He falls. His legs twitch and finally become still. She drops the scissors and screams.

The focus here is on the action—the drama—because movies are primarily visual. Yes, there are notable exceptions, but you are wise to use the strength of the medium for which you have chosen to write. Inner conflict is great, dialogue is important to bring out interpersonal conflict, but make your screenplay visually powerful. *Showing* through action usually works better than *telling* with dialogue. Even in character-driven "dialogue" scripts, add visual touches.

THE IMPORTANCE OF BEING STRUCTURED

Your screenplay must be well structured because the director and other collaborators are going to take your work of art and make it their own—you want the story to survive. This is one reason William Goldman emphasized in his book *Adventures in the Screen Trade* that "screenplays are structure."

Art is a union of form and content, whether it's a painting, a vase of flowers, a rock ballad, or your story. Accordingly, the *content* of your story requires a dramatic structure or *form* to give it shape. Structure is the skeleton on which you hang the meat of your story. And without that skeletal framework, your story content falls flat like a blob of jelly, incapable of forward movement.

Most beginning writers just begin writing without any thought of story structure—where it's going or how it will end. Soon, writer's block sets in. One of your first writing steps will be to construct a skeleton, a structural model. Let's discuss that basic model.

Aristotle was right

Aristotle wrote in his *Poetics* that all drama (and that includes comedy, since comedy is drama in disguise) has a beginning, a middle, and an end. You've heard this before. Traditionally, the beginning is about 25% of the story, the middle is approximately 50%, and the end is about 25%. This is the basic three-act structure. If you like to think in terms of four acts, then Act 1 is the beginning, Acts 2 and 3 are the middle, and Act 4 is the end. A seven-act structure still has a beginning, middle, and end. Shakespeare's five-act plays have a beginning, middle, and end, as does the five-act FOUR WEDDINGS AND A FUNERAL.

Because a screenplay is about 110 pages, the beginning is usually the first 15-25 pages. The middle is the next 50 pages or so, and the end is the last 10-25 pages. Obviously, the exact length can vary, but the middle is the biggest section.

All great screenplays have a beginning, a middle, and an end. In the beginning, you set up your story, get the reader's attention, and establish the situation. During the middle, you complicate matters and develop the conflict that rises to a crisis. In the end, you conclude the story and resolve the conflict. This is the payoff for the reader, for the audience, and for you. Put your hero in the proverbial tree, throw rocks at her, and get her out. Boy meets girl, boy loses girl and tries to get her back again, boy gets girl. Beginning, middle, and end. What about DOA? It opens with the ending. Granted, it opens with the end of the central character's life, but not with the end of the story. What is this story really about? It is not about his death, it's about who killed him. The dramatic premise is this: Can he find his killer before he dies? The story ends when he finds his killer. This is just a creative way of using the basic model.

In BACK TO THE FUTURE, the beginning takes place in 1985, the middle in 1955, and the end in 1985 again. A very simple overall framework.

Twists and Turns

How do you get from the beginning to the middle and from the middle to the end? Turning points. They are also called transition points, action points, plot points, and character crossroads. Turning points are the twists and turns of the story. They are the important events that complicate or even reverse the action, such as cliffhangers, revelations, and crises. Structure is the organization of these events into a story.

There may be dozens of turning points in your story, but the two that facilitate the transition from act to act are key to your story's success. The first big turning point ends Act 1 (the beginning) and moves the reader (and the audience) to Act 2 (the middle). It could be called the *Big Event* because it is usually a "big event" that dramatically affects the central character's life.

The second major turning point moves the reader into Act 3 (the end) and the final showdown. This is the *Crisis*. Of all the crises in your story, this is the one that forces the central character to take the last final action, or series of actions, to resolve the story. Let's look at some examples.

In CHINATOWN, detective Jake Gittes deals with extramarital affairs. A woman claiming she is Mrs. Mulwray hires him to spy on her husband. So he takes some photographs of her husband with a girl. These are published in the *L.A. Times*, and his job is done. He celebrates at a barber shop, where he hears a dirty joke. Cheerfully, he returns to his office and tells his buddies the joke. He doesn't see the beautiful woman standing behind him. The tension increases as Jake tells his joke because we know he's going to be embarrassed when he finally notices the woman. Jake tells the joke, gives the punchline, and turns. Surprise. The woman informs him that her name is Mrs. Mulwray and that she never hired him to spy on her husband, and now she's suing him. He's been embarrassed a second time. The first embarrassment foreshadowed the second. There's a beginning, middle, and end in this scene.

Is this not a big event in Jake's life? Jake has big problems now. If this is the *real* Mrs. Mulwray, who was the *first* Mrs. Mulwray? Who set him up and why? And how is he going to save his reputation?

Steven Spielberg said that, in the best stories, someone loses control of his/her life and must regain it. The Big Event causes that loss of control. In GHOST, the Big Event is the murder of Patrick Swayze. In JUNIOR, Arnold Swartzenegger gets pregnant.

Now let's look at an example of the Crisis, or second major turning point, the one that moves us from the middle to the end. In E.T. it is the moment when E.T. is dying, and the men converge on the house. Everything looks bleak. It is the moment when it looks least likely that E.T. will ever get home. This is the Crisis. What follows is the last, final struggle to get home. You have a similar low point in THELMA & LOUISE. How will they ever escape the law now?

In SLEEPLESS IN SEATTLE, you feel pretty low when Meg Ryan announces that Tom Hanks is history and that she's finally decided to marry Walter. You feel even lower when you see the physical distance between the building she's dining in and the Empire State Building Tom Hanks is headed for.

In the PURPLE ROSE OF CAIRO, Cecilia has a crummy life, a crummy husband, a crummy job, and lives during the Great Depression. For relief, she goes to the local theater where this week THE PURPLE ROSE OF CAIRO is playing. She's seen it four times already, and at the fifth showing, one of the fictitious characters in the movie notices her in the audience and walks right off the screen and into Cecilia's life. The Big Event—right?

The Big Event is the clincher in setting up your audience. They're now prepared for the long haul through the second and third acts. They want to know what happens next.

Let's take a closer look at THE PURPLE ROSE OF CAIRO. In the beginning, we are introduced to reality (Cecilia's husband and life) and then to fantasy (the fictitious character and movies in general). So what will happen in the middle? Can you guess? We'll have a rising conflict; in this case, fantasy vs. reality. This conflict will build to the Crisis. What's the Crisis going to be? It's when Cecilia has to choose between her husband (reality) and the fictitious character (fantasy).

The Crisis in this film is not just a low point but an event that forces the central character to make a crucial decision. Once she decides, then she can move into the final act, the Showdown (or climax) and resolution of the story.

In ALIENS, the Crisis is precipitated when the little girl is kidnapped by the alien creatures, and the planet is about to explode. Sigourney Weaver must make a crucial, life-or-death decision. Will she abandon the planet and save herself? Or will she return for the little girl? She demonstrates her choice by igniting her flame thrower.

In TITANIC, the central character is Rose. The Big Event is when she "attempts" to jump off the ship and is saved by Jack. The Crisis is precipitated by the separation of the lovers. Jack is arrested for stealing the Heart of the Sea. Is he stealing Rose's heart as well?

CASABLANCA: The Big Event, which seems subtle enough, is when Ilsa enters Rick's place and says, "Play it, Sam." Sam tells her she's bad luck to Rick but plays "As Time Goes By" anyway. Then Rick enters and tells Sam, "I thought I told you never to play that song." Then Rick sees Ilsa. Obviously, there's a lot of history between these two people.

The Crisis in CASABLANCA occurs as follows: Ilsa must get the Letters of Transit from Rick. It's the only way she and her husband, Victor Laslow, can escape from the Nazis. One night, Rick returns to his room, and Ilsa is waiting for him. She pleads with him, but he will not give her the Letters of Transit. Finally, she pulls a gun on him. He says, "Go ahead and shoot, you'll be doing me a favor." Will Ilsa shoot him? That's her personal crisis in this story.

She can't and Rick realizes that she must still love him. They have their moment together and then Ilsa says that she can never leave Rick again. "I don't know what's right any longer. You have to decide for both of us, for all of us." Ilsa turns the responsibility over to Rick because he is the central character, and as such he should be the most active person in Act 3. Rick accepts by saying, "All right, I will." Here, Rick agrees to make the crucial decision about whom will benefit from the Letters of Transit. The rest of the story—the end, the final act—is the unfolding of Rick's decision.

Several years ago, I discovered the perfect drama: Dickens' *A Christmas Carol*. We meet Scrooge, Tiny Tim, Bob Cratchit, and others. Each has a problem. Scrooge's problem, which he doesn't realize that he has, is that he lacks the Christmas Spirit. The Big Event is the appearance of Marley's Ghost.

During the middle of the story, three more spirits appear to Scrooge, but the Crisis comes when Scrooge sees his name on the tombstone. He asks the crisis question: Is this fate or can I change? The story ends with Scrooge getting the Christmas Spirit and helping the others solve their problems.

Note that we are allowed to catch our breath after each apparition. In other words, this story is well paced. Excitement and action are followed by reflection and reaction, and each turning point creates even more anticipation for the next, so that the story's high points get higher and higher until the end. In terms of dramatic tension and conflict, your story also needs peaks and valleys. Remember that the peaks should get generally higher as the story progresses.

Of mints and men

I'll take a moment here and offer a letter from a student who thanked me for bringing mints to class and demonstrated her clear understanding of basic story structure. She writes:

"It was ironic that I met another writer who shared my addiction to starlight mints. In my case, it began as an innocent habit. I would keep a jar of mints beside my computer so I could have a little pick-me-up at any time during the day. THE SET UP. Then a trip to the dentist revealed I had my first cavity in twelve years. BIG EVENT. Things went from bad to worse as I missed dentist appointments, spent the housekeeping money on starlight mints, and couldn't even kiss my husband because of all the mints crammed into my mouth. PLOT COMPLICATIONS. Until the CRISIS MOMENT, when my husband told me that I had to choose between starlight mints or our marriage. I made the agonizing decision to give up mints. I'm happy now and my marriage is stronger than ever. RESOLUTION."

Does the movie AIRPLANE use story structure? Yes. Any comedy that tells a story has a story structure. AIRPLANE is the story of a man who has lost his nerve to fly and who must regain it to save the people on the airplane. Here's a quote from the writers of AIRPLANE and NAKED GUN, Zucker, Abrahams, and Zucker. (This appeared in *The Hollywood Scriptwriter.*)

"The movies appear to be a kind of screen anarchy, but believe me, the process of getting it up there is much different. I mean, we're not maniacs, we don't bounce off the walls when we write. It gets to be a very scientifically designed process, actually. We spend a lot of time . . . marking off the three acts, concentrating not on the jokes but on the structure and sequence of the story. It's a very dull first couple of months, but that's how we spend them."

Situation, conflict, and resolution—the flow of the story

MAKE A GOOD FIRST IMPRESSION

The first thing your script should be concerned with is hooking the reader and setting forth the rules of that story. If the opening scene captures the reader's interest, it is called the hook. Otherwise, it's called the opening scene.

Obviously, the opening image—the first thing we see—makes your first impression. It implies something about your story—the location, the mood, or even the theme.

BODY HEAT opens with "Flames in the night sky."

APOCALYPSE NOW opens with a jungle aflame and the surreal sounds of helicopters. Superimposed over this is Martin Sheen watching a ceiling fan that reminds him of helicopter rotors. He is recalling his last mission. What this writer/director is doing is setting the standards by which we'll measure the rest of the story. He defines the context of his story. Just as a character should stay in character, so should your story stay in character.

What is the character of your story? It will include the atmosphere or mood, the location, the emotional setting, and the genre. Genre refers to the type of movie; for example, action/adventure, Western, thriller, romantic comedy, sci-fi, family drama, and so forth.

In GHOSTBUSTERS, we see a librarian scared by a ghost and we laugh our heads off. Supernatural comedy. Then we see Bill Murray hitting on a coed. There are probably a thousand ways to portray this, but the writers stay in the genre. Bill Murray pretends the coed has ESP and that she needs his tutelage and support to understand her gift.

In L.A. CONFIDENTIAL, we meet two Los Angeles police officers in the 1950s. The first few scenes define tone, time, and location. And we see a particular police officer dispensing justice before an arrest.

BLADERUNNER opens with a "guided tour" of a definite future place while setting the mood of the story. JERRY MAGUIRE opens with an introduction to the world of sports agenting. In my screenplay TABLOID, we open in the offices of a tabloid newspaper.

SCREAM begins with a long sequence of Drew Barrymore at home alone. Someone calls her, terrifies her, asks her questions about horror movies. The consequences are deadly if she answers the quiz questions incorrectly. She answers incorrectly. The interchange and resulting carnage establishes the genre as well as the hip style of the entire film.

In STAR WARS, the "rules of the game," the nature of the weaponry, the limits of the technology, and the two conflicting sides are all introduced early.

YOUR TWO KEY CHARACTERS

Early in your script, you'll want to introduce us to your *central character*, sometimes called the *pivotal character*. Often this person will appear in the opening scene. Obviously, the primary *opposition character* must be introduced as well. This person does not have to appear as early, but could. Dramatic choice.

The protagonist is the good guy or hero, while the antagonist is the bad guy. Usually the protagonist is also the central character, but sometimes the role of central character goes to the antagonist. In AMADEUS, Salieri, the bad guy, is the main cause of action and, therefore, the central character around whom the story is built. His opponent is Mozart, the good guy.

In THE HAND THAT ROCKS THE CRADLE, Peyton, the nanny, is the central character because she has the goal that drives the story. Claire, the wife, is the primary opposition character even though she is the protagonist. Marlene is a secondary opposition character.

One key to making a drama dramatic is to create a strong central character with a powerful goal, and then provide a strong opposition character who tries to stop the central character from achieving the goal. This assures us of conflict. And conflict is drama.

THE CATALYST

You've heard the horror stories of readers, agents, and executives reading the first few pages of a script and then tossing it on the dung heap. One way to avoid that is for something to happen in the first ten pages. It pains me to be so pointed, but I do so for your own good. Readers need to know what kind of story they're reading, who to root for, and an idea of the direction of the conflict.

I recall how delighted my agent was when he told me about a script he had just read, REGARDING HENRY. "He's shot on page seven! Imagine, shot on page seven!" He emphasized "page seven" for my benefit because I was late getting things moving in the script he was representing at that time.

Somewhere in the first ten or fifteen pages of your script, something should happen to give the central character a goal, desire, mission, need, or problem. I like to call this event the *Catalyst*, although it's often referred to as the *Inciting Incident*. Yes, it is a turning point. No, it's not usually the same as the Big Event, although it could be. This term and many other terms are used in a variety of ways by industry people. One person's Catalyst is another person's First Major Turning Point. The key is to understand the *principle*.

Here's the principle: When a story begins, life is in balance. Yes, your hero may have a problem, but it's a problem he's always had. Luke Skywalker, in STAR WARS, wants to become a pilot, but he's stuck on the farm. It's a problem he's always had. Life is in balance.

Then the Catalyst kicks things out of balance and gives the central character a new problem, need, goal, desire. The rest of the movie is spent getting things back into balance. For Luke Skywalker, the Catalyst is when he tinkers with R2-D2 and accidentally triggers a holographic image of Princess Leia saying, "Help me Obi-wan, you're my only hope." Now Luke has a desire to help Princess Leia and find Obi-wan Kenobi (Old Ben). Luke's life will not find a new equilibrium until the Death Star is destroyed. The Big Event is Luke's return home to find his aunt and uncle have been slaughtered. Now he joins with Obi-wan to fight the empire.

In WITNESS, an Amish boy witnesses a murder. It feels like the Big Event, but it can't be because it doesn't happen to the central character, Harrison Ford. It's the Catalyst. It creates a problem or desire for Harrison Ford. Now he wants to solve the murder. Now the movie's moving. In other words, the Catalyst begins the movement of the story. But the Big Event in WITNESS occurs later.

The little boy peers through the trophy case at the police office and spots a picture of the killer. Harrison Ford realizes that the murderer is on the police force. He goes to the chief and reports. The chief asks, "Have you told anyone else?" Harrison Ford says, "I haven't told anyone." Then when the chief goes home, he's shot. Harrison Ford knows they'll attempt to kill the boy next, so he rushes to the boy and his mother and together they escape to Act 2 and the world of the Amish.

Do you see that the Big Event is bigger than the Catalyst? In CHINATOWN, the first Mrs. Mulwray who hires Jake is the Catalyst. She gives Jake a mission. But the Big Event is when the real Mrs. Mulwray shows up.

In PRETTY WOMAN, Richard Gere and Julia Roberts meet. Catalyst. He pays her to stay with him at the hotel. Big Event.

In TOY STORY, the arrival of Buzz Lightyear creates a lot of buzz in the toy community and certainly qualifies as a major turning point. And now Woody has something of a problem to solve. But it's not until Buzz tumbles headlong out the window that Woody's life really changes.

JERRY MAGUIRE: He sees his client in the hospital, then writes a mission statement. Catalyst. He is fired. BIG EVENT.

INDEPENDENCE DAY: The aliens arrive. Catalyst. They blow up the White House. Big Event.

THELMA & LOUISE: They leave town to go fishing. Catalyst. Louise shoots Thelma's attacker. Big Event.

Here's a more subtle example. In SLING BLADE, Carl is released from the mental hospital and is then befriended by a boy. Meeting the boy does not really change his life, although it will change his life eventually. It's the dominant relationship in the story. The Crisis will come when Carl sees that the boy is in danger. What will Carl do about it?

You may ask: Can the Catalyst also be the Big Event? Sure. GHOST and REGARDING HENRY are two examples. Keep in mind that I am presenting guidelines in this book, not hard-and-fast rules.

A good catalyst, besides giving the central character a new problem or desire, will often reveal something of the main conflict, story premise, or situation. For example, will Harrison Ford (in WITNESS) catch the killer? Will E.T. get home? Will Roy Scheider get Jaws? Will Richard Gere and Julia Roberts find true love in PRETTY WOMAN? Can Diane Keaton have it all—a family and a career—in BABY BOOM?

FORESHADOWING

Because Act 1 is primarily devoted to setting up the story situation, foreshadowing becomes a vital tool. In the first act of ALIENS, we establish early on that Sigourney Weaver can operate a combination loader/forklift. This large contraption works on hydraulics and is literally an extension of her arms and legs. That's the setup. At the end of the movie, she uses it to fight the big mama alien. That's the payoff.

In most James Bond movies, Q gives James the gadgets he'll use later in the movie. They can be pretty ridiculous, but as long as they are established early, we believe them. However, if at the end of the movie James saved himself with a tiny midget missile that carried a 100-megaton nuclear warhead, we'd say, "Where did that come from?" And we'd feel ripped off—right?

Here's the point: You can get away with almost anything if you set it up, or foreshadow it, early in your story. Much of screenwriting is setting things up for a later payoff.

HIGH NOON is a wonderful example of foreshadowing. The audience is made aware of the terrible thing that might happen at high noon. This foreshadowing helps motivate conflicts between Gary Cooper and his wife, and with certain members of the town.

In an early scene of GHOST, Patrick Swayze watches an airline disaster on the news and comments at how quickly life can end. Later he confides in Demi Moore that he is afraid—every time something good happens in his life, something bad happens. There is a foreshadowing here of his imminent death. There is also a suspenseful moment where a statue of an angel is moved into the apartment. Can you guess what this foreshadows?

Here's a partial list of foreshadowed elements in TITANIC. Most are introduced early in the story.

> The sunken ship, rooms, fireplace, safe
> Rose's comb
> Nude drawing
> The automobile where they later make love
> How the *Titanic* would sink
> Heart of the Sea necklace
> How freezing the water is (Jack points this out in the "suicide" scene)
> Spitting lessons pay off later when Rose hocks one up on her fiancé
> The number of lifeboats
> The gun
> Jack: "You jump, I jump."

Jack: "You'll die warm in your bed." This foreshadowing comes late.
The whistle. This is also introduced appropriately late, and its payoff is powerful.

Foreshadowing creates a sense of unity in a story and also become an a tool of economy, providing more than one use for an element.

Look at all we learn in the first scenes of RAIDERS OF THE LOST ARK. The story is about lost artifacts, archeology, and high adventure involving World War II Nazis. We learn that both Belloq and Indiana are resourceful, that Indiana hates snakes, and that he must recover the lost Ark of the Covenant.

A word of caution on the first act taken as a whole: Don't provide too much information or exposition. Only give the audience what they need to understand the story without getting confused.

THE PINCH AND RISING CONFLICT

The beginning ends with the Big Event. The middle focuses primarily on the conflict and complications of the story. The central character emerges from Act 1 with a desire to do something about the difficult situation created by the Big Event. Her action will likely fail, forcing her to take new actions. There will be many setbacks in Act 2 and some breakthroughs or temporary triumphs.

Remember, the long middle section (Act 2) focuses on a *rising* conflict. Your reader will lose interest in a conflict that merely repeats. Strong subplots that crisscross with the main plot will help you avoid repetitive conflict.

At the *Pinch* of the story, about half-way through, another major event occurs. The central character often becomes fully committed. This is when Scarlet O'Hara makes her famous vow before intermission: "I'll never go hungry again." The Pinch can also be the moment when the motivation to achieve the goal becomes fully clear, or the stakes are raised. In GHOST, this is when Patrick Swayze, as a ghost, learns that his best friend is the one who had him killed.

In DAVE, the Pinch is when Dave defies the press secretary and acts as president. This is truly a Point of No Return for Dave, the point when he becomes fully committed.

In TITANIC, the pinch comes when Rose decides to jilt her fiancé and go with Jack. Once she makes this decision to leave her world, there is no turning back. Shortly after, the ship strikes an iceberg.

From the Pinch on, the central character takes even stronger actions, perhaps even desperate actions that threaten to compromise her values. One or more temporary triumphs arouse the opposition, who now shows his true strength. There may be a major setback, followed often by a new revelation or inspiration.

This is when Tom Cruise discovers that Dustin Hoffman, Raymond, is the Rain Man of his childhood, and that his dad protected Tom as a baby by putting the Rain Man (Raymond) in an institution.

The conflict intensifies, the pace quickens until the worst thing that could happen happens. This is the Crisis, the point when all seems lost, or where the character faces a crucial decision. The worst thing that could happen to Indiana Jones is to be locked in a tomb with thousands of snakes while his enemies get away with the world's most important artifact.

THE RESOLUTION

As you know, the Climax or Showdown follows on the heels of the Crisis. Often, someone or something spurs the character on to the Showdown. The goal—everything—is on the line, including the theme or movie message (discussed later) and/or some important value.

In the case of INDEPENDENCE DAY, the crisis is very dark, but a new revelation provides a glimmer of hope that moves our heroes to take one last gamble. Basic American values and global unity are at stake.

There's something you should know about the final act. It's not mandatory to have car chases and explosions in it. In MOONSTRUCK, everyone simply gathers around the breakfast table. It's the big scene at the end—the biggest scene in the movie, where everything comes together. It's the Showdown. The Showdown is bigger than the Big Event. It's the biggest event (or series of events) in the movie because everything, up until now, has led up to it.

Although Hollywood loves a happy ending, some of the most effective and affective stories are bittersweet or end in some sadness; e.g., MY BEST FRIEND'S WEDDING, TITANIC, GONE WITH THE WIND, SLING BLADE, and CASABLANCA.

Avoid the *deus ex machina* ending (literally, "the god from the machine"). In ancient Greece, at the end of a play or opera, the gods would enter in some sort of a contraption and solve all the mortals' problems. Easy solutions are not dramatic; better that your central character do his own rescuing in the end.

Likewise, don't end your screenplay saying, *It was all a dream.* And bring closure to the end; don't leave the ending open or ambiguous. I realize there are exceptions, and the ending of Hitchcock's THE BIRDS worked for me, but I advise you to wait until you're well into your salad days before attempting such an ending.

During this climactic scene or sequence (or just afterward), the central character realizes something new about herself, or we see some visible or spoken evidence of her growth. The central character has been through a crucible, has shown great courage—physical, emotional, and/or moral courage—and now the final result must be revealed to the audience and understood by the central character. We'll discuss this *Realization* later.

Finally, we have the *Denouement,* where all the loose ends are tied together and any remaining subplots are resolved. In BACK TO THE FUTURE, we see how Marty's family turn out, and the professor returns from the future with a stunning new outfit.

• • • • •

Now please don't internalize all of the above as a formula. This is not intended as a write-by-the-numbers text. In PULP FICTION, two stories are told. One is about how the Samuel Jackson character comes to believe that God has a mission for him. At the Showdown, he doesn't shoot the robber because he's going through a "transitional period." The other story is about how the Bruce Willis character refuses to throw a prize fight and comes to terms with his boss while escaping with his life. Each story has a beginning, a middle, and an end, but the events are not presented in exact chronological order. I wouldn't try something as tricky as this for my first script, but it illustrates an unorthodox use of dramatic principles.

Genres vary. Forms vary. There are many ways to tell a story. Your basic structure will likely change or evolve as you write, so be open to new, creative insights. Keep in mind that every story has its own structure, its own life, its own way of unfolding. It uses you, the writer, to express itself.

Note: For a summary review of the function of each of these key turning points, see pages 82-84.

The low down on high concept

A TITILLATING TITLE

Every screenplay and teleplay needs a titillating title. Of course, from the very beginning you'll want a working title to inspire you. The title you choose for your completed work should be short enough to fit on the marquee. Ideally, it conveys something about the concept or theme. Like the headline in an ad, the title must stop the reader and pull him into the story. For example, the title STAR WARS instantly conveys something of the story.

BODY HEAT and IN COLD BLOOD throw light on the subject matter and genre. DIE HARD and DIRTY DANCING are both "million-dollar titles."

SCREAM is almost as good as PSYCHO as a title for a horror movie, and TOY STORY identifies its market as well as the story concept.

SPACE COWBOYS, because of its connotation, is a good title for the recently developed screenplay about astronauts in retirement.

Although a little long, HONEY, I SHRUNK THE KIDS is a superb title. It effectively conveys a feeling for the story. CONTACT is a wonderful title for an intelligent, sci-fi flick.

An example of an ineffective title might be RAIDERS OF THE LOST ARK. I heard Sydney Ganis explain how much he worried about this title. (Mr. Ganis was the marketer of this project.) Is this the football Raiders? Is this Noah's ark? How is this title going to fit on the marquee? Not to worry. The movie had good word of mouth and a heck of an advertising budget, so it didn't matter.

However, an effective and titillating title can make an important first impression for your script, especially if it hints of a high concept.

IT'S GOTTA BE BIG

Jeffrey Katzenberg, in his now-famous internal memo to Disney executives (published in *Variety*, January 31, 1991), preached the following:

> In the dizzying world of moviemaking, we must not be distracted from one fundamental concept: the idea is king. If a movie begins with a great, original idea, chances are good it will be successful, even if it is executed only marginally well. However, if a film begins with a flawed idea, it will almost certainly fail, even if it is made with "A" talent and marketed to the hilt.

Here's Leonard Kornberg: "When a script comes in, it is the concept that gets it purchased."

Jason Hoffs at Spielberg's company said, "Probably eighty percent of the spec scripts this year were bought for concept and not execution."

According to Robert Kosberg, "Screenwriters usually focus on the craft of screenwriting . . . plot, developing characters, but these all fall aside if the initial concept is not clear. Find great ideas. Keep asking yourself, do you have a good idea here?"

These quotes should not surprise you when you consider that producers, distributors, and exhibitors need a simple, easy way to sell the movie to their audiences. The concept sits at the core of every pitch, regardless of who is pitching to whom. So let's discuss what makes a good concept. Here are a few snippets I've gleaned from Hollywood pros.

- Easily understood by an eighth-grader
- Can be encapsulated in a sentence or two
- Provocative and big
- Character plus conflict plus a hook (the hook is often the Big Event)
- Sounds like an "event" movie with sequel potential
- It has legs—it can stand on its own without stars
- It will attract a big star
- A fresh and highly marketable idea
- Unique with familiar elements

May I summarize all of that? *When I hear a good concept, I immediately see a movie that I can sell.* Does your concept say, "This is a movie!"? I realize there is an element of subjectivity here, but that should come as no surprise. And there is an *implied structure* in good concepts.

For example, here's the concept of HOMEBOY, a spec script that Fox Family Films paid $500,000 for a few months ago. *Two black brothers are out to adopt a younger brother to mold into an NBA player and get rich. They find only a white country bumpkin, then bring him to their neighborhood to make him a star.*

You can almost see the beginning, the middle, and the end. You see the conflict. You see the fun. It's a subjective evaluation to be sure, but that's a good movie concept.

Concept comes in many forms. For example, it can be presented as a *premise question*: *What if Peter Pan grew up?* (HOOK.) Or: *What if the devil had a son?* (ROSEMARY'S BABY.)

The concept can be expressed as a *logline*. The logline is the *TV Guide* one-sentence version of the story. *Terrorists hijack Air Force One.* (AIR FORCE ONE.) Here's the logline for CHAIN LETTER, a spec script sold to Touchstone for around a quarter of a million dollars.

A legal secretary, after being fired and getting dumped by her boyfriend, receives a chain letter, then sends it to the people who wronged her only to find them dead the next morning.

You know it's a movie. It grabs you—hook, logline, and sinker. Most importantly, you (as a producer) know just how to sell it to the public. And that's the key. You know you can sell it to your particular market. You see the theater ad in the paper. You see the video jacket at Blockbusters.

The concept is always a *hook*, which is any brief statement, premise, or logline that hooks someone into the story. *What's the worse thing that could happen to a babysitter? Lose the kids.* (ADVENTURES IN BABYSITTING.) Or: *TOP GUN in a firehouse.* (BACKDRAFT.) Or: *A man dies and becomes his wife's guardian angel.* (GHOST.)

Considering the large number of teenagers who go to movies, here's a strong concept: *A teenage computer hacker breaks into the Pentagon computer system. In the end, he prevents World War III.* (WAR GAMES.)

The concept is important for another reason. It's what you lead with when you pitch your script or write a query letter. We'll cover all of that in Book V. What's important now is this: The concept is what hooks—or fails to hook—the agent or producer.

Also keep in mind that stories are about characters with problems. *My story is about a legal secretary who is fired by her boss and dumped by her boyfriend. Then she receives a chain letter...* And so on.

Some of the best concepts present something extraordinary happening to someone who is ordinary, someone just like us. That something extraordinary is often the Big Event, the first major turning point in the story. Steven Spielberg said, "The best stories are about a protagonist who loses control of his or her life and who must regain it." He or she loses control because of that Big Event.

A sexist actor masquerades as a woman to get a role in a soap opera. As you can see, high concept does not necessarily mean high adventure. TOOTSIE is neither, but the concept is strong, and the character growth arc is implied. (We assume he'll no longer be sexist at the end of the movie.)

A radio talk-show host is out to redeem himself after his comments trigger a psychopath's murderous act. This is the intelligent, character-focused FISHER KING.

The fish-out-of-water concept is always popular; a character is thrown into a whole new situation or lifestyle, as in BEVERLY HILLS COP. SPLASH, for example, is literally about a "fish" (mermaid) out of water.

As mentioned, successful concepts often combine something familiar with something original. The following concept helped sell THE ROTTENS for $150,000 to Avnet-Kerner. Here's the concept:

When the most rotten family moves into a small town and wreaks havoc, the family's youngest son starts to break his parents' hearts when he realizes he wants to live a life of goodness and virtue.

Instead of the familiar black sheep of the family, we have the white sheep of the family. It's a twist on an old idea. In fact, some people might see it as a twist on THE ADDAMS FAMILY concept.

Speaking of a twist on an old idea, you may soon be seeing a high school version of *MY FAIR LADY*, tentatively entitled SHE'S ALL THAT, sold for low six figures.

TEXAS LULLABY is *Hamlet in a trailer park*, and sold for a six-figure amount.

Can you see why this next concept sold? *A teenager is mistakenly sent into the past, where he must make sure his mother and father meet and fall in love, then he has to get back to the future.* It presents a clear beginning, middle, and end. It's about a character with a problem.

Here are three more concepts from recently sold spec scripts (all of which sold for six figures), just to give you a flavor:

RODOLPHO—An illegal immigrant tries to get deported when his sister dies back home.

DAVE THE OX—A bustling sports agent goes to Texas to recruit the local high-school football star and winds up coaching the team.

DIAMOND HEAD—The case of a detective's career comes to a head on his wedding day.

Some (probably most) of these scripts will never be produced. In fact, only about one in fifteen or twenty of the scripts purchased and developed are ever produced. Even million-dollar scripts are sometimes not made; e.g., THE CHEESE STANDS ALONE and THE TICKING MAN.

A good concept has universal appeal. Most everyone can identify with it. Some concepts give us a peek into a special world. We all want an insider's look. Here's the concept of a script that sold for $1 million. It's called BLADES.

A news helicopter pilot is deputized by the police after the president's helicopter, Marine One, is taken over by terrorists. He has to save the president as the terrorists try to manipulate the news media to their advantage.

What are the special worlds we're getting an inside look into? News helicopter pilots, politics, and the news media.

Of course, not all production companies are looking for high-stakes action. You would not pitch *DIE HARD in a mall* to Samuel Goldwyn or Fine Line. But regardless of the company, they all are looking for an angle they can use to sell the kind of movie they want to produce.

One of the pluses of having a powerful concept is the execution of the concept into a screenplay does not have to be superior, it just has to be good. For a lesser concept, the writing has to be superior. In other words, the higher your concept, the more forgiving they will be with your script.

However, If you're writing a sweet, little, character-driven story with no car chases and bombs, wonderful! LOOK WHO'S TALKING is just a simple love story, but the premise is *What if babies could talk?* And that's hot. And many of the concepts listed above are for character-driven stories. When Steven Spielberg divined the idea for ET, he thought of it as his "little movie."

Stories that are offbeat or provocative stand an excellent chance of being purchased if they're easily visualized and encapsulated in a few words. Regardless of how non-mainstream your story is, ask yourself, What is at the core of my story? What makes my story stand out? What is the concept that will help the people understand what it's about?

ADAPTATIONS

Don't adapt it until you own it. This is one of my few carved-in-stone rules. Don't adapt a novel or play unless you control the rights to the property. We'll discuss the acquisition of rights to true stories, books, and plays in Book IV. There are basically three steps to writing an adaptation.

1. Read the novel or play for an understanding of the essential story, the relationships, the goal, the need, the primary conflict, and the subtext.

2. Identify the five to ten best scenes. These are the basis for your script.

3. Write an original script.

Adaptations are not as easy as that, of course; they're difficult assignments. A script cannot hope to cover all the internal conflict that the novel does, nor can it include all the subplots that a long novel can. Novels often emphasize theme and character. They are often reflective, but movies move. These are all reasons why novel lovers often hate movie versions.

Jurassic Park is a novel that was adapted to the screen. The book's central character is the billionaire, with the mathematician as the opposition character. The book is science-driven, an intellectual experience as much as an emotional experience. Spielberg saw the high concept: What if you could make dinosaurs from old DNA?

It's interesting to note the changes that transformed this book into a movie. First, the central character becomes the paleontologist. This provided a more youthful hero. Our paleontologist is given a flaw he didn't have in the book—he doesn't like children. He grows to like them by striving for his goal. There is no love interest in the book, but Laura Dern fills that role in the movie. Although the character development in the movie is thin, these changes make for a more visual and emotionally accessible film. The focus of the movie, of course, is on the dinosaurs, the T-Rex in particular. Hey, movies are visual.

My favorite scene in the book—the moment at the end when the paleontologist realizes that the velociraptors want to migrate—is simply not visual enough for the movie; plus it doesn't have a strong bearing on the main action plot. I think the right choices were made.

Story layering, plot, and genre

Now that we have a basic understanding of how a story works, let's expand on that and deepen the story.

GOALS AND NEEDS

In every story, the central character has a conscious goal. The goal is whatever your central character outwardly strives for. Of course, opposition makes it *almost* impossible to reach the goal. That opposition usually comes in the form of a person who either wants the same goal or who, in some other way, directly opposes your central character's goal.

Beneath it all looms a great unconscious *need*. The need has to do with self-image, or finding love, or living a better life—whatever the character *needs* to be truly happy or fulfilled. This yearning sometimes runs counter to the goal and sometimes supports or motivates it. The Crisis often brings the need into full consciousness.

Usually the need is blocked from within by a character flaw. This flaw serves as the inner opposition to the inner need. This character flaw is obvious to the audience, because we see the character hurting people, including himself. The flaw is almost always a form of selfishness, pride, or greed.

Where does the flaw come from? Usually the backstory. Something happened before the movie began that deeply hurt the character. Now he acts in inappropriate or hurtful ways. Let's see what we can learn about goals and needs from TWINS.

Danny DeVito is the Central Character. His conscious, measurable goal is $5 million. There is a strong outward opposition to this goal—a really bad guy wants the money as well.

DeVito also has a need that he himself is unaware of. He needs the love of a family. Blocking him is his own greed and selfishness—he's out for himself. This is the character flaw, and it is motivated by his backstory. His mother abandoned him, and he learned early that all people are out to get him, so he'd better get them first. DeVito can never have what he truly needs until he gives up his selfish point of view.

This is a neat little story because the goal and the need happen to oppose each other at the Crisis. DeVito must choose between the two. He can escape with the money (his goal), but someone holds a gun on his brother (his need). What will Danny DeVito decide?

At this crisis moment, he finds himself unable to leave his brother. Why? In a later scene, we learn that he really cared and didn't fully realize it until the Crisis. That's why he turned around and willingly gave up the money to save his brother's life. Danny DeVito reformed. He gave up something he wanted for his brother. Fortunately, in the end, he gets both a family and the money. The writer gives the audience what they want, but not in the way they expect it. Don't you love those Hollywood endings?

TWO STORIES IN ONE

Screenplays often tell two main stories. The *Outside/Action Story* is driven by the goal. It is sometimes referred to as the *spine*.

The *Inside/Emotional Story* usually derives from a relationship and is generally driven by the need. It is sometimes referred to as the *heart of the story* or the *emotional through-line*. To find the Inside/Emotional Story, look in the direction of the key relationship in the story. Sometimes there is no inside story, no flaw, no need, as in many thrillers, action/adventures, and horror movies. James Bond has no flaw or need, only a goal and an urge.

Each story—the Outside/Action Story and the Inside/Emotional Story—has its own turning points and structure. One is the main plot; the other, a subplot. Hopefully, the two stories are intertwined synergistically.

Again, TWINS serves as a good example. The Outside/Action story is driven by the $5 million goal, and the Inside/Emotional Story is driven by his need for a family. The action is what keeps us interested, but the emotion is what touches us. Although there are exceptions, the Inside/Emotional Story is what the movie is really about. The movie is really about a relationship.

In GONE WITH THE WIND, Scarlet has several goals. She wants to be seen by all the boys. She wants to get married. She wants never to eat radishes again. She wants to save Tara. And she wants Ashley, which is probably her main goal. Rather complex. It may even sound confusing until you realize the story is really about what she needs—Rhett Butler. Scarlet is outwardly striving for all the things just named, but she is not consciously after Rhett. Nevertheless, the movie belongs to Scarlet and Rhett.

In ROMANCING THE STONE, what is Kathleen Turner outwardly striving for? She wants to find the stone so she can save her sister. Is this a clear and visual goal? Yes. Is she consciously aware that this is what she's after? Yes. Is her goal opposed by anyone? Yes. Zolo wants it, as do the kidnappers. And Michael Douglas wants the stone so he can buy a boat and sail around the world.

What does Kathleen Turner need? Romance. Is she striving for romance? No. She writes out her fantasies in her romance novels. Her flaw is simple indifference—she won't try. In this story, she gets what she needs by striving for the goal.

In my script-consulting work, I receive many scripts that are completely missing a goal. To illustrate, let's pretend I was a consultant for Diane Thomas when she first started writing. She tells me she has a script about a woman who goes on vacation to South America and falls in love with an adventurer. Sounds interesting, but it's not compelling enough. So I ask Diane about the goal.

"Happiness is her goal," she responds.

"Happiness is not a goal. It's too vague."

"Well . . . romance is her goal. That's it."

"That feels more like a need than a goal. It's actually part of your Inside/Emotional Story. You need an action track for this inside story to roll on."

"Well, vacationing is her goal. She consciously wants to have a good vacation. She deserves it after all that writing."

Diane relaxes. It appears as though she has a complete story now, but I disappoint her. "Technically, vacationing is a goal," I say, "but it does not stir my heart nor does it set up strong opportunities for conflict. Something has to *happen*."

"I know!" Diane states triumphantly. "What if her sister is kidnapped and she has to save her?" Now Diane has a strong Big Event and a story.

This problem is so common that I strongly urge you to stop and examine your story. Are you missing an action track for your wonderful inside story to roll on?

Variations on the action and emotion tracks
In BACK TO THE FUTURE, the outside story plot, as you would expect, is action-oriented. It is driven by Marty's goal to get back to the future. So far so good. The inside story plot, however, is driven not by a need, but by a second goal: Marty wants to get his mom and dad back together again.

This results in twin crises at the end of the story, side by side. First, can Marty get his parents to kiss before he disappears into oblivion? This is the Inside/Emotional Story built around a relationship. Once resolved, Marty races from the dance to the Outside/Action Story: Can Marty, in the DeLorean, hit the wire at the same moment that lightning strikes the tower?

Is there an inner need in this movie? Yes, Marty needs a better family, and that's just what he gets in the end.

MOONSTRUCK: Cher's goal is to marry by the book. This goal is represented by Danny. She was married once before and it was unlucky because they didn't do it right, so "this time, Danny, you've got to have a ring and get on your knees and propose, and we're going to a priest." She's doing this marriage by the book.

Cher *needs* to marry for love. This need is represented by Ronnie. This is not fully in her consciousness until she goes to the opera with Ronnie. Blocking her need is her character flaw—she's going to marry someone she doesn't love. This character flaw is motivated by her backstory of having an unlucky marriage. At the breakfast-table scene in the end, she admits that the need is more important to her than the goal.

HOME ALONE's Kevin strives to protect the house and himself from the Wet Bandits. That's the main action plot. The emotional story? He needs his family's acceptance, his mother's in particular. Two flaws block him. One, he's a brat; two, he is incompetent—he can't even tie his shoelaces. These are subplots. The first flaw hooks the parents in the audience—he becomes a son who learns to appreciate his mother and family. The second flaw hooks the kids—he becomes competent fighting the adult bandits. This is a coming-of-age subplot.

The mother's goal is to get home. Her need and flaw are similar to her son's. In fact, they are mirrors of each other. Another subplot involves the man with the shovel who wants to become reconciled to his son. It's not hard to see that the underlying theme of this flick is family reconciliation.

MY BEST FRIEND'S WEDDING: Julianne wants to break up her best friend's wedding, but needs to accept it and let life go on.

KRAMER VS. KRAMER: The goal? Custody. The need? To be a loving father. In this screenplay, the goal and the need oppose each other, creating a crisis. Dustin Hoffman loses custody in a court battle and wants to appeal. His attorney tells him: "It'll cost $15,000." No problem. Hoffman wants to go ahead. "You'll have to put Billy on the stand." Well, to put Billy on the stand could deeply hurt him. Hoffman loves him too much. He chooses to give up custody rather than hurt the child. He overcomes his selfishness and abandons his goal for custody.

There's another way to look at this. Think of yourself as the next great screenwriter creating this story from scratch. You know the story is going to be about Hoffman becoming a father, learning to love his son. So you, the writer, give Hoffman goals, behaviors, and desires that are flawed. You give him a main goal of gaining custody because you know it will eventually contrast with what he really needs, to unselfishly love his son. So Hoffman's goal in this story is flawed—it's not the best way to love his son or satisfy his inner drive to be a father. In the end, he becomes a father by giving up custody, by giving up the goal. In other words, he changes his method and grows into full fatherhood.

In THE WIZARD OF OZ, the main goal is Kansas; the need is to realize there's no place like home.

JERRY MAGUIRE wants a big contract for his only client, Rod. In the process of working with Rod, he manages to accomplish his mission and even finds intimacy with his wife. Let's take a closer look at this story, since it has not one but two flaws and two growth arcs. (Naturally, the flaws are related.)

	Action story	**Emotional story**
Flaw	Self-doubt.	Can't love and be intimate.
Catalyst	Client suffers in hospital; client's son accuses Jerry of not caring.	Meets woman who believes in him.
Big Event	Fired.	Goes on a date.
Pinch	Jerry accuses Rod of playing without heart; Rod accuses him of marrying without heart.	Proposes marriage.
Crisis	After refusing contract, Rod is apparently injured.	Wife separates from Jerry because he doesn't love her.

Showdown	Rod plays well, not injured, gets interviewed, and gets big contract.	Jerry returns to his wife.
Realization	At the two interviews, Rod recognizes Jerry: Jerry has fulfilled his mission, no longer doubts himself, and wants to be with his wife.	

PRETTY WOMAN: Here we have two people who need love, but who are prostituting themselves. Their behavior does not harmonize with their need. In the end, they give up their old ways and thus fill their need. They grow.

My favorite romantic comedy is SOME LIKE IT HOT. Tony Curtis, posing as a millionaire, uses Marilyn Monroe. He *needs* to love her. Marilyn Monroe's goal is to marry a millionaire. She chases after Tony Curtis because she thinks he is one. Her unconscious need, however, is to marry for love. The Crisis comes when Tony Curtis is forced by Spats Columbo, a gangster, to leave Marilyn. At that point, Tony realizes he is actually in love with Marilyn. He realizes what a jerk he is and vows to get out of her life. He'll do what's best for her and leave without her. Marilyn, however, realizes that he's the one, even though he's not really a millionaire. She chases after him. Together for the right reasons, they sail off into the sunset.

In love stories, one or both characters is willing to give up something in the end for the other. That something is often a goal related to their flaw. In PRETTY WOMAN, Richard Gere not only gives up his questionable business practices, but he also overcomes his fear of heights. Love stories are essentially about two people transforming each other and learning to love each other. PRETTY WOMAN is pretty good at doing just that.

PLOT

Up until now, we've explained the outside/action plot and the inside/emotional plot. I'm using the word "plot" as a noun here. The verb *to plot* is a creative process that uses character and story structure. When all the plotting is over, you end up with a *plot* and several *subplots*.

Plot comprises the important events in a character's story. The words *plot*, *structure*, and *story* are often used interchangeably. Plot grows from character because everything starts with a character who has a goal. Since the goal is opposed, the character takes action. The resulting conflict culminates in a crisis. Will she win? Will he lose? Will he grow? Will she decline? The answer to those questions determines the kind of story—the kind of plot—you're writing.

There are basically two kinds of stories: plot-driven stories (which I prefer to call goal-driven stories) and character-driven stories. In goal-driven stories, the focus is primarily on the character's goal and the action—the spine of the story. In character-driven stories, the focus is primarily on character dynamics, a need, and a key relationship—the heart of the story. First, let's look at some examples of goal-driven stories.

• **The character wins.** In this plot model, the character strives for a goal and wins. Very simple and very common. Examples include: INDEPENDENCE DAY, ROCKY, THE TRUMAN SHOW, DIE HARD, THE FUGITIVE, MEN IN BLACK, SILENCE OF THE LAMBS, A FEW GOOD MEN, TOMORROW NEVER DIES, UNDER SIEGE, RUDY, TRUE LIES, SPEED, and THE KARATE KID.

• **The character loses.** With this plot, a moral victory of some kind often results despite the failure of a very sympathetic character. SPARTACUS fails to achieve his goal for the slaves and is crucified, but sees his wife and child escape to freedom. In TITANIC, Rose loses Jack but her heart will go on. THELMA & LOUISE never get to Mexico, but in the attempt they achieve a certain freedom.

Other examples are BRAVEHEART, ONE FLEW OVER THE CUCKOO'S NEST, FROM HERE TO ETERNITY, THE MISSION (here, they flat-out lose), and JFK (the Jim Garrison character).

• **The character sows the seeds of his own destruction.** What Goes Around, Comes Around. Examples include: FRANKENSTEIN, DANGEROUS LIAISONS, ALL THE KING'S MEN, MOBY DICK, and SCREAM (the perpetrators).

The following plot models seem more focused on character dynamics, and on the Inside/Emotional Story.

• **The character grows by doing the right thing.** Here, the character is about to do the wrong thing, but transforms into someone who overcomes his or her flaw, and does the right thing. Very popular everywhere. In CASABLANCA, Rick wants to get even with Ilsa; in the end, he does the right thing and helps her and her husband escape. Tom Cruise, in RAIN MAN, wants his inheritance; in the end, he tears up the check and does the right thing for his brother.

Other examples include: EMMA, ON THE WATERFRONT, MY BEST FRIEND'S WEDDING, JERRY MAGUIRE, THE SCENT OF A WOMAN, BIG, THE DOCTOR, AN OFFICER AND A GENTLEMAN, GROUNDHOG DAY, SCHINDLER'S LIST, and THE CRYING GAME.

Romantic comedies usually fit this plot model because one or more of the lovers give up something for the other. In PRETTY WOMAN, both characters give up their careers. In SOME LIKE IT HOT, the lovers stop using each other. MIDNIGHT RUN is a love story without the romance—both Robert DeNiro and Charles Grodin give up their goals for each other in the end.

• **The character grows up.** Here the character comes of age while striving for one or more goals that are either achieved or not achieved—it doesn't matter which. We don't really care whether the boys are first to find the body in STAND BY ME. What we care about is the relationship and growth of the boys. The goal is only there to give the relationship a track to roll on. In some character-driven stories, the goal may change. And that's fine as long as the conflict intensifies and rises to a crisis and showdown.

Here are more examples of characters growing up: GOOD WILL HUNTING, RISKY BUSINESS, HOOK (Peter Pan grows up), BREAKING AWAY, PLATOON, AMERICAN GRAFFITI, SUMMER OF '42, and FALLING DOWN (the Robert Duvall character).

• **The character learns.** Here, the character learns what he or she needs to be happy. Jimmy Stewart realizes he has a wonderful life in IT'S A WONDERFUL LIFE. David Niven learns what's important in life in THE BISHOP'S WIFE, that the people in the cathedral are more important than the cathedral itself. Harold, in HAROLD AND MAUDE, discovers that life is worth living.

In THE WIZARD OF OZ, Dorothy finds out there's no place like home. She also achieves her goal of returning to Kansas. (An argument could be made that the main plot is a Character-Wins Plot and that the realization of her need is merely a subplot that supports the goal.) Other examples: THE PRINCE OF TIDES—Nick Nolte learns he wants to live with his family. In CITY SLICKERS, Billy Crystal finally figures out the meaning of life.

• **The character fails to learn.** Here, the character fails to learn what he or she needs to learn to be happy. In this plot, the character does not grow, but the audience learns the lesson. Examples include WAR OF THE ROSES, GOODFELLAS, and RAGING BULL. In BUTCH CASSIDY AND THE SUNDANCE KID, Paul Newman and Robert Redford never figure out that they are in the wrong line of work and need to change with the times.

• **The character declines,** often by striving to achieve a worthy goal. Here are your examples: LAWRENCE OF ARABIA, UNFORGIVEN, CITIZEN KANE, and FALLING DOWN (the Michael Douglas character). In the beginning of THE GODFATHER, Michael (the central character) is something of a patriot who doesn't want a part of the family business. In the end, he *runs* the family business, but his rise is also his decline, which is demonstrated in the final scene where he lies, straight-faced, to his wife.

These broad plot models are presented to help you understand how stories work. They are not all-inclusive.

In virtually all stories, there is one main plot. Everything else happening in the character's life is a subplot. In addition to the central character's plot and subplot, each of the other characters in the screenplay has his or her own plot with a goal, action, crisis, and resolution. These are all subplots.

Furthermore, each character's crisis may come at a different juncture in the script, or may converge at the same crisis moment, depending on the story. The great secret to master-plotting is to bring the various subplots and main plot into conflict. In other words, most or all of the subplots should cross the central character's main purpose. One purpose of the step-outline on pages 89-90 is to accomplish this. You should find the Character/Action Grid on pages 94-99 to be helpful as well.

When two characters are at cross purposes, you have a *Unity of Opposites*. To ensure a conflict to the end, you need a unity of the central character's main plot and the opposing character's plot. The unity exists when the two plots are in direct opposition to each other, and compromise is impossible, ensuring a struggle to the end. For example, in FATAL ATTRACTION, a married man has an affair with a beautiful blonde and wants to terminate the relationship with her, but he can't because she carries his baby and is fixated on him. There exists a *Unity of Opposites*. He wants to end the relationship. She wants the relationship to grow. Compromise is impossible.

GENRE

Another element to consider in plotting is genre. This is because each genre carries with it certain characteristics.

Love stories

In a romantic comedy, the lovers meet (Catalyst), are forced to be together or choose to be together (Big Event), fall in love (Pinch), are separated (Crisis), after which one or both will change in some way, reform, and return to the beloved (Showdown). Most often, this results in a Character-Grows-by-Doing-the-Right-Thing Plot.

This category includes "date movies," a term popularized by Jeff Arch and Nora Ephron's SLEEPLESS IN SEATTLE. In fact, in the film itself, *guy movies* are distinguished from *chick flicks*. A date movie is a movie that appeals to both guys and chicks. In the case of SLEEPLESS IN SEATTLE, women presumably see this as a love story, while men see a widowed father getting a second chance.

Action/adventure

Make sure there is plenty of action and adventure. These stories usually open with an exciting action sequence, followed by some exposition. Although these can be suspenseful, the key to this genre is exciting action. These stories follow a Character-Wins Plot and usually end with a chase and/or plenty of violence.

William Martel, quoting Shane Black in *Scriptwriters Network Newsletter* (June, 1992), writes the following:

> The key to good action scenes is reversals . . . . It's like a good news/bad news joke. The bad news is you get thrown out of an airplane. The good news is you're wearing your parachute. The bad news is the rip cord breaks. The good news is you have a backup chute. The bad news is you can't reach the cord. Back and forth like that until the character reaches the ground.

Thrillers

Thrillers focus on suspense more than action. In a thriller, an ordinary man or woman gets involved in a situation that becomes life-threatening. The bad guys desperately want the *MacGuffin*, a name Hitchcock gave to the plot-device that often drives the thriller. In NORTH BY NORTHWEST, the MacGuffin is government secrets. In CHARADE, it's $250,000 in stamps.

Although the characters are after the MacGuffin, the audience cares more about the survival of the central character. This is because she cannot get help, has been betrayed in some way, and cannot trust anyone. The primary motivation is one of survival, so there's not much of a Character Realization in the end.

Many thrillers don't have a MacGuffin, but all thrillers isolate the central character, put her life at constant risk, and get us to identify with her fears.

Horror

Scary movies differ from the thriller in that the opposition is a monster, or a monster-like human. This genre leans heavily on shock and surprise. Examples include JAWS and SCREAM. ALIEN also relies on surprise, but the sequel, ALIENS, was wisely written as an action/adventure story, not another horror movie. Instead of scaring us, James Cameron thrills us with exciting action. Naturally there are horror elements in ALIENS, but the focus of the movie is on action.

Science fiction

Yes, ALIEN and ALIENS were science fiction movies, but the horror and action/adventure genres dominated in each respective case. Thus, we have hybrid genres: Horror/sci-fi and action/sci-fi. BACK TO THE FUTURE is a fantasy family drama, or a sci-fi comedy, or a combination of all four. The point is that most science-fiction takes on the characteristics of another genre and moves it to another world or time.

Traveling angel

This is a story about a character who solves the problems of the people around him. He doesn't grow much himself because he's "perfect," but other characters do; and once they have, the angel rides off into the sunset. MARY POPPINS, SHANE, and PALE RIDER are examples. Percy in THE SPITFIRE GRILL redeems virtually everyone. In the case of THE BISHOP'S WIFE, the traveling angel really is a traveling angel.

Detective/mystery

The murder mystery opens with a murder. Then, the police officer, private detective, or retired novelist solves the case. Since solving the case is primarily a mental exercise, there is often a voice-over narration so we can be privy to the central character's thoughts, as in MAGNUM, P.I. If this central character is a private detective, he will usually be portrayed as one who operates on the fringes of the law, such as Jake Gittes in CHINATOWN. Often, detectives uncover a small corruption that leads to a larger one. Many detective stories contain elements of "film noir."

Film noir

Film noir (literally, "night film") describes both a genre and a shooting style—shadowy, cynical, and realistic—and a storyline that features ordinary people in over their heads, no heroes and villains per se, but generally a struggle between good and evil within the central character, often ending unhappily. DOUBLE INDEMNITY, THE LADY FROM SHANGHAI, TOUCH OF EVIL, THE BIG SLEEP, DOA, THE POSTMAN RINGS TWICE, BODY HEAT, and L.A. CONFIDENTIAL are examples.

Fish-out-of-water

This is a popular genre because it creates so much potential for conflict and fun. A character is abruptly taken out of her element and forced to adjust to a new environment. Thus, Arnold Schwarzenegger, the cop, becomes a kindergarten teacher in KINDERGARTEN COP. And Eddie Murphy goes to 90210 in BEVERLY HILLS COP. In THREE MEN AND A BABY, three Peter Pans suddenly must care for a baby. PRIVATE BENJAMIN could be pitched as *Jewish American Princess joins the Army*.

I suppose you could say that Marty in BACK TO THE FUTURE is a fish-out-of-water when he drops into 1955 culture. So maybe that film is actually a sci-fi/fantasy/fish-out-of-water/family comedy.

Obviously, there are many genres and combinations of genres: Revisionist Western (DANCES WITH WOLVES), Screwball comedy (BRINGING UP BABY), Historical epic (7 YEARS IN TIBET, LAWRENCE OF ARABIA), Buddy picture (OUTRAGEOUS FORTUNE), Milieu (ALICE IN WONDERLAND, MIDNIGHT IN THE GARDEN OF GOOD AND EVIL), Action/romance (ROMANCING THE STONE), and on and on. Once you choose your genre, watch several representative films. You are not researching your story but understanding what makes the genre work.

MYTH

Beyond genre and plot is myth. In any story you write, it may help you to understand the mythological journey. The "hero's journey," as presented by Joseph Campbell, follows a particular pattern that may be weaved into the fabric of any story, regardless of its genre. Many stories contain elements of this mythological journey, while a few, like STAR WARS and THE WIZARD OF OZ, can be called myths because the central character passes through each stage of the hero's journey. Briefly, these are the stages in the hero's journey:

The hero lives amid ordinary surroundings. The Catalyst is actually a call to adventure, but the hero is reluctant to heed the call. This could be the moment when the hero receives her mission. She is given an amulet or aid of some kind by an older person, a mentor. For example, Dorothy is given the ruby red slippers by a good witch. Luke is given the light saber by Obi-Wan. Many stories feature mentors, e.g., Robin Williams in GOOD WILL HUNTING and Tommy Lee Jones in MEN IN BLACK.

The central character travels to the extraordinary world. This is followed by a series of tests and obstacles. The hero often undergoes a death experience and enters the secret hideout, the witch's castle, the deathstar, the belly of the whale, or the innermost cave.

Finally, the hero seizes the treasure and is chased back to the ordinary world, where this treasure blesses the people. The grail heals the land. The hero may be resurrected in some way. Luke and Han are honored at an awards ceremony. Dorothy returns to her family. The LAST STARFIGHTER is transfigured in front of the townspeople. Oskar Schindler is resurrected in a ring ceremony.

As a writer, you may have heard a call to action, a call to write, but hesitated. You must heed the call. As you struggle, as you learn, and as you write, you may very well walk the path of the hero, overcome obstacles, gain allies, and become the next great screenwriter. The hero's journey may very well become your personal odyssey.

Note: This is a good time to do Steps 1, 2, and 3 in the workbook (Book II).

Ten keys to creating captivating characters

Your central character requires ten things from a writer. Keep in mind as we review these that virtually all of them apply to supporting characters, and even minor characters, as well as to your main characters.

A GOAL AND AN OPPOSITION

Your character wants a goal. A dramatic goal is specific and measurable. Dealing with life is not a goal. Happiness is not a goal. Seeking $10 million worth of doubloons on an old Spanish shipwreck off the Florida Keys is a goal. Winning the Pan American Ballroom Dance Competition is a goal. Getting the broomstick of the wicked witch in order to return to Kansas is a goal. The nature of the goal reveals a lot about your character.

Whatever the goal is, it should not be easy to attain. There must be opposition to the goal. Opposition creates conflict, and conflict makes drama. Conflict reveals character and motivates people to learn. Ask yourself, *What does my character want and what does she most fear?* The opposition will force her to face her fear.

The opposition should be an individual. If it is an organization, let someone represent that organization. In GHOSTBUSTERS, the Environmental Protection Agency is represented by a man who makes it his personal business to bust the Ghostbusters.

To demonstrate the importance of an opposition, here's a story I'm paraphrasing from William Froug (*American Writers Review*, January 1997, p. 17). It concerns the classic SOME LIKE IT HOT and how Billy Wilder and I.A.L. Diamond solved their writing problem. They had a funny idea of two men joining an all-girl band. They weren't able to develop a story from it because they didn't have a motivation for the two men to join the band, and they didn't have an opposition.

One day, Diamond walked into the office they shared on the studio lot to find Wilder waiting for him. As soon as he entered the office, Wilder shouted out, "St. Valentine's Day Massacre!" and Diamond shouted back, "That's It!" They made the two men accidental witnesses to the famous gangland killing. Now, in order to escape from both the law (represented by one individual cop) and the mob (represented by one individual mobster), they become cross-dressers so they can join an all-girl band. Once on the road with the band, they become opposition characters to each other (they both want the same woman). Now that's a movie.

In situations where a group opposes the central character, such as a gang, focus on one person in that group who stands as the greatest personal threat to the central character. Personalizing the opposition will create greater drama and will elicit the audience's sympathy for the central character. The hero is often defined by his/her opposition. And that opposition need not be evil; you just need someone who has a good reason to block your hero's attempt to achieve his goal.

It is possible to have a nonhuman opposition, such as the forces of Nature, or even a monster (such as the Great White in JAWS). If you do have such an opposition, consider adding a human opponent as well. In JAWS, the mayor of Amity serves as a secondary opponent to Roy Scheider. In ALIENS, Burke is a strong secondary opponent. In fact, a well-written story often features three opponents.

In addition to the goal, you may wish to give your character some related inner drive or yearning that either supports the goal or is in opposition to the goal. This inner need may be inwardly blocked by some character flaw. This was discussed more fully in the preceding section.

MOTIVATION

Your character must be motivated. Ask yourself this question: *Why* does my character want what he wants? The answer to that question is the motivation. And the more personal, the better. In fact, the more personal it is, the more the audience will identify and sympathize with the character. It's the emotional touchstone between your audience and your character.

What is Rocky's goal in the first ROCKY movie? His goal is very specific. He wants to go the distance with the champ—fifteen rounds. Why? *To prove he's not a bum.* It's the personal motivation that gives the story its power. Personally, I hate boxing. I could care less who won the Thrilla in Manilla. And yet I've watched four of the Rocky movies. Why? Well, it's not for the boxing scenes. It's for the motivation behind those boxing scenes.

In the second ROCKY movie, his wife goes into a coma. Then she blinks her eyes open and says, "Win." Now Rocky has a motive for winning.

In ROCKY III, Mr. T has a tiff with Rocky's manager, Burgess Meredith. Meredith suffers a heart attack and dies. Does Rocky want to clean Mr. T's plow? Absolutely, and so does everyone in the theater.

In RAIN MAN, Tom Cruise's perception of his father's past harsh treatment of him motivates his goal of collecting the inheritance. In other words, he wants the inheritance to get even with his father.

JAWS is a horror movie complete with body parts and a monster. The only personal motivation needed here is survival, but the writer adds something very personal. When Brody fails to close the beach, a boy is eaten by JAWS. At the funeral, the mother slaps Brody's face in front of the entire town and says, "You killed my son." Now Brody wants not only to protect the town, but redeem himself.

In JERRY MAGUIRE, our character is fired and humiliated when he leaves the office. He is also motivated by his employee/wife, who is the only person who supports him.

Like Jerry Maguire, Rose, in TITANIC, is motivated by two things: She is imprisoned by a lifestyle where no one "sees her" as she is, and Jack is the only person who really does "see her." This is why she literally reveals herself to him.

The motivation often grows with the conflict. It becomes stronger as the story progresses. In AMADEUS, Salieri has many reasons for disliking Mozart. It seems that whenever they are together, Mozart finds a way to insult Salieri, even if it's innocently done. These accumulate over time.

The clincher, however, is when Mrs. Mozart visits Salieri. She brings her husband's work with her and confesses that they need money and wonders if Salieri will help them. Salieri scrutinizes the manuscripts, and sees that these are first and only drafts of music, and notices no corrections. From Salieri's point of view, Mozart must simply be taking dictation from God. Salieri takes it personally. He goes to his private room and throws his crucifix into the fire. "From now on we are enemies," he says. Why? Because God chose a degenerate like Mozart over him, Salieri, whose only wish has been to serve God through music. So here we have the goal—to fight God by killing Mozart—and the motivation—because God is unjust.

A BACKSTORY

Before page one of your screenplay, something significant happens to your central character. That event is called the *backstory*.

In ORDINARY PEOPLE, the backstory involves two brothers, teenagers, boating on a lake. A storm capsizes the boat and one drowns. The other blames himself and tries to kill himself. The script begins when he returns from the hospital.

IN SLEEPLESS IN SEATTLE, the backstory is the death of Tom Hanks' wife.

In the above examples, we are given quick glimpses of the backstory. Most often, the backstory is not seen by the audience, but it is there, haunting the central character and affecting his actions.

In THELMA & LOUISE, Louise was raped in Texas. It's what makes it possible for her to shoot Thelma's attacker. This backstory is not revealed to Thelma or the audience until much later in the story.

Hana in THE ENGLISH PATIENT is troubled by the notion that everyone she loves dies.

In UNFORGIVEN, Clint Eastwood was a killer before his wife reformed him.

In STARMAN, the backstory is the death of Karen Allen's husband.

Sometimes only the writer knows the backstory (as in AS GOOD AS IT GETS), but because he knows it, the characters seem fuller on the page.

The backstory can be subtle. For example, in FOUL PLAY, Goldie Hawn was once in love and it ended badly. It's as simple as that. At the beginning of the movie, we see a cautious Goldie Hawn, a person not quite ready for a new lover, particularly if it's Chevy Chase. It's easy to see how the backstory gives rise to the flaw that blocks the need. In the case of Goldie Hawn, she needs to feel safe with a man. She's not approachable because she's afraid.

In ORDINARY PEOPLE, Timothy Hutton's need is to forgive himself for his brother's accidental death. His flaw is that he tries to control his feelings too much and is self-accusing. This all emerges from his backstory.

In STARMAN, Karen Allen's need is to learn to live again now that her husband is dead.

In the CHINATOWN love scene, Mrs. Mulwray asks Jake why he avoids Chinatown. He explains, "I thought I was keeping someone from being hurt and actually I ended up making sure she was hurt." Jake is referring to his backstory, a traumatic event that transpired before the movie began. In the climactic showdown, Jake tries to keep Mrs. Mulwray from getting hurt and, in so doing, inadvertently facilitates her death. The backstory foreshadows the resolution.

SILENCE OF THE LAMBS: When Jodie Foster was a little girl, her dad, a police officer, was killed. She went to live on a ranch. One night they were slaughtering lambs and they were crying. She picked up a lamb and ran, but she wasn't strong enough. They caught up with her and slaughtered the lamb. Her need became to silence those cries. When a woman is captured by Buffalo Bill and placed in a pit, that woman becomes a crying lamb that Jodie Foster wants to save. But is she strong enough? She is. After she saves the woman, she gets a call from Dr. Lector. "Well, Clarice, have you silenced the lambs?" That's the *Realization*. We know she hasn't. They'll always be crying, but now she is strong enough to save them. (Some of my students dispute this, maintaining she *has* silenced the lambs of her past. What do you think?)

In THE SPITFIRE GRILL, Percy's dark past involves the death of her baby and a five-year prison sentence.

Fox Mulder, in the *X-Files* TV series, is haunted by a single, traumatic event. When he was young, his sister was (apparently) kidnaped by aliens. This event deeply affects his actions and personality. He's not just an FBI man, but a person with a life and a past.

Occasionally, the audience is actually shown the backstory. In FLATLINERS, we see each main character's backstory at the appropriate moment in the script. The films CONTACT, THE PHILADELPHIA STORY, BACKDRAFT, and VERTIGO open with a backstory.

In CASABLANCA, the backstory is revealed in a flashback. In NUTS, Richard Dreyfuss must unravel Barbra Streisand's backstory to win the case.

THE WILL TO ACT

How do you judge a person? By words? Or by actions? Don't actions weigh more heavily than words for you? As the saying goes, "What you do sounds so loud in my ears, I cannot hear what you say."

Action reveals character, and crisis reveals his true colors, because a person does what he does because of who he is. Problems and obstacles reveal what he's made of. Since actions speak louder than words, your character will generally reveal more through action than through dialogue. Yes, dialogue can tell us a lot, particularly about what is going on inside, but actions tell us more. Dialogue can be action. When Darth Vader tells Luke that he is his father and that he should join him, that's an action.

Running Bear is a Sioux hunting buffalo on the wide prairie. This is interesting action. The buffalo are the opposition. But how can we make this more dramatic? Suppose the white settler's son is in the buffalo's path. The white man is Running Bear's enemy. But now Running Bear must make a decision that will reveal his true character. He decides to save the boy. Now he has an action—to save the boy from the herd.

Okay, let's take this one step further. The boy's father looks through the window and sees his son, and the buffalo; then to his horror, he sees his enemy, Running Bear. He thinks Running Bear is trying to kill his son. He grabs his rifle and races outside. Now we really care about the outcome. This is drama—characters in willful conflict. Note that each has a different view of the facts. That leads us to our next point.

A POINT OF VIEW AND ATTITUDES

Everyone has a belief system, a perception of reality that is influenced by past experience, a point of view that has developed over time. Our current experience is filtered through our past experience. This means two people may react in totally different ways to the same stimulus. It depends on their perception. Their point of view is expressed in attitudes.

Some time ago, I was in a department store. I found a little three-year-old who was alone and crying. I tried to calm her down so I could find her mother. The problem was her mother found me, and guess what she thought I was? That's right, Chester the Molester. Her perception was understandable, given the times we live in; but it was not reality. We don't see reality the way it is, we see it through the filter of our past experience.

Your character also has a past. We're going to discuss how to create that past shortly, but for right now realize that your character has a point of view expressed through attitudes. What is your character's point of view about life? What is your character's concept of love? How does he or she view the opposite sex? What is your character's attitude toward growing old? sex? falling rain? grocery shopping? dental hygiene and regular professional care? Is happiness a warm puppy or a warm gun?

Sol Stein recommends that you "give each character a separate set of facts. Don't give them the same view of the story." Your character will act from his or her point of view or belief system, regardless of how that point of view squares with reality. Salieri believes that great music comes from God. Therefore, Mozart must be God's creature on Earth.

In STARMAN, an alien creature crash-lands in Wisconsin. He is a being of light who floats over to Karen Allen's house. Karen has withdrawn from life because her husband was killed. The alien finds a lock of her husband's hair and clones himself a body. Now he looks just like her husband. He then makes her drive him to Arizona, which is where his mothership will pick him up. The alien's motivation for this goal is to get home. (This is "E.T. meets IT HAPPENED ONE NIGHT.") His point of view of life happens to be *life is precious*.

Karen Allen's goal is to escape. Her motivation is to be safe from the alien and also to be safe from her past. And the alien looks just like her past. The writer has taken her inside problem and put it on the outside to make it visual. Karen's point of view of life or belief is that life is scary: Husbands die (the backstory) and aliens kidnap you (the action story).

At the Pinch, Karen observes the alien as he brings a dead deer to life. This action emerges from his belief that life is precious. Touched by this action, her goal of escape is displaced by a desire to help Starman. This new goal is motivated by his inspiring action. Her point of view of life changes as well. Life is not so scary.

This story uses the deer as a metaphor. Karen Allen is the dead deer that Starman brings back to life (the emotional story). Her perception of life changes. And that's the key. When a character's point of view changes, that's character growth.

ROOM TO GROW

Your central character also has a point of view of herself. This point of view of self is called self-concept. *I'm a winner, I'm a loser. I'm clumsy, I'm graceful.* All of us act from this point of view of ourselves, and so do your characters. Here's what happens in the well-written story:

Metaphorically speaking, your character is a fish. The Big Event pulls him out of the water. He tries to swim. It's worked in the past, but it doesn't work now. And so he is forced to take new actions, different actions, but things get more and more difficult right up to the Crisis. Mustering all the courage and faith he has, he takes the last final action; then he emerges from the climax with a new self-concept—he's a fish no longer.

This moment is the *Realization*—the character *realizes* a change has taken place. Usually the Realization follows the Showdown (or climax), but it can take place during the Showdown or just before. It's a key emotional moment for your audience.

In GHOST, Patrick Swayze's growth is demonstrated at the end when he's finally able to say "I love you" to Demi Moore, instead of "ditto." Swayze also grows in another way—from mortal to guardian angel to heavenly being. Beginning, middle, end.

In A CHRISTMAS CAROL, Scrooge needs the Christmas Spirit. His attitude toward Christmas is neatly summed up in two words of dialogue: "Bah, humbug." The story is about transforming his belief. In the end, the change of character is revealed through his charitable actions and words.

Dustin Hoffman states his realization in TOOTSIE as follows: "I was a better man as a woman with you than I was as a man. I just have to do it without the dress."

In THE WIZARD OF OZ, Dorothy is asked pointblank, "Well, Dorothy, what did you learn?" And then Dorothy tells us all the ways her perceptions and attitudes have changed. Most important, her attitude toward home has changed. She realizes now that "there's no place like home."

At the end of CASABLANCA, Louie observes, "Rick, you've become a patriot."

In CITY SLICKERS, after Billy Crystal battles the river, he declares, "I know the meaning of life. It's my family."

When Holly Hunter goes overboard with the piano (in THE PIANO), she realizes she wants to live.

JERRY MAGUIRE brings many elements together in the Realization. At Rod's interview after the game and on television later, Jerry realizes he has achieved his mission statement. This is never directly stated, but he has given Rod personal attention and treated him as a person and now Rod is thanking him. The audience also realizes Jerry has succeeded with his outside goal when the terms of Rod's new contract are announced in the interview. Finally, during all this, Troy Aikman, quarterback for the Dallas Cowboys, mentions to Jerry that he likes his memo, referring to the mission statement. Is Troy going to let Jerry represent him now? Looks like it to me.

In MR. HOLLAND'S OPUS, Mr. Holland is rewarded by all of his students who return and play his composition for him. He realizes that he has touched all of these students.

In GROUNDHOG DAY, Bill Murray goes through the five stages of grief—denial, anger, bargaining, depression (the Crisis), and acceptance—and then is presented to us at the town dance and bachelor auction. The town likes him, Rita likes him, and (at long last) he likes himself.

Oskar Schindler is presented with a ring at the end of SCHINDLER'S LIST. He realizes the good he's done (though he regrets not doing more) and that maybe he is a good man after all. He has grown from sinner to saint.

In the beginning of FALLING DOWN, we identify with Michael Douglas, but soon lose affection for him as he declines. Robert Duvall, however, grows. So our affections shift to him. At the end, these two characters square off, both realizing what they've become. Robert Duvall has become a good cop and a man. Michael Douglas has a different realization. He says, "You mean I'm the bad guy?"

How does growth come about? Only through adversity and opposition, and striving for a goal. Only through conflict, making decisions, and taking actions. "True character is revealed," the proverb goes, "when you come face-to-face with adversity."

In defining your character's growth arc, ask yourself how your character grows or learns. Often, your character will grow from some form of slavery to some form of freedom (TITANIC), but it can be from death to life (STARMAN). A character can learn to love (RAINMAN) or overcome pride (DRIVING MISS DAISY) or become more principled (AN AMERICAN PRESIDENT). As already stated, all growth can be defined as a changed perception of self, life, others, or something else.

As a footnote, let me reiterate that in some action/adventures, thrillers, and other stories, the central character may not grow. James Bond doesn't grow; he just accomplishes his mission. However, in most genres, character growth of some sort is desirable, and even essential. One reason I enjoyed DIE HARD was that the writer gave action hero Bruce Willis room to grow in his relationship with his wife.

BELIEVABILITY

One reason dramatic characters are interesting is that they are generally single-minded and focused. Humans have more things going on in their lives and tend to run off on tangents. Your job as the next great screenwriter is to make your dramatic and comedic characters seem as human as possible. In other words, your job is to make us care about them. Here are some ways to accomplish that.

Give them human emotions
As you know, people watch movies to feel emotion vicariously. Whether it's love, revenge, fear, anticipation, or what-have-you, you can only touch these moviegoers if they are able to relate to how your character feels. This doesn't mean that your character should blubber all over the place but that we need to see your character frustrated, hurt, scared, thrilled, in love, etc. Often, we empathize with a character more when she fights what she feels rather than when she expresses it.

RAIN MAN is a remarkable film because one of the main characters is incapable of emotionally connecting with another person. I admire the writers, who dealt with this problem by giving Dustin Hoffman a desire to drive a car. "I'm an excellent driver," he would say. If your eyes became misty, it was at the end, when Tom Cruise lets Hoffman drive the car on a circular driveway.

Give them human traits
First focus on the core of your character—her soul. Who is she? What is her strongest trait? It is important to identify this dominant trait. Then look for a flaw that might serve as a contrast, to create an inner conflict.

When SNOW WHITE AND THE SEVEN DWARFS was being developed, the dwarfs were seven old guys who looked alike and acted the same. Then Walt Disney decided to give each dwarf a human trait and to call him by that trait. What a difference a trait makes.

You don't have to reveal a character's traits all at once. Ideally, each scene reveals something new about your central character. Each contact with a new character sheds new light until the central character is fully illuminated. You will want to introduce your central character in normal circumstances before the Catalyst upsets that balance so that we have a feel for who this person is. Occasionally, this is done by other characters talking about the central character. For example, in CASABLANCA, everyone talks about Rick before we meet him.

It is also important to include characteristics, problems, and imperfections that are familiar to all humans. He's a grouch. She can't deal with people until she's had her morning coffee. Inconsequential human imperfections will make your dramatic or comedic character more believable and more human. An opposition character's imperfections might be more irritating than endearing.

Some writers determine their characters' astrological signs for them. You could give your character one of many psychological and personality tests. Is your character primarily visual, auditory, or kinesthetic? Since you want difficult people in your story, you might avail yourself of a copy of *Coping with Difficult People*. The book describes certain difficult personality types.

Give them human values
Now let's take a moment to consider the Corleone family. It's doubtful that you'd invite these guys over for dinner. And yet, in the GODFATHER movies, you actually rooted for them. Why? Well, for one thing, these guys are loyal. They have a code of honor, a sense of justice. They have families and family values just like you and me. We like people with positive values.

If *your* central character happens to be a *bad guy*, make sure he's morally superior to the others in the story. If your character breaks the law, make him less corrupt than the law. The Corleones had a code of honor—they didn't sell drugs. Sure, extortion, protection rackets, murder, prostitution, gambling, but hey—they didn't sell drugs.

Other ways to create a little sympathy for your character is to give her a talent for what she does, and/or an endearing personal style in how she does it. Give her a moment alone to reveal her goodness. In such a moment, Rocky moves a wino out of the street and talks to a puppy.

Confront your character with an injustice, or place him in a difficult situation or in jeopardy. Be careful not to make him too much of a victim. In GODFATHER II, the Corleones are immigrants in an unfair situation. We sympathize. They take action. We may not agree with their choices, but we admire their fortitude.

Give them human dimension

Your characters, and particularly your central character, should have dimension. Avoid cardboard characters and stereotypes. Occasionally a stereotype works, particularly in a comedy or action script, but your main characters will play better if they have depth. No one is totally evil or perfectly good. The bad guy loves his cat, while the good guy kicks his dog once in a while.

Writers have a tendency to make their favorite characters flat, lifeless, and passive. We're afraid to bloody their face or to give them flaws. Don't fall into that trap. By and large, the most loved characters in film have depth and dimension. Yours should, too. Even sitcom characters tend to have some dimension to them. They may not be terribly deep, but you'd be hard pressed to name a favorite TV character who is not flawed.

Heroes and villains

Depending on the nature of your story, your character lies somewhere between real life and a cartoon. Some heroes are swashbucklers with hardly a flaw. And some villains are bad all the way through. Often, that works for special-effects action movies like STAR WARS. (I say that without any intent to denigrate such movies. Each movie should do what it does best.)

Other films go deeper. In such stories, the hero is often an ordinary man or woman who become a hero on his or her way to something entirely different. An ordinary person becomes an extraordinary person or an extraordinary person comes to realize who he really is or finally finds his way.

Likewise, the opposition character does not need to be a classic villain. Who is the villain in AS GOOD AS IT GETS or GOOD WILL HUNTING or KRAMER VS.

KRAMER? Yes, there is plenty of opposition, but no villain among the main characters, just people.

Generally, the best villains or opposition characters believe they are doing the right thing. In other words, they wouldn't characterize themselves as a villain. Even the fiancé in TITANIC (who is rather one-dimensional) would be able to justify his actions, but he cannot respect Rose's point of view. The opposition character often has difficulty recognizing another person's view of reality or needs.

DETAILS

Details are the little things that mean a lot. Think of them as characterization tools or aspects of character. Idiosyncracies, habits, quirks, imperfections (as discussed) and other characterizations will add a lot to a character. They help make the character a distinct individual. What would Columbo be without his crumpled overcoat? What would Jack Nicholson be (in AS GOOD AS IT GETS) without his obsessive compulsions? Even when he's under pressure to get a coat so he can have dinner with Helen Hunt, he cannot bring himself to step on a line.

Personal expressions can make a difference. The Emperor in AMADEUS concludes his pronouncements with, "Well, there it is," and Raymond the Rainman says, "I'm an excellent driver." Holly Hunter just cries periodically in BROADCAST NEWS, and Roger Rabbit has an endearing way of stuttering when he says, "Please."

In WHEN HARRY MET SALLY, Sally orders her food in a certain way, and she drops letters into the mail box one at a time.

In CONTACT, Jodie Foster sits the same way both as an adult and a child. These are tiny characterizations that add to the believability and definition of a character. How does your character handle the little things?

If right for your character, give him a specialized knowledge or skill, such as Matthew Broderick's computer-hacking skill in WAR GAMES, and Luke's knowledge of The Force in STAR WARS.

In THREE DAYS OF THE CONDOR, Robert Redford is a full-time reader for the CIA. It's easy to believe in his intelligence and knowledge when he's forced to the streets.

Props have been used with good effect. Jack Nicholson's baggies in AS GOOD AS IT GETS. Captain Quigg's ball bearings. Kojak's lollypop. Captain Hook's hook. James

Bond's gadgets. The weapons in MEN IN BLACK. Whenever Indiana Jones gets into trouble, he has his whip. He uses the whip to get himself out of trouble. (The whip, of course, does not save him. He uses the whip to save himself. That's an important distinction.)

It follows that coincidences should generally work against your central character. Make it increasingly difficult for her to achieve her goal. Don't bail her out at the end (*deus ex machina*). She should be the most active character in the final act.

A WRITER WHO CARES

Every character hopes for a writer who cares. Your central character must have a life and a voice of his own. He can only get that from a writer who cares. You show that you care by researching.

The main purpose of research is to come to really know your characters. Once you know who they are, you can observe them emerging on the page as real. One of the most beautiful experiences you can have is when your characters take over your story and tell you what they want to do.

Research is observing people, taking notes in your little writer's notebook when things occur to you. Research is searching your mind, your own experience, people you've known who can serve as character prototypes, places you've seen, and so forth.

Research is investigating, exploring, and creating your character's background. For instance, your character has an educational background; ethnic, cultural, and religious roots; a professional (or work) history; past and present social connections; and a family of some kind. Your character also has a particular way of speaking.

What kind of character would Forrest Gump be if little thought were put to his background, psychology, traits, imperfections, idiosyncracies, and moral character?

Research is trips to the library for information, or to a place of business to understand your character's occupation. Research is interviewing someone of a particular ethnic group, or even visiting a neighborhood. Don't assume you can get by because you've seen other movies that have dealt with the same subject matter.

It's easy to get interviews. Recently, I interviewed a petroleum geologist. I told him I'd buy him lunch if he'd let me ask him some questions. He was thrilled for several reasons. One, he could tell the guys at work, "Hey, I can't go to lunch with you tomorrow. I got a writer interviewing me for an upcoming movie." Two, he was getting a free lunch. Three, he was proud of the job he does. The benefit to me was that I learned many things, unexpected things that I could use in my screenplay to lend authenticity and authority to it.

A struggling student on the East Coast tells me she didn't really understand her story until she interviewed a blackjack dealer in Las Vegas. Another from the heartland benefited immensely from a quick jaunt to the library to investigate fencing and other kinds of sword fighting. A client informed me that most private investigators are employed in family and marital disputes, and by insurance companies. They use clipping services. They sit on the passenger side of the automobile because there's more space. He also learned that it's legal to go through someone's garbage.

Research is writing a character biography or completing a detailed character profile. Of course, much of this information will never make it into your script, but since your character will be alive to you, he or she will appear more fully drawn on the page.

Although your character's physical description is very important to you, it will be of little importance to the script. All actors want to see themselves in the part, so only include physical details that are essential to the story. When you describe a character in your script, it will be with a few lines or words that really give us the essence of the character. Something the actors can act.

But you, the writer, the creator, need to see this person in detail, because a person's physiology affects his psychology. What kinds of emotions does your character have? What is her disposition? How does he handle relationships?

Identify complexes, phobias, pet peeves, fears, secrets, attitudes, beliefs, addictions, prejudices, inhibitions, frustrations, habits, superstitions, and moral stands. Is your character extroverted or introverted, aggressive or passive, intuitive or analytical? How does he solve problems? How does she deal with stress? In what way is he screwed up? And so on. Have fun with this!

Research is reflecting, and asking questions.
- What are my character's values?
- What does my character do when she is all alone?
- What's the most traumatic thing that ever happened to my character?
- What is his biggest secret?
- What is her most poignant moment?
- What are his hobbies?
- What special abilities does she have?
- What is his deepest fear?
- What kind of underwear does she wear?

- Which end of the toothpaste tube does he squeeze? (Well, you don't have to go that far, although it's not hard to guess which end Felix Unger squeezes.)
- What is the worst thing that could happen to my character? (Maybe this will be the crisis.)
- What is the best thing that could happen?
- What is my character doing tonight?

Research is creating unique aspects to your character that makes her stand apart from all other movie characters. Part of this may be giving your character a contradiction or traits that exist in opposition, such as the beautiful woman who's as clumsy as an ox, or brave Indiana Jones' fear of snakes. You may wish to identify one or more loveable imperfections as well.

As this research progresses, certain things will stand out. After all, in the actual script, you will only be able to emphasize certain aspects of your character, so you will want to select those that say the most about your character and relate the best to your story. The work you've done will reveal itself in the unique and multi-faceted character that you have created from the dust.

When do you do this research? Some writers like to do it early in the process; others prefer later in the writing so the characters can be created to fit the demands of the script. Most need to be thorough with this. A thumbnail sketch of the main characters is seldom sufficient.

A STRONG SUPPORTING CAST

A screenplay is a symphony and a symphony requires orchestration. Your character is just a lonely solo without other characters. Obviously, you'll want to do some thinking here as well. In the well-written story, relationships are emphasized. Some relationships work because of opposite personalities. The ODD COUPLE is an excellent example. Some because each can fill the other's need and they transform each other. Some relationships work because the characters are rivals. Some work because of similar interests or goals.

In your cast of characters, you want one central character, at least one opposition character, and a confidant (or sidekick) whom your central character can talk to. This is one way to reveal your central character's thoughts, feelings, and intentions. The confidant sometimes performs the additional function of lending contrast to your central character. In dramas, the confidant sometimes creates necessary comic relief, although this function (if needed) can be performed by another character.

You will probably want a love interest, who may function in another role as well.

Occasionally, you see a thematic character, someone who carries the theme or message of the story, such as the mathematician in JURASSIC PARK.

Sometimes a shapeshifter adds a twist to the story. For example, the central character's friend betrays her. In THE VERDICT, one of Paul Newman's aids works for the opposition.

You want characters with contrasts, and you can contrast characters on many levels, from attitudes to methods to social status. As you add characters, remember that each character in your story must perform a specific function in moving the story forward.

Note: This is a good time to do Step 4 in the workbook (Book II). You will also find Step 7 to be helpful.

Dialogue, subtext, and exposition

WHAT DIALOGUE IS

Dialogue is not real-life speech; it only sounds like it. It is more focused, less rambling than real-life speech. Yes, it contains fragments and short bits, but anything extraneous is pulled out, including the *ans* and *uhs*. You might say that dialogue is *edited* speech. It is organized and has direction, but it retains the style of real-life speech.

Dialogue should be lean and short. Avoid long speeches. Try to keep to one or two lines. Remember that in a movie, people have to understand what's being said the first time through. In a novel, a passage can be reread, but a movie keeps "reeling" along.

Take a look at your script and ask yourself: Is there a better, leaner way to say this? Am I writing more but the audience enjoying it less? I'm not saying you can't write long speeches; I'm only saying they must be justifiable.

Be patient in writing dialogue. Sometimes it takes a while for your dialogue to break through. With many professional writers, dialogue is often the last thing written, so don't panic if your dialogue isn't working at first. The key here is to know your characters well enough that they speak with a voice of their own. That voice consists of eight elements.

1. The text, or words
2. The subtext, or the meaning of the words
3. Grammar and syntax
4. Vocabulary
5. Accent and/or regional or foreign influences
6. Slang
7. Professional jargon
8. Speaking style, including rhythm and sentence length.

IT'S NOT WHAT YOU SAY, BUT HOW YOU SAY IT

Mama was right—the subtext (how you say it) has more impact that the text. Of the eight elements of dialogue, subtext is the one that gives writers the most fits.

What is subtext? Subtext is what's under the text. It's between the lines, the emotional content of the words, what's really meant. When an actor wants to know her motivation in a scene, she wants to understand the emotions going on within the character. She wants to know the subtext.

Usually, the dialogue's context in the story suggests the subtext. For example, in the "fireworks" scene of TO CATCH A THIEF, Grace Kelly seduces Cary Grant, a reformed jewel thief. That's the context. Does she talk about sex? Does she say, "Come on, Cary, let's go for a roll in the hay?" Of course not. This moment requires finesse. She talks about her jewelry, and wouldn't he do anything to steal such beautiful works of art? "Hold them," she says, "the one thing you can't resist." Clearly, she's not talking about jewelry here. The subtext is, "I'm the jewelry, you're the thief—take me." She says one thing by saying something else. The subtext is always obvious to the audience.

In a previous section, we discussed goals and needs—your character not only has an outside goal but some inner need. The goal is the *text* of the story and the need may be thought of as the *subtext* of the story, or emotional through-line. It follows, therefore, that the subtext of the dialogue in a scene will often derive from the character's underlying need or drive in the scene.

In the MOONLIGHTING TV show, a woman hires David and Maddy to find her runaway husband. David and Maddy then argue over the motives of the husband for running away. What are they really talking about? Their own relationship. It's more fun to listen to them when they are indirect.

Subtext has to do with the true intention of the character. The PRINCESS BRIDE is the story of a grandfather who wants to convert his young grandson to a kissing book. A kissing book is one where the boy and the girl actually kiss in the end—yuk! The grandson is sick in bed and is forced to listen to his grandfather read him this kissing book. The grandfather begins reading something like this:

"Once upon a time, there was a boy and a girl. And the girl used to torture the boy by asking him to do things for her, and every time the girl asked the boy to do something for her, he would say, 'As you wish.' But what he was really saying when he said *as you wish* was *I love you*."

I can't think of a better explanation of the relationship between the spoken word and the subtext than this grandfather's explanation.

At the end of this movie, the grandson is converted to this kissing book—he likes it—and as the grandfather leaves, the boy asks him if he could . . . well maybe . . . come by tomorrow and read it again. And the grandfather says, "As you wish." Wouldn't you agree that this indirect statement, loaded with subtext, is much more powerful than the more direct *I love you*? And it's a lot more fun as well.

Which works better? "I'm very fond of you, Ilsa." Or: "Here's looking at you, kid."

Here's a dramatic situation: A cop confronts a robber who holds his gun to an innocent woman's head. Which line works better? "If you shoot her, I'll be real glad, because I'm gonna enjoy killing you." Or: "Go ahead, make my day." In this case, less is more.

In DOUBLE INDEMNITY, Fred MacMurray, the insurance salesman, uses an automobile metaphor to express his sexual interest in Barbara Stanwick. She replies, "There's a speed limit in this state, Mr. Neff. Fifty-five miles per hour." He asks how fast he was going and she tells him, "About ninety." Then he says, "Suppose you get down off your motorcycle and give me a ticket." She says, "Suppose I let you off with a warning." The subtext is steaming off the words.

How do you show that someone's parents don't understand their teenage daughter? One client handled this with the following simple exchange.

```
                    GIRL FRIEND
          Did your parents like your poem?


                    SUZANNE
          They don't understand poetry.
          They think it's dumb.
```

When writing dialogue, keep in mind the character's attitudes, point of view, feelings, thoughts, and underlying need or drive. Try to say one thing by saying something else. This does not mean that every line of dialogue must have a subtext. However, most beginning scripts have too little subtext.

WRITING BETTER DIALOGUE

Here's a technique that will improve your dialogue. Read your dialogue out loud or have members of your writers' group read it to you. With the spoken word, it's easier to detect errors. You will hear what works and what doesn't. Is the dialogue too *on the nose*, too direct? without an implied meaning or subtext?

Also be aware of the rhythm. Some characters are terse and staccato; some are lyrical and elegant. Each character has a style of speech. (If a character speaks with a dialect or accent, just give us a flavor of it.) Avoid VOICE OVER narration. Avoid chitchat. *Hi, how are you? Fine, and how about you?* Also, avoid introductions. *Hi, this is Clark. Clark, this is Lois.* In the well-written story, when introductions are made, there's some clear and overriding dramatic purpose. It's not just cheap exposition.

Dialogue should also move the story forward, just as scenes do, and reveal something about the character's attitudes, perceptions, and values. Every dialogue scene should involve some conflict, even if it is just passive resistance. Back and forth, like a contest or competition.

In FIVE EASY PIECES, Jack Nicholson stops at a diner. He wants toast, he orders toast, but the waitress won't give him toast because it's not on the menu and she doesn't "make the rules." He tries several approaches. She fends him off every time, each time the tension building, the conflict escalating. Finally he orders a chicken salad sandwich, toasted. And tells her to hold the butter, lettuce, and mayonnaise, and to hold the chicken between her knees. She kicks him out, so he clears everything off the table and onto the floor. The exchange of verbal blows creates the rising tension of this classic scene. The theme underneath the dialogue has to do with "the rules."

EXCITING EXPOSITION

Another purpose of dialogue is to communicate the necessary facts of the story. These facts are called *exposition*. Your job is to make the exposition exciting.

Most of the exposition comes out in the beginning of the story. For example, the audience needs to understand how Indiana Jones' mission will benefit the world. Don't give the audience any more information than necessary to understand the story. Be careful not to reveal too much too soon as in THE TRUMAN SHOW. Let your characters keep their secrets as long as they can. Often, saving up exposition and using it in crucial moments will make it more exciting, and even transform it into a turning point.

Some exposition can be creatively planted in love scenes, action scenes, or comedy scenes, because at those moments you already have the audience's attention. In any case, the exposition should come forth naturally and not be tacked onto a scene. Seldom should you allow one character to tell the other something he already knows: *We've been married ten years now, honey.*

Be careful not to get *too* exciting. In the second INDIANA JONES movie, the main exposition is presented through dialogue at a bizarre dinner. The food is so disgusting that the audience's attention is diverted from the characters' dialogue.

In the first INDIANA JONES movie, the exposition is handled more effectively. The opening sequence is so exciting that we are riveted to the screen for the succeeding sequence, where most of the necessary information about the Lost Ark of the Covenant is communicated through dialogue.

Another way to make exposition exciting is to have characters argue over it. Some exposition can be handled without dialogue. This is even better. In the opening sequence of WAR GAMES, we are shown how the U.S. nuclear-missile firing system works. This information not only underscores the danger and prepares us for a thrilling ending, but also makes the story more believable.

Flashbacks
About ninety-five percent of the flashbacks in unsold scripts doesn't work. Usually, the flashback is used as a crutch, a cheap way to introduce exposition. This has given rise to the industry bias against them in spec scripts. Seldom does it move the story forward. And that's the key—use a flashback only if it moves the story forward. Don't give exposition in a flashback unless it also motivates the story, as in JULIA and CASABLANCA. Do not take us to the past until we care about what's happening in the future. Otherwise, a flashback becomes an interruption.

Avoid long flashbacks and dream sequences. They are high-risk. If you must have a flashback, use a transitional device: an object, place, song, visual image, color, phrase, or incident. Quick flashes are the safest, such as the momentary glimpses of the backstory we see in ORDINARY PEOPLE.

My advice on flashbacks is to find a more creative way to communicate exposition. To illustrate, put yourself in the place of the writer of STAR TREK II: THE WRATH OF KHAN. You have a problem: Khan, the opposition character, is Kirk's superior physically and mentally. How can you make it believable that Kirk can defeat Khan?

One solution is to *flash back* to the days when Kirk was a cadet. He takes a field test called the Kobiashi Maru, which presents a no-win scenario. Kirk, however, beats the no-win scenario by re-programming the test computer so that he can win.

You, however, reject this idea of a flashback for one that is more creative. You decide to open the story with a starfleet captain on a ship that is in trouble. Soon we learn that this captain is really a cadet and that she is taking a test called the Kobiashi Maru. She is bothered by her performance. Kirk tells her not to worry, that there is no correct solution—it's a test of character. So she asks Kirk how *he* handled it. He won't tell her.

You have made it a mystery that is touched on throughout the story—how *did* Kirk handle the Kobiashi Maru? The audience wonders. You, the next great screenwriter (and an adept one at that), have created suspense.

CUT TO: Late in the story. It appears as though Kirk and his friends are trapped in an underground cavern with no way out, and with no apparent way to contact Spock, who is somewhere in the universe. At that moment, the female cadet once again asks Kirk how he handled the Kobiashi Maru. Bones tells her that Kirk reprogrammed the computer. "You cheated," someone says.

Then Kirk surprises everyone by pulling out his communicator and contacting Spock: "You can beam us up now," he says. Ah-ha, so Kirk had it all pre-arranged, but to do it, he broke Federation rules. He has cheated Khan and has surprised everyone else. That's when Kirk explains: "I don't believe in the no-win scenario. I don't like to lose." Not only have you explained how Kirk could defeat a superior being, you have also given us the *key* to Kirk's character. And this plays much better than a flashback.

Theme

Did you know there is something inside you that is motivating you to write? There is something that you want to say. This thing inside you is not a little alien creature, it is the *movie message*, sometimes called the *premise*, sometimes called the *theme*.

Regardless of what it is called, think of it as the *moral* of your story. This moral is not a sermon and it is not preached. Often, you don't know what this moral or message is when you start scripting your story. Not to worry—you'll know before you're through. Just keep writing. CAUTION: There is a danger in focusing on the movie message. You run the risk of writing a preachy script.

The resolution of your story will verify the acceptability of your message. This message or theme could be expressed as a universal statement that could apply to anyone. It's something you've been wanting to say. For this reason, it can be thought of as the *point of view* of your story.

WITNESS has a point of view. *Love cannot bridge the gap of two different worlds.* In THE AFRICAN QUEEN, the opposite is true. *Love **can** bridge the gap of two different worlds.* As you can see, the movie message isn't necessarily true in real life, just true in your story. And it should never be communicated in a heavy-handed way.

The message of CHINATOWN is this: *You can get away with murder if you have enough money.*

WHEN HARRY MET SALLY suggests that *men and women cannot be "just friends."*

Times are a-changin', and you have to change with them if you want to survive. This thematic statement, or movie message, suggests characters who are fighting time (the conflict) and who will not succeed. Can you name the movie? BUTCH CASSIDY AND THE SUNDANCE KID.

In THE SPITFIRE GRILL, Percy is an apparent Christ figure who gives her life in the end. The theme is *Christ redeems and heals.* Notice how most of the characters have Bible names. And the name of the town is Gilead from the bible passage that asks, "Is there no balm in Gilead?" The Balm of Gilead is what heals and that is what Percy becomes, a healing balm.

John Truby suggests that theme is the writer's view of how people should act in the world. For example, in GHOST and ROMEO AND JULIET, *great love defies even death.* And in CASABLANCA, *self-sacrifice gives life meaning.*

Theme is what your movie is about. According to Patrick Sheane Duncan, ". . . a movie is generally about one thing, one theme or idea, and every scene and every character is formed from that fountainhead." (*Screenwriter Quarterly*, Fall 1996.)

In MR. HOLLAND'S OPUS, *life is what happens when you are making other plans.* Each scene and the conclusion in particular points to that idea. In NICK OF TIME, it is simply *how do I save my daughter?* That question is the controlling idea. And *life goes on* in MY BEST FRIEND'S WEDDING.

Now stories can also deal with *thematic material.* For example, WITNESS explores themes of violence and non-violence. BROADCAST NEWS discusses substance versus style. BABE presents issues of self-worth, class structure, and personal identity. UNFORGIVEN compares false reputation (Bob and the kid) with true reputation (Will and Bill). (For more examples of theme, check the general index.)

In a few stories, it may be effective to create a thematic or symbolic character: someone whose purpose is to carry a theme, a value, or even the story message. This character is seldom the central character. For example, the mathematician in JURASSIC PARK and Kathy Bates in PRIMARY COLORS.

How to make a scene

Screenplays are composed of acts, acts break down into sequences, sequences into scenes, and scenes into beats. A scene is a dramatic unit consisting of the camera placement (INTERIOR or EXTERIOR), a location, and time. When one of these three elements changes, the scene changes as well. In this discussion, I am using the term *scene* loosely. The points that follow could apply to any dramatic unit consisting of one or more scenes.

KEYS TO GREAT SCENES

- Each scene should move the story forward in terms of both plot and character. In other words, the scene you are now writing should be motivated by a previous scene, and it should motivate a scene coming up. One creates anticipation for another in a cause-and-effect relationship.

If the central character gets more involved in some way, that means your scene is probably moving the story forward. All scenes should direct us to the Showdown at the end, which is the biggest scene, or sequence of scenes, in the movie. Ask yourself: What is the payoff for this scene? Why do I need this scene? What is my purpose for this scene? Does the scene reveal something new about a character and/or the story? At the end of this scene, does the audience want to know what happens next?

- Never tell what you can show. Be as visual as possible. Rather than two ladies at tea commenting on the fact that Darla skydives for relaxation, *show* us Darla actually jumping from a plane, or show her coming home with a parachute and trying to stuff it into the closet.

Do you recall the barn-raising scene in WITNESS? When the workers pause for lunch, the eyes of the elders are on Kelly McGillis, who is expected to marry an Amish man, but who likes Harrison Ford. Without a word of dialogue, she makes her choice by pouring water for Harrison Ford first.

In MY BEST FRIEND'S WEDDING, Julianne (nicknamed Jules) and Michael (her best friend) have a moment together. The setting was visual: A boat on the Chicago River and not a couch in an apartment. They both want to tell each other how they feel about each other, but they fight it (which makes the audience empathize with their feelings more strongly than if both characters just blurted out what they were thinking).

Julianne wants to tell Michael she loves him. As they both approach the moment where they might say what they feel, they approach a bridge. The dialogue continues as follows:

```
                    MICHAEL
          Kimmy says, when you love someone,
          you say it.  You say it out loud.
          Right now.  Or the moment...

He pauses.
                    JULIANNE
          ...passes you by.
```

And now they are under the bridge, silent, and then past the bridge. And that visual cue tells us that the moment has passed for her to say she loves him. The visual cue brings the message home and makes for a stronger moment.

- Avoid talking heads. John and Mary argue over breakfast. One head talks, then the other. Make this more interesting by beginning the argument at breakfast, continuing it while in the car racing to the club, and concluding it during a racquetball match. Each statement a character makes is punctuated by the whack of the racket or the whop of the ball slamming against the wall. Now the action complements the dialogue, plus you give yourself the opportunity to characterize your characters by how they play racquetball, how they drive, what they drive, etc.

- Every dramatic unit has a beginning, a middle, and an end.

- Start the scene as close to the end of the scene as possible. In other words, once your scene is fleshed out, evaluate it and lop off anything at the beginning that is unnecessary. (In fact, cut the fat anywhere you can.)

Imagine a cowboy riding up to a log house in the middle of the prairie. No one for miles around. He quietly dismounts, grabs his rifle, and gingerly approaches the cabin. He peeks through the window. There she is. Young, beautiful, and alone. Inside the cabin, the woman turns. The door is kicked in. The cowboy steps inside and points his rifle right at the woman. He wants the money and he wants her. She reaches behind for a knife and throws it at the cowboy.

Does this scene remind you of the opening scene of ROMANCING THE STONE? It is, except the final version of the scene begins at the moment the door is kicked in. Everything preceding that moment was cut. The writer started the scene as close to the end of the scene as possible.

In terms of scene length, challenge any scene that runs over two pages. Many great scenes are long, and some scenes should be long. Nevertheless, if you challenge your long scenes, you may find ways to improve them and shorten them. This will strengthen the pace of the story.

- Pace your scenes. Provide peaks and valleys of emotion and tension, with the peaks ascending toward a climatic conclusion. Follow action scenes with dialogue scenes. Contrast heavy scenes with light scenes. Make sure the pace quickens as you close in on the Crisis and Showdown. In HOME ALONE, we have the reflective scene in the church just before the madcap slapstick sequence at the house.

Pacing does not need to focus on action and events, such as in LETHAL WEAPON; it can focus on details as in STEEL MAGNOLIAS.

- Scenes should culminate in something dramatic. This could be a decision or an imminent decision. It could be a reversal, a cliffhanger, or a revelation—some event that makes us want to see what's going to happen next. Keep in mind that twists and turns in the plot are essential. You cannot allow your story to progress the way your audience expects it to. Scenes should end with a punch, with some kind of tension that leads us to another scene, such as when Rose's mother orders her to never see Jack again. Throughout the scene, Rose's mother tightens Rose's corset. Note how that adds visually to the tension of the scene. The pressure is tightening around Rose.

In GOOD WILL HUNTING, Will confronts a college kid who is hitting on a coed (Minnie Driver). After the long scene, Will flashes the coed's phone number at the college kid, showing he has won. It punctuates the scene.

In dialogue scenes, generally the last line should be the strongest line. In the very last scene of SOME LIKE IT HOT, Jack Lemmon, who is still posing as woman, must convince Joe E. Brown that he can't marry him. The wonderful conflict is created by Brown's subtle resistance to Jack Lemmon's attempts to achieve his goal of getting out of the wedding. First, he tells Brown that he can't get married in his mother's dress because they aren't built the same way. "We can have it altered." Then Jack Lemmon confesses that he is not a natural blonde. "Doesn't matter." Then Lemmon admits that he smokes all the time. "I don't care." Then Jack tells him he's been living with a saxophone player. "I forgive you." With feigned remorse Jack announces that he can never have children. "We'll adopt some." Finally, Jack removes his wig, speaks in his male voice, and admits that he is a man. The response? "Well, nobody's perfect." And that's the *punch* line that ends the movie.

- Strive to create effective transitions between scenes. I'm not referring to tricky cuts and arty dissolves—leave editing directions to the editor. Find ways to fit the scenes together. For example, one scene ends with a roulette wheel spinning. The next scene begins with a car wheel digging into the mud.

Early in 2001: A SPACE ODYSSEY, a prehistoric man throws his tool into the air. It's a bone that becomes a spaceship, a tool of modern man.

Here's an effective transition from Bruce Joel Rubin's JACOB'S LADDER. In it, Rubin uses sound and images to move us from Vietnam to New York.

```
As he spins around, one of his attackers jams all eight
inches of his bayonet blade into Jacob's stomach.  Jacob
screams.  It is a loud and piercing wail.

From the sound of the scream, there is a sudden rush
through a long, dark tunnel.  There is a sense of enor-
mous speed accelerating toward a brilliant light.
```

```
The rush suggests a passage between life and death, but
as the light bursts upon us we realize that we are pass-
ing through a subway far below the city of New York.
```

This would be followed by INT. NEW YORK SUBWAY - DAY, and the scene would continue.

This kind of transition is the exception rather than the rule. It is important in this screenplay because of the theme. This is the story of how a man comes to accept his own death, very much like Rubin's prior screenplay, GHOST.

You are not required to link your scenes with transitions. You do this occasionally, when appropriate.

Transitions can be visual, verbal, thematic, and so on. Is it okay to sharply contract scenes? Absolutely. If it moves the story forward, use it. Keep in mind that a straight cut from one scene to the next is not only correct, but the norm. The object is not to get fancy but to give the story cohesion.

- Each scene should contain a definite emotion or mood. Focus on that emotion as you craft the scene. Ask yourself: What is my character's intention or goal in this scene? What is my character's feeling? What is my character's attitude? Asking this will help give the scene direction and the dialogue subtext.

- Focus the scene on a well-motivated conflict. Even in less dramatic scenes, a conflict should exist, regardless of how minor or how subtle it is. Often, two people with the same goal will disagree over methods or procedure, or just get under the other's skin: Bones and Spock, James Bond and Q, Butch Cassidy and Sundance. Even in love scenes, there may be some resistance at the beginning. Conflict is one of the tools you can use to build suspense.

For examples of scenes, see Books III and IV.

Suspense, comedy, and television

Building suspense is the art of creating an expectation of something dramatic that is about to happen. Since we go to movies to feel emotion vicariously, putting us in suspense simply builds emotion as we anticipate the outcome. Here are ten tools to thrill and manipulate us.

TOOLS FOR BUILDING SUSPENSE

Evoke emotion

Create characters we like. They must be believable since they act as a conduit through which emotion can pass to us. We need to sympathize with them and feel what they feel.

Create conflict

As mentioned earlier, rising conflict creates suspense. Since conflict is drama, two committed forces in conflict will always heighten suspense. Remember grade school? Two boys would start fighting and everyone would make a circle around them. No one tried to stop the fight. (This is very irritating if you're the smaller boy.) No one stopped it because we were all in suspense, wondering if blood would squirt out someone's nose, and betting on who would win.

Provide opposition

Give your central character *a powerful opposition*; then force your character to battle this foe. The opposition should be in a position of strength, capable of doing damage. In STAR TREK II, Khan serves as an excellent example, because he is superior to Kirk physically and mentally. We all go through the extreme mental duress of wondering how Kirk is going to survive, let alone defeat, this "giant."

The "giant" in FATAL ATTRACTION is Glenn Close, the lover. She is in a position to do damage to Michael Douglas.

The formidable foe in MY BEST FRIEND'S WEDDING is Kim, the fiancée. She has the emotional leverage on Michael, Julianne's best friend. Besides, she's adorable. How can Julianne compete with that?

Build expectation
Create an *expectation for trouble*. Do you recall the baby carriage in THE UNTOUCH-ABLES? In this scene, Elliot Ness must face off with Capone's boys at the train station. He's ready and in position, but a woman is having difficulty moving her baby carriage up the stairs. We get nervous—we just "know" she is going to get in the way. The suspense builds.

Consider also the scene from FATAL ATTRACTION where Michael Douglas returns home and finds his wife conversing with his lover. There is an expectation that the wife might realize that this blonde she is talking to is actually a woman who is having an affair with her husband. In this case the jeopardy is emotional, not physical. When the wife introduces the lover to Michael Douglas, the subtext is powerful because they have already met. The lover says such lines as, "Don't I remember you?" "We've definitely met." "I never forget a face." The subtext is, *You're not getting away from me. I'm going to make you pay.*

At the Showdown of GHOSTBUSTERS, our heroes confront the goddess Gozer. Gozer tells them that the destructor will come in whatever form they choose with their thoughts. Dan Aykroyd has obviously thought of something and the other characters try to figure it out because the destructor is coming, but we don't know what it is. Comedic suspense builds as Aykroyd points to his head and says, "It just popped in there." What just popped in there? And then we catch glimpses of something huge and white moving past the buildings, but we still don't know what it is. Aykroyd babbles, "It can't be, it can't be." The anticipation peaks and finally Aykroyd admits, "It's the Stay-Puft Marshmallow Man." And then we see the huge figure.

Increase tension
Put the audience in a *superior position*. Take, for example, a couple we care about. While they are out to dinner, someone sneaks into their apartment and places a bomb under their bed. Later, our happy couple returns and they hop into bed. *We* know the bomb is there, but they don't. We, the audience, are in a superior position.

Imagine a small child playing in the yard. The mother steps inside the house. The child wanders toward the busy street. We are in a superior position to the child *and* to the mother. We are the only ones who are aware of the danger, and that builds suspense.

64

Use surprise

Throw in an occasional nasty twist, or sudden turn of events. Do you recall WAIT UNTIL DARK? Remember Alan Arkin leaping from the shadows at Audrey Hepburn? You couldn't hear the rest of the movie for all the screaming in the theater.

In PSYCHO, Hitchcock kills Janet Leigh early in the now-famous shower scene. This nasty twist serves the purpose of creating an expectation of *more* violence. Indeed, Hitchcock once remarked, "At this point I transferred the horror from the screen to the minds of the audience." Interestingly enough, there is only one more violent act in the entire movie, and yet we are held in suspense throughout.

Create immediacy

When *something vital is at stake* for the character, that *something* becomes vital to us, the audience, as well. It can be the physical safety of the world or the moral redemption of a juvenile delinquent. It can be the emotional fulfillment of two lovers who find each other, the protection of a secret document, or the triumph of a value. The higher the stakes, the more intense the suspense.

Establish consequences

Closely related to the above is the establishment of terrible consequences if the central character does not achieve her goal. When the Challenger space shuttle exploded, there was a lot of grief and sadness. A couple of years later, we sent up another shuttle. Do you recall the suspense you felt as the countdown proceeded on this later shuttle mission? That heightened suspense was due to the prior establishment of terrible consequences.

Limit time

Put a ticking clock on it. "You have only twenty-four hours to save the world, James. Good luck." Deadlines, such as the one in THE PAPER, create suspense because they introduce an additional opposition—time. You can probably think of a dozen movies where a bomb is about to explode, and the hero must defuse it before the countdown reaches zero. The torpedo-firing sequences in THE HUNT FOR RED OCTOBER were particularly thrilling because of the element of time.

Likewise, when the wicked witch in THE WIZARD OF OZ captures Dorothy, she turns over the hour glass. "This is how long you have to live, my little pretty." Although we are never told how Dorothy is going to die, we still worry. Apparently, Hitchcock was right when he said that "the threat of violence is stronger than violence."

You can easily create an artificial deadline. The damsel is tied to the railroad tracks. Can Dudley Doright save the damsel before the train runs over her? Here you have an implied deadline. Other effective uses of the ticking clock include HIGH NOON and the rose petals in Disney's BEAUTY AND THE BEAST. In TITANIC, can Rose reach Jack and get him out of his handcuffs before the room fills with water?

Maintain doubt

Finally, if there is a reasonable doubt about how the scene or movie is going to end, the suspense is intensified. In the opening scene of THE UNTOUCHABLES, one of Capone's boys leaves a briefcase full of explosives in a store. A little girl picks it up and it explodes. At this point, we realize that anyone in this movie can die, and we fret over Elliot Ness's little girl and wife the entire movie. Why? Because there is genuine doubt about their safety.

LEAVE 'EM LAUGHING

Have you ever watched a comedy and laughed for about twenty minutes and then grown restless? The probable reason for this is that the comedy had a weak story structure with poorly drawn characters. The comedy may have relied more on gags than on character and story.

Comedy is drama in disguise. And there is no comedy without conflict. That means virtually everything in this book applies to comedy as well as to drama. Here are a few points that apply particularly to comedy.

Comedy requires clarity and good timing—a *sense* of humor.

Love situations and other personal situations are easy for us to identify with and are ripe for comedy. That's one reason the family situation comedy has done so well. As psychologist Abraham Maslow stated, "That which is most personal is most general." Comedy reveals our secret desires and yearnings so that we can laugh at them.

Comedy makes good use of surprise and reversals, in revealing the truth about people, situations, and life.

Comedy generally takes an unusual point of view through use of exaggeration, deception, overstatement, understatement, contrast, parody, a ridiculous point of view, or obsession.

Comedy characters need to present the same contrasts that dramatic characters do. In GHOSTBUSTERS, we have a rational, cerebral type (Harold Ramis); an emotional, enthusiastic child (Dan Aykroyd); and a cool dude who understates almost everything (Bill Murray). This is a good mix. The fourth ghostbuster was brought in as an afterthought and doesn't really add to the comedic mix.

Comedy presents people with pretenses or façades, then removes them little by little. One scene from PLAY IT AGAIN, SAM features Woody Allen preparing for a blind date (a situation we can all relate to—right?). He goes to extremes to impress her. He thinks he can score the first night, and that's his pretense. He impresses her, all right, but not the way he had hoped. It's a reversal of what he expected. He's brought back to earth. And it's funny.

Another example of two characters with a pretense appears in CELEBRITY WEDDING, a screenplay by Yours Truly and Greg Alt. Sam and Natalie pretend not to like each other (that's the pretense). They have just seated themselves on a plane, thinking they have escaped from the bad guy, Novaks.

Immediately, Sam spots Novaks, who hasn't yet spotted them. Somehow, Sam must find a way to hide Natalie's face so that Novaks doesn't recognize her. They have to act quickly. Watch how the pretenses are removed and the truth of their feelings for each other are revealed.

(As you will read in Book III, the dash is normally used for interruptions of thought and the ellipsis for continuation of thought. An ellipsis at the end of a sentence normally means the character did not continue her thought.)

```
INT. PLANE - DAY

Sam and Natalie quickly throw themselves into two back
seats.  Sam leans into the aisle and spots Novaks headed
their direction, searching the passengers.

                    SAM
          He's coming.

Sam turns to Natalie.  Gets eye contact.  She responds with
a short gasp.  He kisses her long and hard, hiding her face
from Novaks.

Novaks glances at them in disgust, then turns back.

Sam releases Natalie, who is momentarily paralyzed.

                    SAM
          Ah sorry.  I -- ah, couldn't
          think of anything else.
```

                    NATALIE
          Right -- I mean, I mean under the
          circumstances it was good.   I
          don't mean <u>good</u> good, I mean
          well....

                    SAM
          We really didn't have any other --

                    NATALIE
          -- Exactly. And if we had --

                    SAM
          -- We certainly would've -- or
          wouldn't've....

                    NATALIE
          Absolutely.

                    SAM
                (overlapping)
          Naturally.

A brief, unbearable silence. Face to face. Instantly, they
both reach for the same in-flight magazine.

                    SAM AND NATALIE
                (simultaneously)
          Go ahead.

Disgusted with himself, Sam rips the magazine from the seat
pocket and buries himself in it.

Natalie pulls out the emergency flight card and fans herself.

In this scene, the kiss comes as a surprise. The situation is readily identifiable in the
sense that we've all embarrassed ourselves at one time or another in the presence of
someone we were interested in. The scene ends with a visual subtext that implies Natalie
is "hot."

TELEVISION

As you can imagine, television comedy writing is less visual than screenwriting, with less action. There may be only one or two locations. And so the emphasis is on inter-personal conflict and dialogue. The best situation for a sitcom is one that forces the characters to be together. They live together, work together, or belong together.
Sitcoms thrive with a *gang of four*, four main characters where each can easily be at cross-purposes with any of the others, creating more possibilities for conflict. In other words, they can play off each other.

Structurally, the sitcom opens with a teaser that says, "Boy, this is going to be really funny. Don't change the channel during the next two minutes of commercials!" Act 1 introduces the secondary storyline and the primary storyline in succession. (Sometimes one of these is introduced in the teaser.) Act 1 ends on a turning point that is either the most hilarious moment in the episode, or is very serious. The second act resolves the primary story, then the secondary story. This is followed by a tag at the end that usually comments on the resolution. Some sitcoms present three stories or plot lines.

The hour-long TV drama or comedy also opens with a teaser or prologue. Act 1 establishes what's going on, Acts 2 and 3 develop it, Act 4 pays it off. Most shows add an epilogue. If the show is relationship-driven, an arena is created in which the story can play. The arena for ER is a hospital emergency room.

The *long form*, or Movie-of-the-Week (MOW), contains seven acts and about 100 pages. That means six turning points must be carefully planned. It might be simpler to write this as a screenplay. In fact, the best way to break into television of any kind is with a feature script that you can use as a sample. It shows you can create characters from scratch and write a story around them. Being the next great screenwriter, it's a challenge you can meet.

It goes without saying that the principles of drama that we have covered up until now apply to writing for television as well.

Note: This is a good time to do Step 5 in the workbook (Book II). Next, read the formatting and style guide (Books III and IV). Then do Steps 6 and 7 in the workbook. Finally, use the marketing plan in Book V to sell your screenplay, consulting the resources in Book VI.

7 STEPS TO A STUNNING SCRIPT

BOOK II

A Workbook

About this workbook

This workbook takes you through the seven steps of the writing process. I've tried to make it simple and easy to follow.

Each step is marked with checkpoints to keep you on track. In all, there are 26 checkpoints and more than 150 key questions to help you evaluate your progress. Not every question needs to be answered. Not every checkpoint needs to be reviewed in the order it's presented. These are not hard-and-fast rules, but fluid guidelines to help you craft a stunning script. In fact, many writers like to begin the process by developing their characters; if you are one of those, you may want to do Step 4 before Steps 2 and 3.

This workbook becomes a more effective tool if you've studied the primer (Book I) first and have started or have the nascent concept for a script.

Take a moment now to congratulate yourself. You are embarking on a great journey. I hope you enjoy the adventure of creating movie people and plotting the events of their lives. May success be yours.

Step 1—Summon your Muse

Before the workshop began, two writing students were into it. "Writing is purely a creative endeavor," Sheila insisted.

"But *screen*writing is a scientific process," Sam argued.

Back and forth they went. Finally, Robert, my teacher's pet, chimed in. "Stop! You're both right. Screenwriting is both an art and a science. The professional writer uses the head as well as the heart."

Sheila and Sam shot doubtful glances. "You can't have it both ways," Sheila replied.

Sure you can, and here's why:

The writing process begins with the creative urge, a desire to express something. Like a tiny seedling, an idea emerges from your heart and pushes its way through the soil of your subconscious. Often, several ideas will sprout. Like any birthing process, this can happen at any time and any place. And with the emergence of your idea comes that wonderful creative feeling.

How do you nurture that young seedling of an idea? What makes it grow? Thought and hard work make it grow. You think about the possibilities. Then, you blueprint the core story, which consists of a beginning, a middle, and an end. All this head work will act like a shot of adrenalin to your heart. More ideas will flow, and the story will evolve until it matures.

Every writer has two natures: the heart and the head. The heart is the passionate creator, the emotional artist, the child, the intuitive subconscious. The head is the detached critic or editor, the parent, the logical and analytical scientist or surgeon. And quite conscious.

Good writing utilizes both natures but operates like an alternating current between the two. When you're in the creative, artistic mode, you shut off the head. You encourage the creative flow. You don't correct the spelling or improve the grammar. You just play in your sand box. There are no rules or restrictions. But once that energy is expended, the parental side takes over and cleans up the mess.

Back and forth you go. You write from the heart. You edit from the head. Back and forth until the head and heart agree (or you've become a schizophrenic).

The good Lord gave our brain two hemispheres. Both are important. Sheila is right-brained and focuses on the intuitive, artistic side of creativity. Sam is left-brained and focuses on the analytical, scientific side of creativity. Each should use his or her greater talent without abandoning his or her lesser talent.

I sometimes worry about writers who search for formulas, who want to make writing purely a science so that they can write by the numbers. They may want inflexible rules so they can be in control of the process. This is to be expected. Our educational system inculcates this into our brains. The secret to great writing is to be part of the process. You can't control it. In truth, the story knows from the beginning where it's going. There is no sweeter moment than when your characters take over and tell you what they want to do and say.

I also worry about the purists who may insist that anything written from the heart is perfect just the way it comes. That which comes easily is not necessarily good. They may be loathe to edit their work for fear of breaking some divine law. If this were true, no one would ever revise anything. There would be no second drafts, no rewriting. So, just because it felt good when you wrote it doesn't mean that it is ready for market.

Writing is an evolutionary process that must be trusted. You must believe that there is a story within you. You must believe that it will find its way out. And you must believe in your talent to nurture it into a stunning script. If you believe, and act on your belief, your Muse will come to you.

THE WRITING PROCESS

Becoming part of the writing process is like "getting religion." For some writers it is almost a mystical experience. Let me provide a suggested framework for this process.

First you start off with a creative jolt, an idea that's about a 7.0 on the Richter scale. Then you do a lot of hard thinking—hammering out a good dramatic premise—beginning, middle, and end. You write the *TV Guide* logline in terms of character, action, opposition, and resolution. What's the concept?

Then, on wings of song, your Muse comes down from Olympus and whispers sweet things. You write all these gems down.

You visualize the one-sheet, the poster that will adorn the movie theater walls in just a couple of years or so. You ask: Do I have a story? Do I have an original concept that will pull people in? If everything feels right up till now, you begin your research.

You develop your characters using both sides of your brain. Remember, even though your characters are within you before you ever begin, once they emerge, they must take on a life of their own.

With an understanding of your story and characters, you now construct the all-important story outline. This outline, sometimes called the step outline, is comprised of paragraphs, one paragraph for each scene, anywhere from 30-100 steps in all. (This figure can vary, depending on genre.) Many writers use 3" x 5" cards, a card for each scene, and pin these cards against the wall. This is when you chart the sequence of your story, alternating between your creative/intuitive nature and your evaluative/practical nature.

Whenever you think you're getting off base, you write a short treatment—about three pages—to get back on track.

By now, your creative pump is primed. You write your first draft from the heart. Some of these scenes are already written from previous bursts of creative joy. Intuitively, creatively, the draft takes shape. The second draft is written from the head, analytically. Death and regeneration.

Even as you approach the end of the process, the story is fluid, evolving into what it eventually wants to be. Don't force the process by being too rigid about scenes you have fallen madly in love with. Don't feel confined by your original outline. Remain open to your Muse.

Now this is just one way to write a script. You will find the way that works best for you with experience. Some writers prefer to just write and allow things to manifest themselves in the writing. The most important thing is to trust the process and believe in yourself. The story is inside you; you must let it out in one way or another. So what are you waiting for? Come on. Let's create a masterpiece!

Step 2—Dream up your movie idea

What if you don't have any ideas? Here are a few tips that will help you get those creative juices flowing.

1. Put your mind in a relaxed state through meditation or deep breathing. Visualize a natural setting where you feel safe, or drift off to the setting of your script. The right brain, the Inner Creator, always works best when the left brain, the Inner Critic, has been tranquilized.

2. Rely on the Inspiration Cycle: Input, Incubation, Inspiration, Evaluation. After a few days of jamming your brain, relax and tell yourself you need a breakthrough, then incubate. In other words, wait. It may take a few days. Soon enough, while falling asleep or taking a shower—Eureka!—the inspiration comes. You're flying. It may continue to flow for some time. But don't stop when it does. Evaluate it (the Inner Critic has been waiting for this moment) as a means of bringing on the next cycle of inspiration.

3. Stimulate the senses. Engage in a physical activity such as gardening, chopping wood, shoveling snow, fishing, dancing, aerobics, kneading clay, washing the dishes, tinkering with the car, and so on. Physical activity not only relaxes you, but it stimulates the senses and sensory details will stimulate your writing. It also occupies the left brain, freeing your child-like right brain.

4. Stir your creative desire by inventing writing rituals. Acquire a ball cap and imprint or embroider the word "writer" on it. Whenever it's time to write, you can tell your loved ones, "I'm wearing my writer's cap tonight." I know a writer who begins every session with an herb tea ceremony, instructing her "analytical brain to sleep so that the creative brain can come forth with a masterpiece." Speaking of ceremonies, why not conduct opening and closing ceremonies for the Writer's Olympics, starring you? Writing should be fun, so have a good time.

When I need to drop into the creative mode, I often play stimulating music, usually soundtracks and classical music, because they stir my emotions and imagination. You may find it helpful to look at a painting, photo, or object that suggests theme, character, or location to you, something that pulls you into your story. I know someone who closes her eyes and types as she visualizes.

5. Reflect on and dip into your past. The research has already been done on your life and your world. It's all inside you. You can draw from this well, especially when you need to feel the emotion your characters are feeling, but beware the quagmires of autobiographical writing.

I'm often asked: Is it true I should write what I know? Can I base my script on something that happened to me years ago? How true to life should my characters be? Can I use myself and people I know? The answer is you need just enough distance from these characters and incidents that they can take on a life of their own.

Writing that is too autobiographical is usually flat, with the central character often becoming an observer of life instead of an active participant. Once I read a script about a wife who was abused by her husband. The wife did nothing but complain for ninety pages. On page 100 a neighbor rescued her. The only reason I read this all the way through was because I was paid to evaluate it. I thought to myself, This is often how real people behave, but movie people are willful and active.

The writer had painted herself into a creative corner. She was too close to the truth. She needed to use the energy of her personal experience and create a drama with it. Even "true" stories combine characters and condense time for dramatic purposes.

The problem with autobiographical writing (and all writing, of course, is partly autobiographical) is that we love our central character. We make her perfect. We're afraid to bloody her nose. Solution? Use yourself and people you know as a basis for the fictional characters you create. Be as autobiographical as you want—you need that energy—but create enough distance to be objective. It's a razor's edge that every writer must walk.

6. Carry around a tape recorder or notebook. (There's never been a writing instructor or adviser who hasn't recommended this helpful tip.) When you carry around a notebook or a microcassette recorder, you are asking your subconscious to find ideas for you. Armed with one of these tools, you'll be more observant and open to wandering ideas looking for a home. Write down, or record, these ideas and bits as they occur to you.

7. See movies in your genre. In fact, see eight good films and two dogs. Read a screenwriting book. Read screenplays—yes!—read screenplays. Page through old movie books or books of foreign films. Attend a seminar or workshop. Remember, don't stop learning in order to write; and don't stop writing in order to learn.

8. Steal. Shakespeare did. Are you greater than he? Look to the classics for plot and character ideas. Creativity is not creating something out of nothing; it's a new twist on an old idea. It's making new combinations of old patterns. It's converting the Big Dipper into the Little Ladle. Creativity is disrupting the regular thought patterns to create a new way of connecting. Gutenberg took the wine press and the coin punch and created the first printing press.

Read fairy tales, folklore, mythology, and history. Many classic plots can be easily adapted. *Romeo and Juliet* became WEST SIDE STORY. *Faust* became DAMN YAN-KEES, ROSEMARY'S BABY, WALL STREET, and BLUE CHIPS. Homer's *Odyssey* became FALLING DOWN. *The Tempest* has been transformed into several movies. How many *Frankenstein* plots can you identify? How about *King Midas, Jack the Giant Killer,* and *Cinderella*/PRETTY WOMAN plots? Maybe it's time for your character to take the Hero's Journey (page 35). Try variations and twists of plots. How about a modern update of *Moby Dick* or some other classic? Just make sure that any work you adapt is in the public domain.

9. Visit parks, airports, parties, court rooms, crisis centers or other places where people are likely to congregate or be in some kind of transition. This will help you look for character and story details. You may even find someone to be a character in your script.

10. Read the news. "Giant White Caught Off New England Coast" was the headline that inspired JAWS. "80-Year-Old Widow Weds 17-Year-Old Boy" inspired HAROLD AND MAUDE. TV and radio talk shows can give you ideas for topics that are current.

If you are aware of a true story that would work for a Movie-of-the-Week (and if it's not a big story that has already attracted producer-types), then buy an option to the rights of that story and write the script.

11. Understand dramatic structure. This needs to be said. Sometimes you're stuck because you've violated some principle of dramatic structure. Use this in connection with #7 above. I've heard many writers credit a book or seminar for helping them work through a writing problem.

12. Be open to radical change. Be flexible. I once changed the gender of my central character to awaken a tired story. Maybe you should open your story on your current

page 30 instead of page 1. Ask questions. Ask the "what if" question. What if an alien child was accidentally left behind on Earth? What if my central character's mother is a jackal? Be open to any ideas, and any criticism. Everything goes. Nothing's written in stone until the shoot wraps.

13. Write what you care about, what you have passion for. What type of movie do you like to watch? This may be the type of movie you ought to write. Discover and follow what fascinates you.

Use the energy from pet peeves and gripes. Writing what you feel strongly about will help you keep going when the going gets tough. And keep in mind that the process of writing one script will generate ideas for other scripts and will grease the works for future creative success.

14. Try clustering. It's a technique that naturally summons your creativity and eliminates anxiety. Get a clean sheet of paper and write your story problem, concept, or character about half way down the page. Draw a circle around it.

Now brainstorm, using free association. Whatever comes to mind, write it down, circle it, and connect it to its parent (or simply make a list). Go with any ideas that float by, regardless of how bizarre or strange. Keep your hand moving. If you have a moment when no idea comes, doodle in the corner until it does. Within about five minutes, you'll have a feeling of what you're supposed to do. An insight will come, the solution will be revealed, or a new idea will leap into your mind. If nothing happens, just stay relaxed. This is something that can't be forced.

15. Confront your blocks. List all your barriers to writing and communicate with them; that is, turn your barrier into an object or person and write a dialogue. In this free-writing exercise, an insight will come to you. Yes, you can overcome the barrier.

Keep in mind that the master key to overcoming writer's block is to realize that it's no big deal, just an occupational hazard. The real problem is when you panic. Blocks are just part of the writing process. In fact, a block is a blessing in disguise because now that your "head" is stymied, your subconscious is free to break through. So relax. Have fun. Trust the process.

Once you have a hat full of story ideas, you can search for the nuggets, the genuine movie concepts, the premises that have commercial potential.

CHECKPOINT 1

- How solid is your story idea, premise, or concept?
- Will it appeal to a mass audience?
- Is it fresh? original? provocative? commercial?
- Does hearing it make people say, "I want to see that!"?
- Is it large enough in scope to appear on the silver screen?
- Does it have "legs"—stand on its own as a story without big stars?

CHECKPOINT 2

- Do you have a working title that inspires you?
- Will this title titillate the audience? Is it a "grabber"?
- Does it convey something of your story concept or theme?
- Does it conjure up an image or an emotion?
- Is it short enough to appear on a marquee? (Not always necessary.)

CHECKPOINT 3

Imagine how your movie will be advertised. Then on a sheet of paper, sketch out the one-sheet (movie poster) for your movie.

- Is there a striking visual image that will stop passersby?
- Is there a headline that plays off the title or conveys a high concept?
- Will people want to see this movie?

Step 3—Develop Your Core Story

What is your story about? You need to know this and you need to know it now. There are producers who believe that if you can't tell them your story in a sentence or two, there isn't a story. They may be right.

A story presents a character who wants something and who is opposed by at least one other character. This opposition causes conflict and a series of critical events all leading to the Crisis and Showdown at the end. Here are the critical events in virtually all dramas and comedies:

CATALYST

Your story starts out in balance, but the Catalyst upsets that balance (hopefully by page 10-15), giving the central character a desire, problem, need, goal, mission, or something to do. The story now has direction and movement. In WITNESS, the catalyst is the Amish boy witnessing the murder. It gives Harrison Ford something to do—try to find the killer.

BIG EVENT

This is an event that changes your central character's life in a big way, thus the Big Event. It comes in around pages 20-30. This is where Marty travels to 1955 in BACK TO THE FUTURE.

PINCH

About half way through the script, there is another major plot twist. It is often a point of no return for the central character, or the moment when the character becomes fully committed, or when the motivation is strengthened or becomes clear. It's when Scarlet O'Hara vows never to go hungry again in GONE WITH THE WIND.

CRISIS

This is an event that forces a crucial decision. Often it is simply the low point in the story, the moment when all looks lost, or when the lovers are separated. In E.T., it's when the men converge on the house and E.T. is dying. How will he ever get home now? In about 15-30 pages, we'll find out.

SHOWDOWN

Commonly called the climax, this is when the central character and opposition character square off. It's the final battle in STAR WARS, the breakfast-table scene in MOONSTRUCK.

REALIZATION

Just after the Showdown, or during it, or occasionally before it, the audience realizes that your central character has grown, changed, or figured something out. This is when the scarecrow asks Dorothy what she has learned. She knows now that there's no place like home. It's when the family admires and accepts Kevin at the end of HOME ALONE. Let's look at examples from four movies.

DAVE

Catalyst:	Dave is asked to pretend he's president
Big Event:	The real president dies; Dave "becomes" president
Pinch:	Dave acts as president and defies the press secretary
Crisis:	The press secretary implicates Dave in a scandal
Showdown:	Dave defeats the press secretary at a joint session of Congress
Realization:	I can *help people find jobs*—Dave runs for office

THELMA & LOUISE

Catalyst: Louise takes Thelma fishing
Big Event: Louise shoots and kills Thelma's attacker
Pinch: Louise tells Jimmy good-bye
Crisis: It becomes apparent that Thelma and Louise will die
Showdown: They are pursued to the Grand Canyon—there's a standoff at the rim
Realization: We've *achieved a certain freedom together.*

TWINS

Catalyst: Danny meets his brother Arnold
Big Event: Danny is saved by his brother, so he takes him in
Pinch: Danny meets the scientist; believes Arnold really is his brother
Crisis: Danny must choose between his brother and $5 million
Showdown: Together, Danny and Arnold trick the bad guy
Realization: *I'm not genetic garbage*—Danny finds his mother

THE HAND THAT ROCKS THE CRADLE

	Peyton (Central Character)	Claire (Protagonist)
Catalyst:	Hub's suicide; no family	Molested by doctor
Big Event:	Gets Claire to hire her	Hires Peyton
Pinch:	Gets Solomon kicked out	Fires Solomon
Crisis:	Kicked out of the house	Asthma attack
Showdown:	Battle with Claire	Battle with Peyton
Realization:	None	*I trust my instincts* (trusts Solomon w/ child)

CHECKPOINT 4

Write the *TV Guide* logline for your story.

- Who is your central character?
- What is his/her main goal? (This is the goal that drives the story.)
- Why is the goal so important to him/her?
- Who is trying to stop your character from achieving the goal?

CHECKPOINT 5

Identify the parameters of your story.

- What is the genre? (Action/adventure, thriller, romantic comedy, etc.)
- What is the time and setting?
- What is the emotional atmosphere, and the mood?
- What, if any, story or character limits exist?

CHECKPOINT 6

- What is the Catalyst that gives your central character a direction?
- What Big Event really impacts your character's life?
- Is there a strong, rising conflict throughout Act 2?
- Does the conflict build? or just become repetitive?
- Is there a Pinch, a twist in the middle, that divides Act 2 in half and more fully motivates your character?
- What terrible Crisis will your character face?
- Will the Crisis force a life/death decision, and/or make the audience fret about how things will turn out in the end?
- How does your story end? What is the Showdown?
- In the end, does your character learn something new?
   Or, is his/her growth (positive or negative) made apparent?
   Or, does he/she receive any recognition in the end?

CHECKPOINT 7

Now write out your core story in three paragraphs, one for the beginning, one for the middle, and one for the end. Paragraph 1 will end with the Big Event; paragraph 2 with the Crisis. Obviously, you cannot include all of the characters in this brief synopsis. Once this is done, re-evaluate your story.

Step 4—Create your movie people

Your central character wants something specific. That something is the goal. The character, who is conscious of this desire, strives for it throughout most of the story. Of course, the character is opposed by at least one other person.

In most stories, the character also has an inner need, something she may not be consciously aware of until the Crisis. This need is a yearning for the one thing that will bring true happiness or fulfillment to the character. The need is blocked by a flaw, usually a form of selfishness. The flaw emerges from a past traumatic event—the backstory.

The main plot of most movies is driven by the goal. It's the Outside/Action Story.

The main subplot is driven by the need. It's the Inside/Emotional Story. It is usually focused on the primary relationship in the story. It's concerned with character dynamics.

The Outside/Action Story is the spine; it holds things together. The Inside/Emotional Story is the heart; it touches the audience. To make the Outside/Action Story and Inside/Emotional Story work, you need to understand your movie people and how they function.

CHECKPOINT 8

Does your central character have the following?

- An outside goal that the audience will care about?
- A powerful, personal motivation for achieving the goal?
- An opposition character in a position of strength, capable of doing great damage?
- The will to act against opposition, and to learn and grow?
- Human emotions, traits, values, and imperfections that people can identify with?
- A particular point of view of life, the world, and/or self, giving rise to attitudes?

- Details, extensions, idiosyncracies, and/or expressions that are uniquely his/hers?
- A life and voice (dialogue) of his/her own?
- A key event from the past that has given rise to a character flaw?
- An inner need that he/she may be unaware of at first?

CHECKPOINT 9

Evaluate your other main characters (and especially your opposition character) by the criteria of Checkpoint 8. Each should have at least a goal or intention in the story. The more depth you can give them, the more interesting they will appear.

CHECKPOINT 10

Your movie people have sociological, psychological, and physiological characteristics. Use the following to provoke your creative thought.

Sociology

Occupation	Education	Criminal record
Birthplace/upbringing	Ethnic roots	Religion
Past/present home life	Political views	Social status
Hobbies	Affiliations	Private life
Work history	Work environment	Personal life

Physiology

Height/weight	Build or figure	Attractiveness
Appearance	Hair/eyes	Voice quality
Defects/scars	Health/strength	Complexion
Clothing	Physical skills	Athletic ability

Psychology

Fears/phobias	Secrets	Attitudes
Prejudices	Values/beliefs	Inhibitions
Pet peeves	Complexes	Addictions
Superstitions	Habits	Moral stands
Ambitions	Motivations	Temperament
Personal problems	Imagination	Likes/dislikes
Intelligence	Disposition	

CHECKPOINT 11

These are questions to ask of any of your movie people:

- How do you handle stress, pressure, relationships, problems, emotion?
- Are you extroverted or shy? intuitive or analytical? active or passive?
- What's your most traumatic experience? most thrilling experience?
- Essentially, who are you? What is at your core?
- What is your dominant trait?
- What do you do and think when you're alone and no one will know?
- How do you feel about yourself?
- How do you feel about the other people in the story?
- Who are the most important people in your life?
- How do you relate to each?
- What's the worst (and best) thing that could happen to you?
- What are you doing tonight? tomorrow?
- Where do you want to be ten years from now?

CHECKPOINT 12

- How does your central character grow or change throughout the story?
- How is your character different at the end of the story?
- What does he/she know at the end that he/she did not know at the beginning?
- What is your character's perception of reality?
- Does that perception change by the end of the story?
- Is your protagonist likeable?
- Will the audience identify with your central character on some level?
- Does your central character have depth, with both strengths and weaknesses?
- Will the two key roles attract stars?

CHECKPOINT 13

- What is the theme or message of your story?
- What are you trying to say?
- Will the end of your story say it for you without being preachy?
  (The theme may not be evident to you until later in your writing.)

CHECKPOINT 14

Revise your three-paragraph synopsis to incorporate any changes to your story.

Step 5—Step out your story

This is where you find out if your story is going to work or not. Here, you outline your story. This work will make the actual writing much easier than it would ordinarily be.

CHECKPOINT 15

Plot the action of your story. Identify your central character's action plot and emotional subplot. Look at your other movie people; identify their goals. Their goals will drive their individual plots (actually subplots). Do these various plot lines intersect, resulting in adequate conflict for drama or comedy?

CHECKPOINT 16

Write a four-page treatment (double-spaced). Summarize the beginning of your story in one page, the middle in two pages, and the end in one page. Focus on two to four main characters, the key events (plot points), and the emotional undercurrent of the story. Although somewhat difficult, this exercise will help tremendously in laying a strong foundation for your story. Now answer these questions:

- Is the central conflict of the story clearly defined?
- Are the character's goal and need clear?
- Are the stakes of the story big enough for a commercial movie?
- Does the story evoke an emotional response?
- Will the audience cry, get angry, laugh, get scared, fall in love, get excited, etc.?
- What makes this story unique, fresh, and original?
- Is your story too predictable? Have we seen this before?
- Are the facts of the story plausible? (They don't have to be possible, just plausible.)
- Will people be emotionally satisfied at the end?

CHECKPOINT 17

Step out your script. This is a crucial step. Traditionally, the step outline consists of a series of 3" x 5" cards, one card for each scene or dramatic unit. Consider attaching these cards (or post-it notes) to a wall, table, or cork board to see the entire story at once.

At the top of each card write the master scene heading, then summarize the action of the scene in a sentence or short paragraph, emphasizing the essential action and purpose of the scene. Some writers like to list the characters appearing in the scene in the lower left-hand corner of the card. That way, they can see who is where at a glance.

You can use the lower right-hand corner for pacing and tracking plots. Some writers use a highlighter and identify plots by color. Blue is the action story, red is the love story, and so on.

You can identify scenes as fast or slow, action or dialogue. If you discover that you have four dialogue scenes in a row, all with the same characters, you can adjust this pacing problem by moving scenes around, cross-cutting with action scenes, condensing, or even omitting an unnecessary scene.

If additional ideas come to you, jot them down on blank cards. You'll end up with 30-100 cards, depending on the nature of the story.

Of course, you don't have to use 3" x 5" cards. You can step-out your story on your computer—whatever works for you. Once completed, your step outline will become the basis for writing your script.

CHECKPOINT 18

Now that your step outline is complete, ask yourself these questions:

- Are your scenes well paced?
- Do the major turning points come at about the right time?
- Do things just happen, or is there a cause-and-effect relationship between character actions?
- Do the subplots intersect with the main plot, creating new complications?
- Are your characters' actions motivated, or do they exist just to make the story work?
- Does action, conflict, and dramatic tension build, or just repeat and become static?
- Are your central and opposition characters forced to take stronger and stronger actions?
- Does the conflict rise naturally to a crisis/climax?

Step 6—Write your first draft

Write your first draft from the heart. Keep your head out of it as much as possible. It's okay to change the story. It's okay to overwrite. It's okay to include too much dialogue. Everything goes, everything flows.

Once this draft is completed, you may wish to register it with the Writers Guild of America. This is optional since you will register it again after your final polish.

CHECKPOINT 19

It is absolutely imperative that you do the following upon completion of the first draft.

1. Take at least two weeks off from your script. Let it ferment for a while. You will be much more objective for the pre-revision analysis (Checkpoints 20-24). During this time you may want to read a book, go to a seminar, see movies of the same genre, or read scripts, or turn your attention to other things.

2. Reward yourself in some way that makes you feel good about being the next great screenwriter.

Step 7—Make the necessary revisions

Before writing the second draft, consider letting your hot property cool off. Sit on it a couple of weeks, then craft your second draft from your head. Here, you become a script surgeon. Whittle down the dialogue; remove unnecessary narration, flashbacks, dream sequences, and so on. You become an analyst in every way you can define that word. Once this work is completed, polish your script until you are ready to present your wonder to Hollywood. The following checkpoints will help you evaluate your revisions.

CHECKPOINT 20

Review Checkpoints 1-19. Do not skip this checkpoint.

CHECKPOINT 21 (the script itself)

- Is your script too technical, too complex, or too difficult to understand?
- Will your script require a huge budget with unshootable scenes, such as herds of camels crossing the San Diego Freeway? Other possible big budget problems: special effects, period settings, exotic locations, too many arenas or locations, large cast, water, and animals.
- Is your script's budget about right for its market?
- Have you followed the rules of formatting and presentation as described in Book III?
- Have you written thoughts, feelings, memories, or anything else that cannot appear on the screen?

CHECKPOINT 22 (dialogue)

- Is the dialogue "too on the nose"?
- Do your characters say exactly what they feel?
- Does each character speak with his/her own voice, vocabulary, slang, rhythm, and style?
- Is the dialogue crisp, original, clever, compelling, and lean?
- Are individual speeches too long or encumbered with more than one thought?
- Does the story rely too heavily on dialogue?
- Are your dialogue scenes too long?
- Are there too many scenes with talking heads?
- Are you telling when you could be showing?
- Is the comedy *trying* to be funny, or is it naturally funny?

CHECKPOINT 23 (exposition)

- Are you boring your audience by telling too much too soon?
- Are you confusing your audience with too little information?
- Are you giving your audience just enough exposition to keep them on the edge of their seats?
- Is your exposition revealed through conflict or through static dialogue?
- Have you used flashbacks as a crutch or as a means to move the story forward?

CHECKPOINT 24 (character and story)

- Will the reader root for your hero?
- Will the reader have an emotional identification with the hero?
- Are your characters believable? Are they humans with dimension?
- Do your characters come across as retreads whom we've seen before?
- Do any of your characters grow or change throughout the story?
- Is there a moment at the end when this growth will be recognized by the reader?
- When will the reader cry?
- Is the story too gimmicky, relying too heavily on nudity, violence, shock, or special effects?
- Will the first 5-10 pages capture the reader's interest?
- Do the first 20-30 pages set up the central conflict?
- Does the middle build in intensity toward the Showdown at the end?
- Is the story, plot, or ending too predictable?
- Are all the loose ends tied up in the denouement (the resolution after the Showdown)?

CHECKPOINT 25

Sometimes it just doesn't work. You have story problems, character problems, and you're not quite sure how to solve them. When you are blocked or you sense something is wrong, what can you do?

1. Don't panic. We all go through this. Realize that you have the ability to solve your problems.

2. Take two weeks off. Don't worry about it. You may get inspiration during this period because you will be more relaxed.

3. Read a book; go to a seminar; flick out. Many of my "breakthroughs" have come on the plane while reading a book about writing.

4. Often you actually know where the trouble is. You have a gnawing feeling inside about something in your story, or perhaps a sense that "something" is wrong, but you ignore it because you don't want to do a major rewrite. In my script-analysis work, I don't know how many times a writer has told me the following: "I kinda knew what was wrong, but I guess I needed you to confirm it." The point is this: You have an inner sense that you must learn to trust, even when it makes the writing process uncomfortable and the rewriting painful. When you read your script through, if you naturally stop reading at some point, that often signals a problem.

5. Get feedback from other writers or consider using a script consultant.

6. Study mythology (Christopher Vogler's *Writer's Journey*) and understand your genre.

7. Revise your four-page treatment. Sometimes this helps you focus and get back on track.

8. Ask stupid questions. Don't be afraid to challenge your own ideas. Ask "What if?" Nothing is sacred. Anything goes. Maybe your hero should be the villain.

9. When revising, if solving one problem also solves another problem, you're on the right track.

10. Create a Character/Action Grid. Essentially, this is a mini step-outline, constructed on a few sheets of paper. Use it to identify each character's purpose and actions in the story. Most writers use it for their five to seven main characters.

On the next three pages you will find a format for the Character/Action Grid, developed by Donna Davidson and me. When Donna read the first edition of my book, she expanded my original tool for her own use. Donna has since published four novels and used the Grid for each. Feel free to photocopy these three sheets for your personal use. As you can see, the Character/Action Grid has two sections: 1) Character and Story (page 96), and 2) Actions (page 98).

Character and story

The sheet on page 96 allows you to develop four main characters on one page. The sheet on page 97 is exactly the same, except it is designed for just one character—it gives you more room to write. Not every cell in the grid needs to be filled. Make this tool *your* tool. Create your own categories. Better yet, create your own Grid.

At the bottom of the Grid page 96, you have room to think through your main turning points in terms of each character. Obviously, not each character will be involved with each turning point.

Actions

You will not be able to plot your entire screenplay on just one sheet of paper (page 98). You may need two or three of these sheets. In the second row of the grid, write the names of your five main characters. Then in the remaining rows and columns simply list each action a character takes. Dialogue can be considered action when it constitutes or creates movement. When Rose tells Jack in TITANIC (after Sunday service) that she cannot see him again and is returning to her fiancé, that is an action.

The Grid allows you to see the entire story on just a few sheets of paper. It helps you notice if a character is static or uninvolved in the action, or if a character's actions are repetitive rather than building. In other words, you can more readily see if you have a rising conflict or a stagnant story.

The Grid helps with pacing and spacing. Is there a major twist every so often? Are the subplots supporting the main plot? Are character actions crisscrossing throughout the story? Are all of your other major characters fully involved in the story? Does a character disappear for half the story? (That can be good or bad, depending on the story.)

I recommend use of the Grid after the first draft or when you are stuck. But you are the captain of your ship. Use it when you wish or not at all.

On page 99, you will find an example of a partially completed Character/Action Grid.

CHARACTER/ACTION GRID—Character and Story				
Title, genre, concept				
Theme or message				
CHARACTERS				
Role, purpose in story				
Occupation				
Conscious goal				
Personal motivation				
Inner need				
Flaw blocking need				
Backstory				
Dominant, core trait				
Other good & bad traits				
Imperfections, quirks				
Skills, knowledge, props				
Point of view, attitudes				
Dialogue style				
Physiology				
Psychology, Sociology				
Relationship w/others				
Catalyst				
Big Event				
Crisis				
Showdown				
Realization				
Denouement				

CHARACTER/ACTION GRID—Character and Story	
Title, genre, concept	
Theme or message	
NAME OF CHARACTER:	
Role, purpose in story	
Occupation	
Conscious goal	
Personal motivation	
Inner need	
Flaw blocking need	
Backstory	
Dominant, core trait	
Other good & bad traits	
Imperfections, quirks	
Skills, knowledge, props	
Point of view, attitudes	
Dialogue style	
Physiology	
Psychology, Sociology	
Relationship w/others	
Catalyst	
Big Event	
Crisis	
Showdown	
Realization	
Denouement	

CHARACTER/ACTION GRID—Actions				

Character/action grid example

I created the following as a small example of how to use the Grid. I created only three characters. I won't take you through the entire grid with them, nor will I outline the entire story. I just want to give you a feel for the Grid's use. You will want to list every important action of your main characters from the beginning to the end of the story.

CHARACTER/ACTION GRID — Character and Story

Char:	Jim	Sally	Max
Role:	Central character/hero	Love interest, 2nd opp.	Main opposition
Occ:	Investigative journalist	Animal rights advocate	Circus owner
Goal:	Exploit Blimpo the Elephant for a story	Save Blimpo the Elephant from exploitation	#1 Circus Act in U.S.
Motiv:	Salvage career	Blimpo saves her life (later)	Prove he's not a loser
Need:	Be more caring	Trust and love Jim	Respect animals
Flaw:	Anything for a story	Only trusts animals	Inhumane

CHARACTER/ACTION GRID — Actions

JIM	SALLY	MAX
Fired, but then gets last chance		
Dumped by Sally	Dumps Jim; can't trust him	Whips Blimpo
	Kidnaps Blimpo; chased	Chases Sally
	Hides Blimpo in Jim's yard	
Next morning: Finds Blimpo		

Continue outlining your characters' actions to the end. When the Grid is completed, you will be able to see your entire story on 1-3 pages. The structure, pacing, motivation, and plot lines will be easier to work with.

CHECKPOINT 26

Before you submit your script, do the following:

- Get feedback from writers' group members.
- Consider hiring a professional reader or script analyst.
- Review Checkpoints 1-24 one last time.
- Make adjustments. Is your script a "good read"?
- Be sure the script looks 100% professional and that it is formatted correctly.
- Register your script with the Writers Guild of America.
- Create a strategic marketing plan (see Book V).

CORRECT FORMAT FOR SCREENPLAYS & TV SCRIPTS

BOOK III

A Style Guide for Spec Scripts

How to use this guide
and its unique cross-referencing tools

This book gives you everything you need to know and only what you need to know to correctly format your screenplay, TV drama, or sitcom script. It also teaches you about writing and writing *style*. Every attempt has been made to simplify the material.

Professional scripts sometimes vary slightly in formatting style, and yet they all look basically the same—they all look like scripts. There are surprisingly few absolutes. These formatting guidelines are like accounting principles—they are generally accepted by the industry. They will increase your script's chances of being accepted by agents, producers, directors, and talent (actors and actresses).

This book is both a textbook and a reference book. It contains clear, how-to instructions and sample scenes. You can easily find information in any of the following ways.

1. Use the **index** (pages 156-158) to quickly find any subject area or term.

2. Read the **body of the text** (pages 110-152) as a style guide. It consists of numerous how-to instructions and explanations, which are easily spotted. Most are also identified by a letter code. This letter *reference code* can be cross-referenced to the same reference code in the sample scenes on pages 106-109. For example, on page 139 in the body of the text, you will find reference code [T] next to an explanation of OFF SCREEN. Using that reference code, you can cross-reference to page 109, where you will find the same reference code [T] next to an example of OFF SCREEN in the sample scenes.

3. Read the **sample scenes** on pages 106-109 and, using the same coding system explained in Number 2 above, cross-reference to an explanation in the body of the text. These codes appear in alphabetical order in the body of the text.

4. Note how the guidelines are grouped, and then go to specific areas that you need to study.

5. Check the glossary on page 155 for terms not defined anywhere else.

Some writers like to mark the first page of the index with a paper clip for fast access. The first page of the sample scene could also be marked with a paper clip.

All sample scenes and excerpts appear just as they would in an actual script, right down to the 10-pitch, 12-point font (see pages 111-112). One last thing to keep in mind before going on—you are writing a *spec* script (on *spec*ulation that you will sell it later) in standard spec screenplay format.

THE *SPEC* SCRIPT—HOW IT IS DIFFERENT

The *spec* script is the *selling* script. You write it with the idea of selling it later or circulating it as a sample. (Once it is sold, it will be transformed into a *shooting* script.) The *spec*-script style avoids camera angles, editing directions, and technical intrusions. You may use these tools, but only when absolutely necessary to clarify the story. Scenes are not numbered in the spec script; that's done by the production secretary after your script is sold.

All the camera and editing directions in the world cannot save a bad story, but too much technical intrusion can make even the best story a chore to read. The main reason you write a *spec* script is to tell an interesting story. So concentrate on the story and leave the direction to the director and the editing to the editor.

Virtually every script you buy from a script service or bookstore, or view in a script library, is a *shooting* script, or a variation thereof. Most screenwriting books contain formatting instructions for *shooting* scripts only. To make matters worse, some professional writers and producers still recommend the *shooting* script format because it's what they've always used and it's what working writers use when they are hired to write directly for a production.

But the *shooting* script is not a joy to read for agents, executives, and readers who must plow through dozens of scripts every week, week after week. The technical directions clutter the script and intrude on the reading experience. That's fine if the script is about to be produced, but it works against you if you want your story to flow smoothly to the reader, enticing him/her to buy or recommend it to the higher-ups.

Both script styles utilize the same standard screenplay formatting rules—master scene headings in CAPS, double-space to narrative description, dialogue indented, and so on. And the *spec* script occasionally employs some *shooting* script terms: MONTAGE, FLASHBACK, INSERT for notes and letters, and INTERCUT for telephone conversations.

The essential difference between the two styles is this: The *shooting* script format requires specific technical instructions so that the director, crew, and cast can more easily perform in the shoot. The *spec* script format emphasizes clear, unencumbered visual writing to sell agents and producers on a great story.

What follows is a sample of a title page (page 106) and sample scenes (pages 106-109) in standard spec screenplay format with the cross-referencing codes mentioned earlier. These samples scenes are followed by pages of explanations and instruction, which often provide alternate examples. After all, there is usually more than one way to apply the formatting guidelines. Last is a glossary and a complete formatting index.

A personal note: In response to the many owners of past editions of this guidebook who have written me concerning the content of the sample scenes that follow, I now feel compelled to explain that the scenes romanticize my teaching policy of tossing a candy mint to any student who makes a brilliant comment or asks a profound question. Yes, now it can be told, I am the perspicacious professor.

THE PERSPICACIOUS PROFESSOR

by

David Trottier

1234 William Goldman Dr.
Hollywood, CA 90028
213/555-6789
dave@clearstream.com

FADE IN: [A]
                    [F]
A large university campus. Students jam the walkways. A sign
on a building reads: "CINEMA DEPARTMENT."   [K]

        [C]
INT. SMALL CLASSROOM - DAY   [B]

Twenty students sit in rapt attention while a handsome PROFESSOR [I]
scrawls "FORMATTING" across the blackboard. Slung over his
shoulder is a leather pouch, the kind used by Sea World trainers,
only this one is filled with candy mints instead of fish.
    [I]
CHARLIE kicks back near a window, raises his hand. Two BUZZING [L]
flies vie for territorial rights to the chocolate on his face.

                    CHARLIE
            How do you handle phone calls?

The professor moonwalks to Charlie's desk carrying a demo phone.

            [R]   PROFESSOR
            Excellent question, my man.

He tosses the grateful boy a candy mint. Charlie catches it on
his nose and BARKS like a seal.   [M]

Outside Charlie's window, a YOUNG WOMAN in pigtails and a   [G]
pinafore yanks someone out of the phone booth and steps in.

    [C]
EXT. CLASSROOM - DAY   [H]
                    [J]
The young woman is CALCUTTA COTTER. With the phone to her ear,
she turns towards the classroom window and frowns at what she
sees -- the professor doing cartwheels down the aisle.   [G]

                    WOMAN'S VOICE (VO)   [U]
            Make him pay, Calcutta.

INTERCUT TELEPHONE CONVERSATION - CALCUTTA AND DEAN ZACK   [V]

The voice belongs to DEAN ZELDA ZACK who stands at her polished
desk with a swagger stick tucked under her arm.

                    CALCUTTA
            It'll work?

                    DEAN ZACK
            Stumps him every time.

The dean chortles. Calcutta smiles, then SLAMS the receiver.

2

INT. CLASSROOM - DAY
                              [N]
The professor's hand SLAMS the receiver of his demonstrator phone.

The students simmer with interest.

The door swings opens. Calcutta steps in and shuffles to her
desk.

                    PROFESSOR
[W]   Remember. It's gotta be lean.
          Description...dialogue.
                    (arching his brow)
          All lean, my pets -- lean!

He pirouettes and clicks his heels, to his students' delight.

Calcutta raises her arm and wags it aggressively.

A hush fades into silence. When she speaks, her lips are not
unlike those of Orson Welles when he said, "Rosebud."

                    CALCUTTA
          The <u>tabs</u>. Where do I set them?

The professor wilts under the heat of Calcutta's challenge. The
students exchange questioning glances as the professor stumbles
dizzily to his desk. He gazes blankly ahead to a spinning room. **[O]**

MONTAGE - THE PROFESSOR'S TRANCE **[D]**

-- The room spins.

-- He jabs at a giant tab key on a keyboard to no effect. In
   frustration, he hurls the computer out the window.

-- Dean Zelda Zack rides up to the same window on her swagger
   stick. He recoils. She transforms into a witch, CACKLES, and
   rides off.

-- The spinning room slows to a stop. **[M]**

BACK TO CLASSROOM

The students are horrified. Calcutta smiles gleefully.

The professor looks like he's just been hit by a Scud missile.

                    CHARLIE
          Our dear professor. What's wrong?

Several students clench the edges of their desks. Can he do it?
                                                        [P]
                          CHARLIE (OS)   [T]
               He's done for.

Murmurs of agreement. The professor stares at his shoes and
makes an attempt at moonwalking. His feet start remembering.

                          PROFESSOR
               Where to set your tabs. Assume
               a left margin at...um...at fifteen.

The students brighten in their seats. Calcutta frowns.

The professor is now in a serious moonwalking stride.

                          PROFESSOR   [S]
                          (the master)
               Dialogue at twenty-five.
               Parentheticals at thirty-one...

Calcutta nervously chews a pigtail.

                          PROFESSOR   [S]
               ...And then the character's name
               in caps! At thirty-seven!

Cheers and kudos. The professor's moonwalk has taken him to
Calcutta's desk where he towers over her limp form.

                          PROFESSOR   [S]
               But why, Calcutta? Why?

                          CALCUTTA
               Cuz everyone else always gets a
               candy, even Charlie, and I don't.

Her shoulders heave in heavy sobs.

INSERT - THE PROFESSOR'S POUCH   [E]

His fingers deftly lift a candy mint.

BACK TO SCENE   [E]

Calcutta lifts her head just as he flicks the candy into the air.
She catches it on her nose, BARKS like a seal, and consumes it
greedily. The students cheer.

As the professor pats her head, her pigtails rise as if to extend
her radiant smile.

The cover, title page, front page, and last page

OVERALL SCREENPLAY APPEARANCE

Physically, a screenplay consists of a front cover (of solid color index stock, at least 65 pound, preferably 110 pound), a title page (or *fly page*), the pages of the script itself (printed on one side only), and a back cover—all 8½" x 11", all three-hole punched. That's it. Nothing appears on the front cover, not even the title. Your script will be placed on a stack. Someone will write your title on the side binding with a magic marker. Don't do it for them.

To bind the script together, use Acco (or some other brand) No. 5 round-head brass fasteners, 1¼" in length. (Some people like to use No. 6 or No. 7.) It is fashionable to place the fasteners (or "brads") in the first and third hole and leave the middle hole empty. Do not bind a script in any other way. The above method makes it easy for producers and others excited about your work to make photocopies to pass around, which is something you want.

Here's a list of NO-NOs in preparing your script for submission to agents:

- No fancy covers, artwork, illustrations, or storyboards.
- Don't number the scenes. This is done after the script is sold.
- No fancy fonts or proportional fonts, only 12-point Courier.
- No justified right margins. See page 112.
- Don't type CONTINUED at the top and bottom of each page.
- Don't bold or italicize.
- Avoid camera and editing directions.
- Don't use a dot-matrix printer. Photocopies are okay.
- Don't date your script in any way. Scripts get old fast.
- Don't write "First Draft," "Final Draft," or any draft.
- No suggested cast list or character list with bios, unless requested.
- Don't include a list of characters or sets.
- Don't include a synopsis unless requested—you are selling your ability to write.
- Don't include a budget.

Your script should be about 100-110 pages—ideally, about 100 for a comedy and 110 for a drama. The latest trend has moved the page limit from 120 pages to 110. Don't "cheat" by using thinner margins, by squeezing more onto a page, by using a smaller typeface, or by widening dialogue lines beyond the standard 3-3½ inches.

The above rules may seem nitpicky, but they're easy to comply with, and adhering to them places you in the realm of the professional writer in the know, and helps you make a good first impression. Obviously, if your script is wonderful, but violates one of these little conventions, it is not going to be rejected. But why not give yourself every advantage to make sure your script is read in the first place?

THE TITLE PAGE

The example you see on page 106 is correct for a script that has not yet found an agent. Nothing else belongs on the page. You may add quotation marks around the title if you wish, or underscore it. If there are two writers and the two worked together and contributed equally, use an *ampersand* instead of the word *and*. For example:

```
                    "NAZIS IN SPACE"

                          by

             Bart Snarf & Buffy Bucksaw
```

When the word *and* is used, it usually means a writer was brought in later to rewrite the first writer's script. In other words, they didn't work together.

Your address and phone number should appear in the lower left or right corner. Once your script has found an agent, then the agent's contact information will appear on the title page. Your agent will be able to show you how to do that.

If you register your script with the Writers Guild or other service, you do not need to indicate as much on the title page. Although you want to register your script, posting the notice is not necessary. In other words, all you need is the title, author, and point of contact. That's it. (For information on the Writers Guild, see Books V and VI, or the index.)

TYPEFACE, MARGINS, AND TABS

Typeface
Always use Courier 12-point font. Do not use a proportional font, such as what is commonly used in typesetting. It compresses letters and characters to get more words on a

line. All books and magazines use a proportional font. The letters are squeezed together. The right margin is justified. It looks great, but it's anathema for screenplays.

Here's what is wanted: A good, old-fashioned PICA (for typewriters) or Courier 12-point, 10-pitch font with a ragged right margin. What is *point size*? This is how tall the letter or character is. What is *pitch*? Pitch refers to the number of characters that fill an inch. In other words, if you were to type ten characters side by side, print, and then measure them on the printed page, they should come to an inch. Let's try and see.

1234567890 — This is a Sabon 12-point proportional font. Ten characters measure less than an inch.

```
1234567890 -- This is a Courier 12-point, 10-pitch font.  It
works.  This is what you use in a screenplay.  It looks like
it's typed using a typewriter.
```

All of the examples in this format guidebook are in Courier so that they appear exactly the way they would appear in a script.

Why all the fuss over a font? Because the 10-pitch font is easier on the eyes of industry people who read dozens of scripts every week. It also retains the "one page equals one minute screen time" industry standard.

Margins

Because scripts are three-hole punched, the left margin should be 1.5 inches, the right margin a half inch. The top and bottom margins should be one inch each. Assuming the standard ten characters per inch (10-pitch font), that would mean a left margin at 15 (1.5 inches from the left edge of the paper) and a right margin of 80 (eight inches from the left edge of the paper). The right margin should be *ragged*.

Tabs

Although variations abound, let these standards guide you in setting your tabs:

- Left margin at 15 spaces (1.5 inches) from the left edge of the page.
- Dialogue at 25 spaces (2.5 inches); that's 10 spaces from the *left margin*.
- Actor's instructions at 31 (3.1 inches); that's 16 spaces from the *left margin*.
- Character's name at 37 (3.7 inches); that's 22 spaces from the *left margin*.

Make sure your dialogue does not extend beyond 60 spaces (6.0 inches) from the left edge of the page (in other words, a line of dialogue should be no wider than 3.5 inches, although some writers limit themselves to 3.0 inches), and actor's instructions beyond 50 spaces. The above guides are not written in stone—some writers indent 12 or 14 for dialogue, some indent 7 for actor's instructions, etc. As mentioned, a ragged right margin is preferred to a justified right margin.

PAGE NUMBERS

Page numbers should appear in the upper right, flush right, after which you double-space and resume your writing. Your first page does not carry a page number. (To those using typewriters instead of computers: If, in your final draft, you double the length of an early scene—say, on page 70—and you don't want to retype all the page numbers on the subsequent pages of the script, consider numbering the "extra" page *70A*. Anyone having a script that is overlong may consider using this trick as well. Just don't use it in the first 50 pages.)

[A] THE FIRST PAGE

Some writers write their title, CAPPED and underscored, at the top of the first page; but the great majority don't. A screenplay begins with FADE IN, as demonstrated on page 107. The example below is also correct, but includes a master scene heading.

```
FADE IN:

EXT. LARGE UNIVERSITY CAMPUS - DAY

Walkways are jammed with students.
```

CREDITS

Don't worry about where to place your opening and closing CREDITS. They're *not* required for the spec script. Besides, it's very hard to judge just how long it will take the credits to roll. If you insist on indicating the credits because you have this neat little opening written, then use this format:

```
ROLL CREDITS.   Or . . .    BEGIN CREDITS.
```

And after the last opening credit . . .

```
END CREDITS.
```

In the above example, CREDITS is treated as a "heading." However, it can also be included in the body of the description. The word TITLES is often used in place of CREDITS. Again, I strongly advise against indicating CREDITS or TITLES.

THE LAST PAGE

At the end of your screenplay, double-space (or triple or quadruple), type *The End*, and center it. As an alternative, double-space, flush right, and type FADE OUT.

Headings

Screenplays and TV scripts consist of three parts: 1) Headings (sometimes called *slug lines*), 2) Description, and 3) Dialogue. This section deals with headings. Headings always appear in CAPS and come in two general categories: Master scene headings and secondary headings.

[B] MASTER SCENE HEADINGS

A master scene heading consists of three parts.

First is the location of the camera. If the camera is located outside or outdoors, then use EXT. for EXTERIOR. If it is indoors, then use INT. for INTERIOR. (See page 123 for a discussion of "Camera Placement.")

Occasionally, the action moves back and forth through a doorway or opening. This can create a large number of master scene headings. Sometimes a scene begins outside, but quickly moves inside (or vice versa). In such cases, the following heading is permissible:

```
INT./EXT. CLASSROOM - DAY
```

The **second** part of a master scene heading is the location of the scene, the place where everything is happening. Usually one or two words will suffice. At code [C] on page 107, the location is a small classroom. I use the word "small" only because I don't want the director using one of those large, semi-circular auditoriums. I want a more intimate scene and perhaps a modest budget. Generally, you want master scene headings to be short and specific.

The **third** part of the master scene heading is the time of day. Most often this will be DAY or NIGHT. Avoid terms like DUSK, DAWN, LATE AFTERNOON, EARLY EVENING, HIGH NOON, GLOAMING, or the time on the clock. Use these only if absolutely necessary.

Occasionally, SAME is used to indicate that the scene takes place at the same time as, or just after, the previous scene. CONTINUOUS is occasionally used for a similar purpose—to show continuity. Sometimes LATER is used to indicate passage of time.

```
INT. KITCHEN - SAME
```

If a scene requires further identification because it is a dream, for example, such a clarification may be added as a **fourth** part of the master scene heading. Suppose your screenplay jumps all over time. In that case, you could additionally indicate the date (or the season) of the scene. Here are two examples:

```
EXT. TOKYO BAY - TWILIGHT - SUMMER, 1945

INT. BEDROOM - NIGHT - MARTY'S DREAM
```

An alternate method reads as follows:

```
INT. BEDROOM - NIGHT (MARTY'S DREAM)
```

Technically, if any of the three (or four) elements of a master scene heading change, you have a new scene, and must type in a new master scene heading with the change. Headings never appear as the last item on a page.

There are many ways to express a master scene heading. Here are the most common.

```
INT. CLASSROOM - DAY

INT.  CLASSROOM - DAY
```

As usual, variations abound, but the general form remains the same.

Recently, I have seen some scripts with master scenes bolded. I suspect this might become common practice in years to come, but until it does, I wouldn't bold anything.

[C] SPACING BETWEEN SCENES

Do you space twice or three times between master scenes? The correct answer is three. Twice used to be acceptable, but not anymore. You want to create as much white space as possible

Do not number your scenes (or shots) in a spec script. This is done by a production person after the final draft is sold and the script has gone into production.

SECONDARY HEADINGS

Master scenes often contain more than one dramatic unit, each of which requires a heading. These can be individual SHOTS (although you will seldom, if ever, use the term SHOT), or side locations, or specific instances that require highlighting. They provide you with ways to break up master scenes. Most of the rules regarding master scene headings apply to these as well.

Never end a page on a heading. Move the heading to the top of the next page.

Headings are always in CAPS. Although you may triple-space between master scenes, you normally double-space before and after secondary headings. Here are the most common uses of secondary headings. Let's start with an example.

In CASABLANCA, much of the action takes place at Rick's Cafe. These scenes can be quite long unless they are broken up into smaller scenes. For example, the master scene would be as follows:

INT. RICK'S PLACE - NIGHT

A few paragraphs into the scene and we go to a specific spot at Rick's place.

AT THE BAR

or

IN THE GAMING ROOM

We are still at Rick's Cafe. If we cut to the same location, but time has passed, we normally have a new master scene, and write:

INT. RICK'S PLACE - LATER

116

But we can probably get away with just:

```
LATER
```

Another advantage of using secondary headings is that you can direct the camera without using camera terms.

Suppose you want to focus on characters in an intense scene. Instead of the common ANGLE ON ILSA or CLOSE ON ILSA, you simply write:

```
ILSA

removes a gun from her purse and points it at

RICK

who stops cold in his tracks.  Looks at her in surprise.
```

Now you are using character names as headings, and the story flows easily without being encumbered by camera directions. Here is an excerpt from my screenplay, A WINDOW IN TIME. Note how this directs the camera without using technical terms.

```
EXT. TEMPLE RUINS - DAY

Abu nods gratefully to the Man in Khakis, then rushes to

THE TEMPLE BASE

where a small hole has been cut into the foundation.  The
Man in Khakis leads Abu into the blackness.

INSIDE THE CATACOMBS

Abu and the Man in Khakis crawl on all fours toward the
torch light ahead, and finally into

A LARGE CIRCULAR CHAMBER

where torches illuminate the stoic faces of a dozen workers
standing back against the single, circular wall.
```

You may have noticed in the above example that I get away without using master scene headings where they would normally be required. It is clear that the catacombs are an INTERIOR and that it's still DAY, and the same is true of the circular chamber. Be careful, however, not to get too creative. You never want to lose or confuse a reader. Your goal is a clear, unencumbered flow of images, sounds, and actions.

Don't end a sentence with a heading.

```
Rick struts into the
```

```
GAMING ROOM.
```

That's a no-no.

Other common secondary headings are the MONTAGE, the SERIES OF SHOTS, the INSERT, and the INTERCUT.

[D] MONTAGE and SERIES OF SHOTS

If I didn't use the MONTAGE sequence on page 108, I would need more master scene headings than Carter has pills. A MONTAGE is a sequence of brief shots expressing the same or similar idea, such as a passage of time, or a stream of consciousness. Here's a common format for the MONTAGE.

```
MONTAGE - SUZY AND BILL HAVE FUN TOGETHER

-- They run along the beach.  Suzy raises her countenance
   against the ocean spray.

-- They bicycle through a park.

-- Bill buys Suzy ice cream at a small stand. She stuffs it
   into his face.  The patrons chuckle.
```

And, of course you would end the montage with BACK TO SCENE or END MONTAGE or a new Master Scene Heading. It's okay to include dialogue in a MONTAGE sequence, but generally the focus is on beats of action.

In a very short MONTAGE, you can simply write the MONTAGE in paragraph form beginning with the word MONTAGE followed by a colon and the narrative description.

Some studios and production companies prefer a MONTAGE format that lists location, then action.

```
MONTAGE - SUZY AND BILL HAVE FUN TOGETHER

-- A beach - They race across the sand.  Suzy raises her
   countenance against the ocean spray.

-- A park - They bicycle down meandering paths.
```

-- An ice cream stand - Bill buys Suzy an ice cream cone. She
   stuffs it into his face. The patrons chuckle.

This style can also be used with the SERIES OF SHOTS.

Similar to the MONTAGE is the SERIES OF SHOTS, consisting of quick shots that tell a story. They lead to some dramatic resolution or dramatic action, whereas a MONTAGE focuses on a single concept (in the professor's case, hysteria or irrational fear). Here's an example of how to format the SERIES OF SHOTS.

SERIES OF SHOTS

A) The classroom spins.

B) The professor, in a panic, jabs the computer tab key.

C) He tosses the computer out the window.

D) He peers out the window, clutching his little dog.

E) Dean Zelda Zack rides up on her swagger stick, hurls the
    computer back at him, and CACKLES.

BACK TO SCENE

The MONTAGE is used more than the SERIES OF SHOTS. Even when the sequence is a true SERIES OF SHOTS, the MONTAGE format is often used. Sometimes the heading MONTAGE is used and then the shots are numbered exactly like the SERIES OF SHOTS example above. The rules are fluid here, and the terms are often used interchangeably. Use both devices sparingly.

Generally, a MONTAGE in the script is scored to music in the movie. For example, the above MONTAGE of Suzy and Bill could be lengthened to be accompanied by a love song—the MONTAGE concept would be "falling in love." The training MONTAGE from ROCKY is another example. Thus, the word MONTAGE often means: *Put the hit song here.* Now, don't *you* indicate the musical selection you'd prefer. In fact, don't refer to music at all. That's someone else's job. (For more on music, see page 134.)

FLASHBACKS AND DREAMS

Since the FLASHBACK is often abused by beginning writers, make sure that your use of it pays off dramatically. In terms of formatting, handle a FLASHBACK like a MONTAGE. (Note that secondary headings are often followed by a space-hypen-space and then an explanation of the heading, as with the example below.)

```
FLASHBACK - THE PROFESSOR'S BEDROOM BACK HOME
```

A much younger professor, in a panic, jabs the tab key of the computer. In frustration, he hurls the computer out the window. He peers out, then clutches his little dog as a young Zelda Zack rides up to the window on a broom. She CACKLES and rides off.

```
BACK TO PRESENT DAY
```

Another way to handle the above is to write the master scene heading as follows:

```
INT. BEDROOM - DAY - FLASHBACK
```

Or

```
INT. BEDROOM - DAY (FLASHBACK)
```

If a FLASHBACK covers several scenes, then indicate it with FLASHBACK SEQUENCE. Once the FLASHBACK SEQUENCE concludes, indicate PRESENT DAY at the end of the next master scene heading.

```
INT. CLASSROOM - DAY - PRESENT DAY
```

Or simply write:

```
BACK TO PRESENT DAY
```

FLASHBACKS, DREAMS, and DAYDREAMS are written in present tense. In fact, all the conventions that apply to FLASHBACKS also apply to DREAMS and DAYDREAMS.

[E] INSERT

The INSERT (also known as the CUTAWAY) is used to bring something small into full frame. This can be a book, news headline, sign, contract, letter, or a leather pouch filled with mints. You use the INSERT because it is important to draw special attention to the item. In the case of a letter or a document with a lot of text, you may wish to use the INSERT as follows.

```
INT. LIMO - LATE NIGHT
```

As Silvester steps into the limo, the chauffeur hands him a letter and bats his eyes like an ostrich.

```
                         CHAUFFEUR
              Your wife, sir.

Silvester tears the letter open as the door SLAMS shut.

INSERT - THE LETTER

              "Dearest Darling Silvester,

              I am leaving for Loon City to start
              a turkey ranch.  Don't try to follow,
              my peacock, or I'll have your cockatoo
              strangled.  There's plenty of chicken
              in the refrigerator.  I love you, you
              goosey duck.

                    Your ex-chick, Birdie"

BACK TO SCENE

Silvester smiles like the cat who ate the canary.

                         SILVESTER
              So long, Tweetie Pie.
```

Note that the contents of the note are indented like dialogue; however, quotation marks are used to quote the letter.

Once you have written the INSERT, it is good manners to bring us BACK TO SCENE (See Code [E] on page 109), although this can also be done with a new master scene heading or secondary heading. In any situation like this, opt for clarity and a smooth flow of the story.

Sometimes an INSERT is unnecessary. That is the case with my insert on page 109. Here is perhaps a more efficient way to write it.

```
Her shoulders heave in heavy sobs.

The professor dips into his leather bag and deftly snatches
a candy mint.

Calcutta lifts her head just as he flicks the candy into
the air.
```

Consistency
Notice that virtually all **specialized secondary headings** take on the same style. They name the special function first and then what it involves. Here's a list:

```
MONTAGE - SUZY AND BILL HAVE FUN TOGETHER

FLASHBACK - THE PROFESSOR'S BEDROOM

INSERT - THE LETTER

INTERCUT TELEPHONE CONVERSATION - CALCUTTA AND DEAN ZACK
```

You could even use this style with the SERIES OF SHOTS.

```
SERIES OF SHOTS - THE PROFESSOR'S DAYDREAM
```

INTERCUT

A full explanation of this secondary heading plus examples can be found under "Telephone Conversations" on page 140 and on page 107.

[F] ESTABLISHING SHOT

At the beginning of a movie or scene, there is often an establishing shot to give us an idea of where on earth we are. Don't use the camera direction ESTABLISHING SHOT; simply describe the image. In my script, we are in a university campus classroom. Note that paragraph code [F] in the script example on page 107 goes from general to specific, from long shots down to a close shot.

Here are two ways to present an establishing shot. The first is incorrect.

```
EXT. NEW YORK CITY - DAY - ESTABLISHING
```

Correct:

```
EXT. NEW YORK CITY - DAY

Manhattan sparkles in the sunlight.
```

The second example is preferred because it is more interesting, plus it directs the camera without using camera directions. It's obviously a long shot of the entire city.

[G] CAMERA PLACEMENT

In the scene beginning at reference code [B] on page 107, the camera is inside the classroom. We know this because the master scene heading is INT. SMALL CLASSROOM - DAY. The INT. means the camera is inside the classroom. However, the camera can SEE (at the first reference code [G]) out through the window to the young woman in pigtails and a pinafore.

Likewise, in the next scene, the camera is outside the classroom (by virtue of the EXT.) "looking" into the classroom as the professor performs cartwheels down the aisle (at the second reference code [G]). Thus, the window is used as a transitional device between scenes. (See page 114 for information on master scene headings and page 131 for information on directing the camera.)

[H]   The master scene heading is EXT. CLASSROOM - DAY. It could as easily have been EXT. PHONE BOOTH - DAY. The reason it isn't is that I felt the relationship between the phone booth and classroom would not be quite as clear. The choice, as always, is yours. Always strive to write clearly so that the reader can easily visualize the images and actions of your scene.

IMPORTANT NOTE

Many writers who are new to the business believe they must use fancy formatting techniques to get noticed by agents and producers. So they add CAMERA ANGLES, clever DISSOLVES, arty MONTAGES, and so on. I have a copy of the original BASIC INSTINCT spec script by Joe Eszterhas—the one he was paid $3 million for. There is not a single DISSOLVE, CUT TO, SERIES OF SHOTS, MONTAGE, INSERT, INTERCUT, or fancy technique in his entire 107-page script. Only scene headings, description, and dialogue—that's it. His focus is on telling a story through clear, lean, unencumbered writing.

Description

Screenplays and TV scripts consist of three parts: 1) Headings, 2) Description, and 3) Dialogue. We will now discuss description.

Narrative description is written in present tense because we view a film in present time. Double-space between paragraphs and do not indent. Keep your narrative description (and dialogue) on the lean side, providing only what is absolutely necessary to progress the story while emphasizing important actions and moments. Be clean and lean. Limit your paragraphs to four lines (not four sentences). Big blocks of black ink can make a reader black out.

As a general rule, allow one paragraph per beat of action or image. When a reader reads your paragraph, she should clearly "see" and "hear" what you describe. The result will be that she will "feel" what you want her to feel.

Beginning at [B] on page 107, there are a few things that I feel are necessary to set up for the sequence to work. First, my professor "looks" different from the stereotypical professor; plus, I establish that this scene is about formatting. Also, the professor has a leather pouch filled with candy mints. The pouch of mints is of tremendous importance to the story, so I take two lines to describe it.

I could have chosen to give the pouch a separate paragraph to give it more emphasis and to imply that the pouch deserves a separate camera shot.

Please notice that I do not describe anything in this classroom or even how the professor dresses. In this scene, I don't need to. Generally, physical descriptions of locations and characters should be sparse. (Please see "Character Descriptions" on page 126.)

In addition, don't write anything that can't actually be represented on the screen. Thoughts, feelings, motives, recollections, and writer's explanations of what's going on must be expressed in terms of action or dialogue, with action often being the better choice of the two.

Important action segments that may take a lot of screen time can be stretched out on the page by using short paragraphs and emphasizing specific images and emotions.

```
Duke sneers at the catcher.  Taps the bat twice on the
plate and spits.  A brown wad splatters on the plate.

The catcher refuses to notice.  Keeps his eyes ahead.

Smiley steps off the rubber.  Nervously works the rosin bag.
Wipes the sweat from his forehead with his arm.

Duke leans over the plate like he owns it.  Allows himself a
self-satisfied grin.
```

For action sequences, the following style (called *stacking actions*) is gaining favor for the simple reason that it is easy to read.

```
Duke sneers at the catcher.
Taps the bat twice on the plate.
Spits a brown wad that splatters on the plate.
Allows himself a self-satisfied grin.
```

Unless important to the plot, incidental actions—such as *he lights her cigarette, she moves to the table, she stands up*—should be avoided. The actions in the above example—*tapping the plate, spitting*—would be incidental if this weren't the bottom of the ninth, two outs, score tied, and a three-two count.

Finally, try not to end a page in mid-sentence or in mid-speech.

[I] CHARACTER FIRST APPEARANCES

The name PROFESSOR (top of page 107) is in CAPS because this is his first appearance in the screenplay. CHARLIE is likewise capitalized because it's the first time he appears in the story. So why wasn't "twenty students" capitalized? Because they weren't important enough to warrant drawing the reader's focus to them. You do not need to capitalize the names of characters who do not have speaking parts, but it is not incorrect if you do. (Please see page 127 for "Characters With More Than One Name.")

When a name in CAPS is followed by a possessive, the *s* is placed in lower case:

```
A BANSHEE's scream shatters the silence.
```

CHARACTER DESCRIPTIONS

When a character first appears in the script, you have an opportunity to suggest something of his/her nature. In most cases we do not need to know the character's height, weight, hair color, or the fact that she looks exactly like Cher. Do not give a driver's license description of your character and do not pin the name of a famous actor or actress on your character because it limits who can star in your screenplay. Here is how my co-writer and I describe our lead in TABLOID:

```
SAM BURNS sports a week's growth and unruly hair.  Every-
thing about him, from his wrinkled suit to his careless
manner, suggests he doesn't give a damn about anything.  In
fact, Sam would pass as a bum if it weren't for that hard,
confident look in his eye that tells you he's a man to be
dealt with.
```

Yes, we take certain liberties here, but so can you. This is one of the few places where you can. Notice that Sam not only has certain clothes, but he carries an attitude. He's been somewhere before he got here—he's a human with emotions and a past. Here is a description of a character in MY BEST FRIEND'S WEDDING:

```
This is DIGGER DOWNES, 36, kind eyes, an intellectual's
mouth, Saville Row's most unobtrusive and conservative
chalk-stripe suit.  He's gay, but you wouldn't guess it.
Loyal and wise, and you might.
```

Notice that the physical description of Digger is qualitative. It characterizes him without forcing an actor to have a certain color hair, eyes, and build. And from SCREAM:

```
BILLY LOOMIS, a strapping boy of seventeen.  A star quar-
terback/ class president type of guy.  He sports a smile
that could last for days.
```

In BODY HEAT, the central character is introduced as follows:

```
...we see the naked back and head of NED RACINE.
```

In the subsequent paragraph, we learn he that Ned is wearing shorts, smoking a cigarette, and gazing at a distant fire. That's it. (Also note my comments on "Visual Characterization" on page 128 and the character descriptions in Book IV.)

CHARACTER NAMES

All of your major characters deserve names as do your important minor characters. Characters with only one or two lines of dialogue *may* be given names, but usually *aren't* given names so that the reader knows not to focus on them.

When you give a character a name, especially in the first twenty or so pages, the reader believes that that character is important to remember. If you present too many characters too fast, the reader can be overwhelmed. For that reason, some minor characters and all characters with no speaking parts should be referred to in terms of their function or characteristics or both. For example, if you have three technicians who only appear in one scene, refer to them as GRUFF TECH, SEXY TECH, SHY GEEK, and so on.

Suppose you have six police officers speaking in a scene. You may choose to refer to them as OFFICER 1, OFFICER 2, OFFICER 3, and so on; but I don't recommend it. First, limit the number of speaking officers to one or two. If any of those six officers is an important character, try to give him most of the lines. If these officers are not important (have no lines, or just have one line, or only appear in one or two scenes), distinguish them in some visual way: MACHO COP, TOOTH PICK, CHUBBY COP. This makes them easier to visualize and signals to the reader that they are not particularly important.

[J] CHARACTERS WITH MORE THAN ONE NAME

CALCUTTA COTTER is in CAPS because although she was first introduced as a YOUNG WOMAN (below [M] on page 107), we are now learning her name for the first time. (See page 125 for more on "Character First Appearances.") If a character has more than one name that is used in the screenplay, you must take pains not to confuse the reader. You may give the character as many names, nicknames, or descriptions (the professor, the teacher, the great communicator, etc.) as you wish in the *description* section of the screenplay. But the character must be *referred* to by the same name in the dialogue caption (I'm not referring to the actual words of the dialogue, but to the character's name that appears in CAPS above the dialogue—that name should be the same throughout the script, with rare exception). (Also see "Character Caption" on page 136.)

VISUAL CHARACTERIZATION

This is a good place to mention that movies are visual, so it doesn't hurt to give your character a visual identification such as Charlie's peanut butter and flies.

Toward the bottom of page 107, Dean Zelda Zack, like the other characters, is described in sparse terms. However, I give her one thing that adds to her character *visually*: a swagger stick.

Also on page 107, I give the classroom its only physical description, and that is the fact that there is a window where Charlie sits. This is mentioned only because of its importance later as a transitional element. (See page 131 for more on transitions, and page 126, "Character Descriptions," for examples of visual characterizations.)

ACTION VERBS

Because a screenplay is written in present tense, it's easy to find yourself writing like this: John *is looking* at Mary. Suzy *is walking* past the cafe. Snake Koslowsky *is seated* on the couch. Replace those progressive forms written in passive voice with simple present tense written in active voice: John *looks* at Mary. Suzy *walks* past the cafe. Snake *sits* on the couch.

Now go one step further and create something even more active and concrete: John *gawks* at Mary, or John *gazes* at Mary. Suzy *scampers* down the sidewalk, or Suzy *sashays* down the sidewalk. Snake *coils* on the couch. Now the reader can more easily visualize the action and gain a greater sense of the character as well. And without a single adverb. Use concrete verbs as characterization tools.

Concrete, specific nouns also help us "see." *Dinghy, rowboat, yacht,* and *pontoon* are more descriptive than *boat.* And no adjectives are needed.

REDUNDANCIES

Avoid saying things more than once.

Redundant:

INT. CLASSROOM - DAY

Calcutta enters the classroom.

Correct:

```
INT. CLASSROOM - DAY

Calcutta enters.
```

Redundant:

```
EXT. OUTSIDE THE CLASSROOM - DAY
```

Correct:

```
EXT. CLASSROOM - DAY
```

Redundant:

```
He glares at her with anger.

                    STEVE
                 (angrily)
       I feel like breaking your nose.
```

Correct:

```
He glares at her.

                    STEVE
       I feel like breaking your nose.
```

...And you might not need the glaring.

[K] SIGNS, NEWS HEADLINES, SONGS, BOOKS, MAGAZINES, NOTES, AND LETTERS

There are many ways to handle signs. I chose to put CINEMA DEPARTMENT in CAPS, which is generally preferred. I could have as easily put it in quotes (like I did at code [K] on page 107), or underscored it, or any combination. Never use italics, however, to set apart anything. Stay with one font throughout.

News headlines, name plates, song titles, book titles, names of magazines, plaques, signs on doors, etc., are usually placed in CAPS. Sometimes the contents of notes, letters, or documents need to be shown. Here, you may want to use the INSERT. The INSERT is explained on pages 120-122.

[L] SOUNDS

The general rule of thumb is to place *important* sounds in CAPS, although you are not required to. This is why I capitalized BUZZING (on page 107). Do not use the archaic: SFX. BUZZING FLIES.

[M] SPECIAL EFFECTS

The climax of this little scene (code [M] on page 107) is Charlie catching a mint on his nose and barking like a seal. This may require a special effect. In the past, this may have been written FX. CHARLIE CATCHING A MINT ON HIS NOSE, but not now. (By the way, FX. and SPFX. both mean Special Effects; and SFX. means Sound Effects.) There is another possible special effect at [M] on page 108.

Don't use FX. or SPFX. unless it's absolutely necessary for the clarity of the story. Since special effects are costly, you don't need to advertise to the studio or producer how expensive your movie is going to be. Sell the script first. After the script is sold, a production person will go through your script and identify all the special effects.

SUBTITLES AND SUPERS

Subtitles are words that are superimposed on the screen to add some special meaning to what we're seeing and/or hearing.

```
EXT. CASTLE ON A LAKE - DAY

A beautiful storybook castle.

SUPER the legend:  "Once upon a time there lived a prin-
cess...."

Or...

A beautiful storybook castle.

The words "Once upon a time there lived a princess" FILTER
INTO VIEW.
```

Or just write SUPER. (See page 181 for an example.) Subtitles and superimpositions are capitalized because they are special effects. (For information on dialogue subtitles, see page 139.)

[N] TRANSITIONS

The SLAMMING of telephone receivers (bottom of page 107 and top of page 108) is a transitional ploy. I am suggesting to the director that once Calcutta SLAMS her phone, that we should CUT immediately to the professor SLAMMING his phone. This situation could also be handled with the MATCH CUT, discussed next.

EDITING DIRECTIONS

If I wrote the transition described above to include the editing direction MATCH CUT, I would have written it as follows:

```
The dean CHORTLES.  Calcutta smiles, then SLAMS the re-
ceiver.

                                             MATCH CUT:


INT. CLASSROOM - DAY

The professor SLAMS the phone receiver.
```

The MATCH CUT is used to match an object or image from one scene to the next. The above transition of Calcutta slamming her phone receiver to the professor slamming his is an example. However, an editing direction is not necessary here because the transition is obvious. Use the MATCH CUT only when the *match* is not already obvious.

The use of CUT TO is seldom necessary. Obviously, one must CUT at the end of a scene, so why indicate it? If such editing tools as the WIPE, IRIS, FLIP, and DISSOLVE are important to the story, then include them in the script, but be judicious. My advice is to not use them. Stay with occasional uses of CUT TO and MATCH CUT, maybe one or two per screenplay. Remember the trend today is toward lean and *clean* scripts.

CAMERA DIRECTIONS

Let's break current convention and rewrite this section utilizing our vast arsenal of camera and editing directions. Note as you read the bad example below how the technical directions detract from the story and slow down the read for the reader. (By the way, CU means CLOSE UP, and ECU means EXTREME CLOSE UP.)

```
INT. CLASSROOM - NEAR SUNSET

CU PROFESSOR SLAMMING the receiver of his toy phone.

PULL BACK and BOOM to ESTABLISH classroom.

PROFESSOR'S POV:   CAMERA PANS the class.

                                        DISSOLVE TO:

LOW ANGLE of the professor -- confident.

WIDE ANGLE of THE STUDENTS as they SIMMER with interest.

ZIP ZOOM TO ECU doorknob opening.   PULL BACK TO REVEAL
Calcutta coming through the door.   DOLLY WITH Calcutta's
SHUFFLING feet as she makes her way to her desk.

CLOSE ON the professor expounding.

SWIRLING SHOT of the professor in increasingly larger con-
centric circles.
```

Please, I beg you, don't do this to your script! First, you may insult the director. Second, it breaks up the narrative flow and makes the script harder to read. Third, you take the chance of showing off your ignorance. Fourth, readers are not pleased. So, go easy. Remember, the story's the thing. Concentrate on that. It's true that most shooting scripts (the scripts you buy to read) contain many such camera directions and technical devices. Keep in mind that these directions and devices were likely added *after* the script was sold to prepare it for the shoot.

There is an acceptable way to indicate all the camera directions your heart desires without using the technical terms. Simply be creative and write the script so that they're implied. On page 108, I write:

```
When she speaks again, her lips are not unlike those of
Orson Welles when he said, "Rosebud."
```

This may not be especially creative, but it is a very definite ECU (Extreme Close Up). At [N] on page 108, I use the word "hand" to imply a CLOSE UP or ANGLE of the phone SLAMMING. If he "surveys" the class, that might imply a POV (Point of View) shot, but certainly it is a MEDIUM SHOT of some kind. The students SIMMERING with interest is a REACTION SHOT of the entire class or REACTION SHOTS of individual students. (See how I give the director a choice!) If it's tremendously important to the scene that Charlie react strongly, I will write that reaction shot in a separate paragraph, as follows:

```
Charlie is so excited that he leaps from his seat and ex-
ecutes a flawless back flip.
```

Although correct, avoid headings like: ANGLE ON CHARLIE, CLOSE ON CHARLIE, and ANOTHER ANGLE. Noting the examples on pages 116-117, you may decide to put the camera on Charlie in this way:

```
CHARLIE

leaps from his seat and executes a flawless back flip.
```

The *spec* script's emphasis is on lean, visual writing. Your goal is to create images while avoiding the use of technical terms. Instead of CLOSE UP OF DARLENE'S TEAR, you write *A tear rolls down Darlene's cheek*. (It's obviously a close up.)

In conclusion, use camera directions and editing directions sparingly, only when they are really needed to clarify the action or add significantly to the story's impact.

WE SEE and TO REVEAL
Writers often use the camera direction WE SEE. Another favorite is PULL BACK TO REVEAL or REVEALING. Although correct, they are seldom the most interesting way to convey the action and details of the scene to your reader. Likewise, avoid WE MOVE WITH, WE HEAR, and other first-person intrusions.

B.g. and f.g.
B.g. stands for *background* and f.g. stands for *foreground*. These terms may be used in your narrative description to clarify action (for example: The T-Rex moves in the b.g.), but I recommend you use them sparingly. If you must use them, just write out the word (The T-Rex moves in the background) or better yet: Behind them lumbers the T-Rex.

[O] POV

Many writers use the POV ("point-of-view") device instead of writing creatively. Since the POV is a camera direction, you want to avoid it in your spec script.

Incorrect:

```
JOJO'S POV - The killer advances toward him.
```

Correct:

```
Jojo watches the killer advance toward him.
```

You're still directing the camera, even though you're not using camera directions. In RAIDERS OF THE LOST ARK, *What he sees:* is used in lieu of the POV.

The heading at Code [D] on page 108 could have been written: THE PROFESSOR'S POV. And that would be technically correct. Instead, I avoided the inclusion of a camera direction, but still made it clear (at Code [O]) that the spinning room is seen from the professor's point of view (POV).

At the second Code [G] on page 107, we see the professor from calcutta's point of view. This could have been written as CALCUTTA'S POV, but that would interrupt the narrative flow.

The PHANTOM POV is used when we don't know the identity of the character sneaking through the bushes toward your unaware hero. Just write: Someone (or something) pulls away tree branches and moves closer and closer to an unsuspecting Giselda.

MUSIC

Don't indicate music in your script unless it is essential to the progression of your story. If music is an integral part of your story—a movie about a rock singer, for example—then you may wish to indicate music in a general way:

A HEAVY METAL RIFF rips through the silence.

Or . . .

Upbeat ROCK MUSIC plays.

Another way to indicate music generically is to describe the sound of it: The radio BLASTS. Keep in mind that since music is a SOUND, you can emphasize it by placing it in CAPS.

A more professional approach is to intimate music indirectly by suggesting an emotional mood. You'll manage this through description, dialogue, and character. The director and composer will pick up on your *vibe*, and select or compose music that matches the emotion of the scene.

Regardless of whether you indicate music or not, the one thing you should *not* do is pick specific songs. Unless you own the rights to the songs, you are creating a no-win situation for yourself and a legal hurdle for anyone interested in buying the script.

[P] AUTHOR'S INTRUSION

In virtually every literary form, author's intrusion is unacceptable. In a screenplay, it is only permissible if it helps tell the story or clarifies something. However, don't overdo it and don't get cute. Don't interrupt the narrative flow of the story. When in doubt, stay out. At code [P] on page 109, I intrude with my sentence, "Can he do it?"

[Q] CONTINUED

In days past, if a scene did not conclude at the bottom of any page, it was customary to double-space and type (CONTINUED) at the lower right (flushed right); and type CONTINUED: at the upper left (flushed left) of the next page, followed by two vertical spaces, after which the writing resumed. This is no longer done. If you own software that writes CONTINUED automatically, disable that function.

SPECIAL NOTES

Once every blue moon you get a creative idea that does not fit any known formatting guidelines. In these few cases, simply write a note in a separate paragraph. You may place the note in parenthesis if you'd like, although it's not necessary. Here's an example from one of my old scripts:

```
(NOTE:  This scene is SHOT in BLACK AND WHITE.  It should
appear old and scratched as if it originated from a 1950's
public information library.  There are intentional JUMP
CUTS.)
```

Dialogue

Screenplays and TV scripts consist of three parts: 1) Headings, 2) Description, and 3) Dialogue. This section deals with dialogue.

The dialogue sections of a screenplay consist of three parts: 1) Character caption, 2) Actor's direction, 3) and Character's speech (the dialogue).

[R] CHARACTER CAPTION

First is the character name or caption, sometimes called the *character cue*. It always appears in CAPS. A character is referred to by exactly the same name throughout the screenplay. In the narrative description, you may use a variety names, but the character cue for a character should be the same throughout the script. (See page 127.)

ACTOR'S DIRECTION

Directly below the character name is the *actor's instructions*, sometimes called *personal direction* or *parentheticals* or *wrylies*. The term *wrylies* derives from the tendency in many beginning screenplays for characters to speak wryly.

```
                    LEFTY
                  (wryly)
         I've had my share of mondo babes.
```

Wrylies can provide useful and helpful tips to the reader, usually suggesting the subtext or attitude of the character. However, keep in mind that wrylies are optional and should be used with moderation. Avoid telling your actors how to act. In most cases, the context of the situation and the character's actions will speak for themselves.

On page 109, I use only one wryly, and you could argue for its omission on grounds that it is redundant—it is already evident by his action (moonwalking) that he is "the master" once again.

Generally, don't use wrylies to describe actions, unless those actions can be described in a few words, such as "tipping his hat" or "producing a stiletto." (See example near code [W] on page 108.)

Actually, this is not a bad tactic since some executives read dialogue only. A few well-placed wrylies can enhance the value and comprehension of a scene. I hasten to add that an executive seldom reads a script until a coverage is written by a reader (story analyst). Most professional readers read the entire script.

Avoid using the word *beat* (a theatrical term indicating a pause). It's usually best not to instruct an actor when to pause. If you must indicate a pause, find a more descriptive word than *beat*. Instead, indicate a small action that accomplishes the same purpose, but which also adds a characterization.

Dull:

```
                COQUETTE
        So why...
            (a beat)
        ...did you come here?
```

Interesting:

```
                COQUETTE
        So why...
            (raising her lips)
        ...did you come here?
```

CHARACTER'S SPEECH

The third part of dialogue is the speech itself, the words to be spoken. Because speech is indented, you do not use quotation marks or italics to indicate the spoken word. Avoid hyphenation and maintain a ragged right margin. Each speech should be as brief as possible, and generally convey one thought. One or two sentences is plenty in most cases. Fragments are welcome. Avoid long speeches.

Write all numbers out except years: "I've told you twenty-five times now that I was born in 1950." Avoid using exclamation points (and making the speech look like a want ad)! Avoid underlining words for emphasis unless it is crucial to understand the story. When working with dialects and accents, sprinkle in bits of dialect and phonetically spelled words just to give us a flavor of the accent or regional influence. Make sure the speeches are easy to read. For information on dialogue punctuation, see page 144. For information on where to set your tabs, see page 112.

[S] CONTINUING AND CONT'D

On page 109, the professor begins to speak, then stops, then continues. In fact, I interrupt his speech three times with narrative description (each continuation of his speech marked with code [S]). In the past, this would have been handled in one of two ways:

```
                    PROFESSOR
                  (continuing)
          But why, Calcutta?  Why?


                    PROFESSOR (cont'd)
          But why, Calcutta?  Why?
```

The above devices have fallen completely out of use. Don't use either *continuing* or *cont'd*.

MORE

When someone's dialogue does not conclude at the bottom of the page, type (MORE) directly below the last line of dialogue.

```
                    BUGSY
          I am at the bottom of the page,
          and I'm running out of room.
                    (MORE)
```

At the top of the next page, continue as follows:

```
                    BUGSY (cont'd)
          I'd like to continue my speech.
```

There is now a trend to eliminate the use of (MORE) and (cont'd) altogether. A better alternative is to simply conclude the speech at the bottom of the page or move it all to the top of the next page. You can cheat occasionally on your top and bottom margins (not on your left and right margins). Avoid ending a page in the middle of a speech and never end a page on any kind of heading.

[T]   OFF SCREEN (OS) and VOICE OVER (VO)

OFF SCREEN, at code [T] on page 109, indicates that Charlie is in the scene—he's at the location of the scene—but that he is not in the camera frame. We hear his voice, but do not see him on the screen. Why do I want Charlie OFF SCREEN? Because I want the camera to focus on the professor, whose back is now to the class. Now, if Charlie is not only off screen but also out of the scene (not in the classroom), and the professor HEARS his voice—say, in his mind—then this is a VOICE OVER as follows:

```
                CHARLIE (VO)
          You're done for, old man.
```

The voice trails off. The professor sees no one.

If Charlie is in the scene and hears his own voice in his head, that's still VOICE OVER.

Narration is VOICE OVER. In cases where a character is on screen and we hear his thoughts or he narrates his own story, use the VOICE OVER. In phone conversations where the person on the other line is not "in the scene" but we hear her voice, this would be a VOICE OVER. (See "Telephone Voice" on page 140.) Recently, I've seen scripts where VO is not used in telephone conversations, and that's okay as long as the script is clear and not confusing. (Note: Some writers write O.S. and V.O.)

OVERLAPPING DIALOGUE

There are two ways to handle overlapping and simultaneous dialogue. One is to simply indicate "overlapping" or "simultaneous" in the parenthetical actor's instructions. A less-preferred method (because it is difficult to read) is to treat the dialogue the same way you treat subtitles. An example follows.

Subtitles
Subtitles are words that are superimposed on the screen to add some special meaning to what we're seeing and/or hearing. Now here's an example of subtitles that are used to translate or otherwise comment on dialogue. This method could also be used for simultaneous dialogue. Simply place one character on the left and the other on the right.

INT. SPACESHIP CONTROL ROOM - NIGHT

Diptar enters the large room and bows before Grand Master.

```
      GRAND MASTER            SUBTITLES
   Raltar.                 Report.
```

```
        DIPTAR                        SUBTITLES
Orf pok etar vespar.        The brain evacuator is ready.
Nit etular orf vorpar       The earth specimens are in
quex glipular.              place.


      GRAND MASTER                    SUBTITLES
     (deeply felt)          Soon we will have complete
Flippar eglip xerox         command of their language,
clinggu, kalipsu...         customs, and...
zzzzzzzzipar.               reproductive techniques.
```

No doubt, you recognize this scene from my classic script RATMAN FROM SATURN.

For another example of simultaneous dialogue and overlapping dialogue, see the comedy scene on page 67-68.

[U]   THE TELEPHONE VOICE

Voices coming through telephones, walkie-talkies, radios, and similar devices are VOICE OVERS. Sometimes I see: *(on phone)* or *(amplified)* or the antiquated *(filtered)* typed adjacent to the name. In any case, the person speaking is obviously not in camera and not at the scene location. At code [U] on page 107, I use a VOICE OVER (VO) for clarity. For a discussion of VOICE OVER and OFF SCREEN, see page 139.

Television

Treat the television set as a separate character. If there is a specific character who is on television, simply indicate as much in your description and type the character's name as the character caption or cue. If you want to be especially clear, add *(on TV)* as follows:

```
        JOCK JIM (on TV)
Hi, Mom.  We're number one!
```

[V]   TELEPHONE CONVERSATIONS

There are many ways to handle phone conversations. At code [V] on page 107, I use the INTERCUT. This indicates to the director that I want to intercut (or crosscut) between the two people who are speaking on the phone. I want to SEE both people (not at the same moment, of course). The INTERCUT example on page 107 is such a short conversation that it is really unnecessary to INTERCUT. I only did it to demonstrate its use to you.

Because the INTERCUT may also be used to present two scenes simultaneously, it can be utilized as follows:

```
INTERCUT - JOHN'S BEDROOM/MARY'S KITCHEN
```

Or, you may indicate INTERCUT, then double-space and describe the scenes or situations in the narrative description. Finally, you'll double-space and conclude with either END INTERCUT or a heading. At the bottom of page 107, my INTERCUT example ends, but I do not indicate END INTERCUT because I "cut" to a heading at the top of page 108.

The INTERCUT device gives the director complete freedom as to *when* to intercut between speakers. (He/she has complete freedom anyway, so why not be gracious?) The reason you use this device is that otherwise you would have to write a master scene heading with each change of speaker. This can become laborious and interrupt the story flow. On the other hand, it may improve the story and give you more control over whom the camera is on at any point in the conversation. Let's rewrite the scene that begins at [H] on page 107 without the INTERCUT, using master scene headings.

```
EXT. CLASSROOM - DAY

The woman in the phone booth is CALCUTTA COTTER.  With the
phone to her ear, she turns toward the classroom window and
frowns at what she sees -- the professor doing cartwheels
down the aisle.

                    DEAN ZACK (VO)
          Make him pay, Calcutta...

INT. DEAN'S OFFICE - SAME

DEAN ZELDA ZACK stands at her desk with a swagger stick
tucked under her arm.  A big sign that says "DEAN, CINEMA
DEPARTMENT" sits on her polished desk.

                    DEAN ZACK
          ...Make him pay.

INT. PHONE BOOTH - SAME

Calcutta's excitement is subdued by doubt.

                    CALCUTTA
          It'll work?
```

```
INT. DEAN'S OFFICE - DAY
```

Zack's confident smile reveals gold caps over her front teeth.

```
                  DEAN ZACK
          Stumps him every time.
```

The swagger stick slashes the desk. The delirious dean
CHORTLES with satisfaction.

```
EXT. PHONE BOOTH - SAME
```

The CHORTLING is heard through the phone receiver. Calcutta
smiles, then SLAMS the receiver.

Now let's take a third tack. Suppose you don't want the camera on Dean Zelda Zack, nor do you want to hear the dear dean. In such a situation, the conversation would read something like this:

```
EXT. CLASSROOM - DAY
```

With the phone to her ear, CALCUTTA COTTER turns toward the
classroom window and frowns at what she sees -- the professor doing cartwheels down the aisle.

```
                  CALCUTTA
          I'll make him pay, all right --
              (turns to phone)
          You're sure it'll work?
              (nodding)
          Beautiful.
```

Calcutta urges a smile, then SLAMS the receiver.

This version also works well. The only thing we're missing is the identity of Calcutta's information source. It may serve the script better dramatically to withhold the name of this person. Ask yourself: What is the best way to move the story forward?

Also, note that instead of using the word *beat* or *pause*, I give Calcutta little actions (turns to phone; nodding) that accomplish the same purpose.

COMPUTER CONVERSATIONS

How do you show e-mail conversations? Do you represent the typed words as dialogue? First of all, only words that are spoken should appear as dialogue. That is what dialogue is. However, if a person repeats out loud what she reads on the monitor, then you could write what she actually says as dialogue. Otherwise, you want to find a clear way that doesn't confuse the reader or slow down the read. Perhaps, you can use a variation of the INSERT.

```
Sid faces his computer monitor, then types on the keyboard.

ON THE MONITOR

Sid's words appear:

          "But Renee, they're tapping my phone
          conversations."

BACK TO SID

who studies Renee's response.

ON THE MONITOR

Renee's response appears:

          "You're being silly, Sid."
```

Notice that the words that are typed are indented like dialogue and appear with quotation marks. You could also go to a shorthand version of the above by simply omitting the phrases "Sid's words appear" and "Renee's response appears." It goes without saying that you don't write something like SID'S POV - THE MONITOR.

MUSIC LYRICS

There may be a rare instance where you'll need to include music lyrics in your script because a character sings them. First of all, never include lyrics from a song whose rights are not owned by you. It's a huge negative when a reader sees music lyrics from a popular song in a script. If you are creating a musical, or quoting a poem or song that is in the public domain, or even have a character who is singing nonsense for comedic effect, then you can write lyrics in two different ways. One is to write them as dialogue (since they are dialogue) in stanza form, just like a poem. An alternative is to use slashes, as follows.

```
                    MCKAY
          Well, you take the high road/and
          I'll take the low road/And I'll
          be in Scotland before you.
```

[W] DIALOGUE PUNCTUATION

The use of the dash (--) and the ellipsis (...) has become very clouded in recent years. Usually, they are used to make dialogue look like...well -- er, dialogue.

There used to be very definite literary rules about these. Today they are used interchangeably and you may use them anyway you like—whatever feels good to you to make your dialogue look conversational. (Be careful not to overuse them.) However, understanding their actual use in terms of writing dialogue can be very helpful in presenting a consistent pattern in your written communication.

> -- The dash indicates a sudden shift or break in thought, or to show emphasis. It is used when one character interrupts another, or shifts his thought, or a character is interrupted by a sound or an action, or a character speaks as if interrupted or with sudden emphasis.
>
> The dash is written two different ways:
>
> > Example 1 -- Space, hyphen, hyphen, space for narrative description and dialogue.
> >
> > Example 2 - Space, hyphen, space for headings.
>
> ... The ellipsis is used for continuity. A character will start speaking, then pause, and then continue. When a character is interrupted, and then continues later, the ellipsis is used instead of the dash.

Here's an example of both the dash and the ellipsis.


```
EXT. BALCONY - EVENING

Coquette dabs her eyes with a handkerchief.  Suddenly, Vivi
blunders through the French doors.  Coquette turns expect-
antly, then puts on an angry face.

                    COQUETTE
          Why did you come here?

                    VIVI
          I came here to --

                    COQUETTE
          I don't want to know why you came
          here...
```

He moves earnestly toward her.   She softens.

                COQUETTE
      So why...
            (raising her lips)
      ...did you come here?

Vivi's lips are now just a silly millimeter from hers.

                VIVI
      I came here to...

His gaze fades into a blank stare, then stupefaction.

                COQUETTE
      You have forgotten --

                VIVI
            (recovering)
      But one kiss and I will remember
      why I came here.

He lays one on her, then looks joyously into her confused face.

                VIVI
      I came here to kiss my
      Coquette -- you!

An equally acceptable way to present an ellipsis in screenplays is to space after the ellipsis as follows:

                COQUETTE
      So why...
            (raising her lips)
      ... did you... come here?

For another example of dialogue punctuation, see the comedy scene on pages 67-68.

How to format TV scripts

This section builds on information in the previous sections of this book. Sample scenes of a sitcom spec script can be found on pages 153-154.

TV MOVIES

A teleplay for a TV movie (called *long form* or *MOW* for "Movie-of-the-Week") is normally seven acts and about 100 pages for a 93-minute TV movie slated for a two-hour time slot. If you write such a teleplay, I recommend you use standard spec screenplay format as discussed in the previous section. That way, you can avoid the pain of delineating acts and pacing the story's major turning points for commercial breaks. Besides, your MOW could actually become a feature movie in the selling process. Just write it as a feature screenplay—this is perfectly acceptable to virtually all MOW production companies. Once your teleplay is sold, then you can convert it into the seven-act format preferred by the production company.

If you're curious about act lengths, these are standard for most MOWs.

Act One:	18-23 pages
Act Two:	12-15 pages
Act Three:	12-15 pages
Act Four:	9-12 pages
Act Five:	9-12 pages
Act Six:	9-12 pages
Act Seven:	9-12 pages

As mentioned before, use standard spec screenplay format. At the end of each act, you will break to a new page and center the act number at the top of that page (ACT ONE, ACT TWO, and so forth). From the act designation, double or triple space and write the next scene. It's as simple as that.

Acts should end on dramatic moments. Acts One and Three should end on particularly strong twists, cliffhangers, or dramatic moments to keep people from switching channels at the first commercial break and at the "end of first hour" break.

PILOTS

It is nearly impossible for novices to break into television with a new series pilot or mini-series. If you have a hot idea that you believe in, write the pilot as a TV movie (using standard spec screenplay format) and market it as a feature script or TV movie. That way, it will be easier to get it read. If it truly is a great series idea, the agent or producer reading it will see that potential.

DRAMATIC SERIES

If you want to write an episode for a one-hour series—whether a dramatic series like ER, or one more humorous like ALLY MCBEAL—you will still use standard spec screenplay form (as used with feature scripts). You do not need to indicate scenes; however, you must designate the four acts, teaser, and tag.

Teaser
This is the brief (about one minute or so) initial section establishing the show. Seldom do you find an episodic series anymore that doesn't open with some kind of teaser. However, it is seldom indicated as a TEASER in the script. Most scripts simply FADE IN just like a feature screenplay.

The four acts
After the teaser, break to a new page and center ACT ONE at the top of the page, triple space, and write out the scenes just as you would in a feature screenplay, using standard spec screenplay format.

Many production companies also request that you add END OF ACT ONE at the end of the act (just triple space and center END OF ACT ONE), after which you break to a new page to the second act, and so on. Some shows, like the *Star Trek* series, have five acts. After each act, break to a new page.

Tag
The tag, often called the epilogue, is the brief (about one minute or so, and often less) ending section that ties up loose ends. In some shows, this is "scenes from next week's episode." Usually, the epilogue or tag is identified as such at the top of the page.

Title page and script length
Your script will be about 54 pages in length.

The title page for any episodic TV show, regardless of length, is similar to that of a feature script, except that the title of the episode is included along with the title of the series. Here is an example from an imaginary series entitled L.A. SCRIPT DOCTORS.

```
               L.A.  SCRIPT  DOCTORS


            "THE PERSPICACIOUS PROFESSOR"
```

The title of the episode, in addition to being set aside in quotes, can be underscored. If you prefer, it can appear in upper and lower case. The point is to distinguish it from the series title above it. Also, you can space twice (as I did) or three times between the series title and the episode title.

It may be worthwhile to acquire a script from the series itself for writing style, number of acts, how acts are labeled, and formatting quirks (keeping in mind that you are writing a spec script, not a shooting script, and that you will avoid camera angles and editing directions in your script.) Also, try to get a copy of the show's bible (see page 280).

SITUATION COMEDY

Situation comedy (sitcoms) utilizes a mutant variation of standard spec screenplay format. Because of the special format, several pages of explanations plus an example follow.

If you want to write for a specific TV show, obtain a copy of one of their scripts, since each show varies slightly in formatting style, as you will see in the explanations that follow. Keep in mind that scripts you purchase are shooting scripts and not spec scripts, but it always helps to become familiar with the writing style of the show. Sitcoms are either taped or shot on film, which is one reason for variations in formatting style. If possible, get the show's bible as well (see page 280).

If you have a series idea for a new sitcom, you face huge obstacles in marketing it. Generally, you need to be somewhat established in the television industry to have a chance. See Book V for more information.

A half-hour sitcom script is about 40-50 pages, but can be longer depending on the show. This differs from standard spec screenplay form, which is about a page per minute of screen time.

The title page for a sitcom script is handled in the same way as a dramatic series script. See example above for L.A. SCRIPT DOCTORS.

A sitcom is simpler than a screenplay, both in structure and content. Comparing the screenplay scene on page 107 to the sitcom scenes on pages 153-154 should prove instructive. What follows applies to sitcom scripts only.

The cast list and sets list
Although these two lists appear in shooting scripts, you will *not* include them in your spec script. They are *not* required. If you are writing a shooting script, the cast list will include any actors already assigned to the series. Usually, the characters appearing every week are listed first, followed by any guest characters. The sets are listed in three categories: exteriors, interiors, and stock shots.

Typeface, margins, and tabs
Like all other scripts, sitcoms are written in Courier 12-point. Margins for sitcom scripts are at 1¹/₂ inches on the left, one inch on the right, and one inch at the top and bottom. Tabs from the left margin are 10 spaces for dialogue (although some scripts indent more) and an additional 12-14 spaces to the character cue (character's name).

Page numbering
Page numbers are typed at the top right corner of each page and are usually followed by a period. Some shows ask you to indicate parenthetically the act and scene numbers just below the page number. That is what I did in my example (pages 153-154). Some shows, such as *Frazier*, ask you to indicate only the letter of the scene below the page number (without indicating the act number). Other shows only require a page number at the top right corner of each page.

Acts and scenes
Sitcoms consist of a teaser, two acts, and a tag. The first act ends on a major turning point, followed by a commercial. Acts are designated in CAPS (for example, ACT ONE) and are centered at the top of the page in the same manner as a dramatic series. At the end of the act, break with END OF ACT ONE, centered two or three spaces below the end of the act.

A teaser is often not included in a spec script, but when it is, it is designated as a TEASER. A tag is designated as the final scene in ACT TWO, or as a TAG, or not included at all. Again, it depends on the sitcom series you are writing for.

In sitcoms, scenes are designated with letters: Scene A, Scene B, and so on. Sometimes the word "scene" appears in CAPS: SCENE A, SCENE B, and so on. Often, you only see the letter without the word "scene": A, B, and so on.

Please note the sample scenes on pages 153-154. Each time you change to a new scene, you break to a new page, come down about a third or a half of the page, and then center your scene designation and place it in CAPS.

On page 154, we have a new scene. Naturally, if this were a continuation of the previous scene, I would have continued the scene at the top of the page.

End scenes with a CUT TO: or FADE OUT, neither of which must be underscored.

Occasionally, you see a script that includes the designation for an act along with each new scene change, as follows:

ACT ONE
Scene D

Only do this if the particular sitcom you are writing for requires it.

Headings

Each scene begins with a master scene heading—indicating exterior or interior camera position, location, and day or night—written in CAPS and underscored, as follows:

INT. SMALL CLASSROOM - DAY

In a few scripts, the characters in the scene are included parenthetically, as follows:

INT. JERRY'S APARTMENT - DAY
(Jerry, Kramer, Elaine)

In either case, you will double space to description.

Description

Narrative description always appears in CAPS and is single spaced. Because a sitcom is really a TV play, the emphasis is on dialogue rather than action, so there will be comparatively less narrative description and more dialogue in a sitcom than in a motion picture screenplay.

Entrances and exits

In situation comedy, there are very few changes in location (sometimes none). To keep the read from bogging down, and because sitcoms are really stageplays written for television, all entrances and exits of characters are underscored. This includes a character movement from place to place within a scene. For example:

ELLEN STEPS OUT OF THE CLOSET AND INTO THE LIVING ROOM

Or

ROZ ENTERS FRAZIER'S BOOTH

Or

BART CROSSES INTO THE KITCHEN

In addition, all first appearances of characters are underscored. Furthermore, at the beginning of each scene, after the heading, establish which characters are in the scene. Do this with the first sentence of narrative description. Note my example on pages 153 and 154.

Sounds

Sounds no longer need to be underscored. However, on occasion, there may be a particularly important sound that you want to emphasize. In such cases, double space and write the sound out as follows:

SOUND: DOORBELL RINGS

Special effects are handled in exactly the same way.

FX: NUCLEAR EXPLOSION

It's hard to imagine much need for a special effect in a sitcom script.

Dialogue

Because there is such an emphasis on the dialogue in television comedy, it is double-spaced for ease of reading. Actor's instructions (wrylies) are used more freely than in a screenplay, and are usually placed within the dialogue block itself. (Sometimes they are brought to the left margin, but they are always enclosed in parenthesis.)

Here's one of my favorite lines from a *Seinfeld* script. (George pretends he is a marine biologist to impress Holly. Suddenly they come upon a beached whale and a crowd.)

                    HOLLY

        (BLURTS) Stop! Everyone, this

        is one of the world's foremost

        marine biologists. (WITH PRIDE)

        This...is George Costanza.

AS ALL EYES TURN TO GEORGE, A MAN WITH A VIDEOCAMERA BEGINS
CAPTURING THE MOMENT FOR POSTERITY.

ACT ONE

Scene A

FADE IN:

INT. SMALL CLASSROOM - DAY

About 8 STUDENTS AWAIT THE PROFESSOR, WHO ENTERS WITH
EXCITEMENT. OVER HIS SHOULDER IS A STRAP SUPPORTING A
LEATHER POUCH, THE KIND USED BY ANIMAL TRAINERS, ONLY THIS
ONE IS FILLED WITH CANDY MINTS INSTEAD OF FISH.

CHARLIE RAISES HIS HAND.

                    CHARLIE

          Hey, Mr. Professor, how do you

          handle phone calls in a script?

                    PROFESSOR

          (SCINTILLATING) A most excellent

          question.

HE TOSSES THE GRATEFUL BOY A CANDY MINT. CHARLIE CATCHES
IT IN HIS MOUTH AND SMILES BROADLY.

                                        FADE OUT

Scene B

INT. DEAN'S OFFICE - DAY

CALCUTTA COTTER SPEAKS WITH DEAN ZELDA ZACK.

                    CALCUTTA

          ...And then the professor gives

          everyone a candy -- all except me.

DEAN ZACK SLAPS HER SWAGGER STICK ACROSS HER POLISHED DESK.

                    DEAN ZACK

          Make him pay, Calcutta, make him

          pay. (PACING) Now do exactly

          what I told you. It stumps him

          every time.

CALCUTTA EXITS.

                    DEAN ZACK

          Now, Mr. Professor, let's see you

          get out of this one.

DEAN ZACK LAUGHS INSANELY.

                                        FADE OUT

Glossary of terms not discussed elsewhere

ANGLE - Directs the camera to a particular person or object. The character's name itself could be written as a heading in CAPS and serve the same purpose. Angles (or SHOTS) can be wide, low, tight, close, high, bird's eye, etc.

AD LIB - This instructs the actors to fill in the dialogue with incidental lines.

ANAMORPHIC LENS - A lens used to shoot a wide-screen film; also, to project it onto the screen.

CRANE SHOT - A moving shot from a camera on a lift.

DISSOLVE - An editing direction where one scene "melts" into another, the former fading out while the latter fades in.

DOLLY or **TRUCK** - Picture this as a camera on wheels. Variations abound: CAMERA IN, PULL BACK TO REVEAL, TRUCK WITH, CAMERA PUSHES IN, etc.

FADE OUT - The image fades to black. This editing direction appears two spaces below the last line, flush right.

FREEZE FRAME - The image freezes on the screen and becomes a still shot. Often used with END CREDITS.

MOS - Without sound. Originated with German director Eric von Stroheim, who would tell his crew, "Ve'll shoot dis mid out sound." Use this to describe action that appears without sound. Occasionally characters will speak MOS in the b.g.

O.C. - OFF CAMERA, a term now used only in television.

OVER THE SHOULDER - Shooting over someone's shoulder from behind.

PAN - A stationary camera pivots back and forth or up and down (TILT).

PINKS - From the expression *fix it in the pinks*. Revisions of shooting scripts are usually done on colored paper.

REVERSE SHOT - When we're looking over Vivi's shoulder to Coquette, then reverse to look over Coquette's shoulder to Vivi.

SHOCK CUT - A sudden cut from one scene to another. (Also SMASH CUT.)

SLOW MOTION and **SPEEDED-UP MOTION** - You know what these are.

SPLIT SCREEN - The picture is divided into two (or more) sections.

STOCK SHOT - A film sequence previously shot and stored at a film library.

SUBLIM - A shot lasting a fraction of a second.

SUPER - A superimposition—one image (usually words) overlaid on another.

WIPE - An editing direction where one image moves another out of frame.

ZIP PAN - A super-fast PAN, creating a blurred image and a sense of quick movement.

ZOOM - A stationary camera with a zoom lens enlarges or diminishes the image.

Formatting index

WRITING YOUR BREAKTHROUGH SPEC SCRIPT

BOOK IV

A Script Consultant's View

The spec script—your key to breaking in

When a writer breaks into Hollywood, it's with a *spec script*. When a writer's paid millions of dollars, it's for a *spec script*. Although *shooting scripts* abound and can be easily purchased, *spec scripts* are difficult to find and little is written specifically about them. And yet, agents and producers alike are searching for the right *spec script* that convinces them you are the next great screenwriter.

Virtually every script you purchase from script services or find in screenwriting books is a *shooting script*. And yet, you must write a *spec script* to break in. (The differences between the two is explained in Book III.)

The main purpose of Book IV is to demonstrate spec writing. A secondary purpose to is to reinforce principles taught elsewhere in *The Bible*. In this book, I will analyze excerpts from two of my scripts that have made a difference in my career. We will also look at scenes from some of my clients and revise them into the current spec writing style. Each example will present new writing problems and provide new insights from the elementary to the complex. We will conclude with a line-by-line analysis of the first ten pages of a screenplay.

AVOID THIS COMMON TRAP

Many writers make the crucial mistake of assuming that they understand spec format and writing. For that reason, some make glaring errors in their scripts that could have been avoided. Because the information in this book on spec writing builds on the foundation laid in Book III, I strongly urge you to read (not skim) Book III if you haven't already. *You will find a great deal of direction concerning spec writing* (in addition to current formatting conventions).

Exercises in revising scenes

Here is a short scene that needs a little help. The three children—Jamie, age 14; Billy, age 10; and Sissy, age 6—stand over the grave of their alcoholic father (Larry). They're on their own now, and it has been established earlier that Jamie has been taking care of the family anyway. How would you revise it?

```
EXT. COUNTY CEMETERY - DUSK

A soft wind rustles the hair on three darkly dressed figures
standing over an unmarked grave.  Eyes fixed on freshly cov-
ered ground.  Everyone there who ever cared about Larry or his
family.  Jamie, Billy, and Sissy stand alone.

                    JAMIE
          We used the last of our savings to put dad
          here.  (pause) There's not much left.

Her conversation is with herself.

                    JAMIE
          I guess we'll have to rely on ourselves.
          (ironically) We've always had to anyway.
          Not much different now.

She regains some composure.

                    JAMIE
               (thinking softly)
          Gotta get some dough.  Fast.
          There isn't much time.

She doesn't even have the luxury to allow herself to mourn for
more than a few minutes.  It's on to the next crisis to solve.
She has been and now certainly is the only one to find the
answers to all their worries.
```

```
                    BILLY
           We gonna be split up now!
```

Have you written your revision? Okay, let's take a close look at the original again. In terms of formatting, the dialogue lines for Jamie's first two speeches are too wide (more than 3½ inches wide) and the wrylies are not written correctly. You caught that immediately.

What is the purpose of the scene? Apparently to show Jamie as the new head of household and to show Billy as worried about being abandoned, which (of course) adds to Jamie's burden. In your revision, you want to make sure the scene focuses on that aloneness and burden (now it's us against the world).

The dialogue is too on the nose. Jamie is saying precisely what she is thinking and feeling. What's worse, her combined lines represent a soliloquy—a must to avoid. How can we improve the dialogue?

Because it is already obvious that they are alone in the world, she does not have to come out and say it. Just them standing alone around the grave would *show* it without her having to *tell* us.

The exposition about the savings being gone might be worth keeping because it adds to the opposition. But let the line come in response to something Billy says or does.

Jamie's last line about needing "some dough" is already implied in the exposition about the savings, so her third speech can be omitted as well.

What does the last wryly, "thinking softly," mean? First of all, how can you think softly? And how can you say a line by thinking softly? So the wryly makes no sense.

The first paragraph of narrative opens with a soft wind. Why do we need the wind? I don't see why, as this is written now, but since the whole world is against these kids, let the whole world come at them like the wind. In my revision, I'm going to use a cold wind (not a soft wind) to subtly represent the opposition in this scene. And I'm going to end my revision with Jamie accepting the challenge of that wind. I think that will help move the story forward a little better.

The last two lines of the first paragraph are confusing. Who is everyone? I assume the writer means that the three kids are the only people in the world who cared about Larry. You cannot afford to confuse your reader.

In the third paragraph, Jamie regains some composure. When did she lose it?

The fourth paragraph is an "author intrusion." The writer is including things that cannot appear on the screen. You cannot *tell* us this stuff, you've got to *show* us through action, sound, and images; or reveal it in dialogue.

Once you have written your revision, take a look at mine. Remember, there is no one correct way to revise this scene. I'm hoping your version is better than mine.

See revision on page 169.

ANOTHER SHORT SCENE FOR REVISION

Here we have the first two paragraphs of a screenplay written by one of my clients before she became a client. The following big blocks of black ink are guaranteed to discourage any reader. Let's see if we can't whittle them down a little while being more specific in describing images and actions. Here's the original.

```
EXT. TRAIN - DAY

We see the skyline of New York from a train.  Painted on the
side of it are words that say, Brooklyn Railroad.  It's going
very fast and has a gray look to it.

INT. TRAIN - DAY

Inside the train are all kinds of commuters.  They are from
every age and ethnic group and they fill the train car clean
up.  They are all headed to work in New York City, as can be
plainly seen from their working clothes.  A bunch of them
cannot find seats and must stand.  One of them is SALLY
STANWICK, who has piercing blue eyes and long, flowing locks
of blonde hair.  She is in her mid twenties and is wearing a
silk blouse with a pink sweater over it and a plain black
cotton skirt.  She senses someone behind her and turns to see
a young man giving her the eye and smiling at her in a very
peculiar way.
```

Let's critique the first paragraph. Avoid "We see" and just describe the scene in a more interesting way. The second sentence contains the pronoun "it." "It" could refer to the train or to the skyline of New York. It is unclear.

Because no paragraph of narrative description should exceed four lines in length, the second paragraph represents a major violation. We need to condense it or break it up.

Why must this woman's eyes be blue and her hair blonde? Unless essential to the plot, get rid of specific physical descriptions. Describing her attire is a good idea, but would be better if that attire commented on her character.

The writer uses too many words to describe the group and its ethnic diversity.

Finally, what does the writer mean when the man smiles "in a very peculiar way"? That's too general. How does the reader visualize it?

Our revision should include only what is essential to move the story forward; and since this is an opening scene, it needs to establish a mood, atmosphere, or something about the nature of this story.

As you know from reading Book III, each paragraph of narrative description, ideally, should present one beat of action or one main image. This is not a hard-fast rule, just a guideline. Let's adhere to that guideline in this revision.

Without using camera directions, let's open with a shot of the train in the foreground and Manhattan in the background. In fact, let's handle this in four brief paragraphs.

1. Our first image will be of the train, establishing departure location and destination (with the train in the foreground and Manhattan in the background).

2. Our second image (and second paragraph) will be of the people in the train car.

3. Our third paragraph will describe Sally and her action.

4. Our fourth will describe the second character.

We will omit Sally's eye and hair color to keep casting options open. The specifics of her clothes are irrelevant, so let's omit them, unless you can describe her in something that comments on her character. I think I'm going to give her a simple cotton dress—this is an uncomplicated young woman.

Let's also make sure the young man's smile says something about him—I think I'm going to use his smile as an action. And let's use a strong active verb, like *assaults*.

Finally, let's make sure our narrative description is as "lean and clean" as possible and makes the reader ask, "What happens next?"

See revision on page 169.

THE CHARACTERS IN A SCENE

Virtually every scene should feature a character with an intention, goal, desire, need, or problem. There should also be some opposition to the central character's actions toward that goal or intention. This creates conflict. The conflict will escalate if the central character continues to be thwarted in his efforts. The character will be forced to act more strongly until an outcome is determined.

This simple scene is from a family comedy written more than a decade ago that became a sample script that I never sold but which found me work. The children are about ten years of age. Just prior to the scene, the Red Hat Bandit was about to do damage to the children, who discovered his hide-out. They defended themselves with wood swords, tree limbs, and rocks to render the Red Hat Bandit unconscious. Here is how the scene breaks down dramatically:

Stinky wants to control the group, be the leader, prove he's smarter than the rest. Everyone calls him Stinky because he likes to "cut the cheese." He even woke up his sleeping uncle once that way (established in Act 1).

Ralph's primary emotion in this scene is curiosity, which leads him to challenge Stinky. Stinky asserts that the bandit is dead, but Ralph is not so sure. So the primary conflict in this scene is between Ralph and Stinky. Both are motivated in their intentions. Note the differences in their speaking styles.

Glodina's primary emotion is fear. She fuels a secondary conflict with the three boys (the Magnificent Three) because she wants to leave and they don't. Her desire to leave creates a little suspense—we suspect something bad could happen if they stick around too long. In fact, Glodina's line "Let's go then before he wakes up" foreshadows the end of the scene.

Seebee is a big fan of "Zombie Busters," a TV show where zombies suck the brains out of their victims (again, established earlier in the screenplay). Although Seebee is the central character of the movie, he is only a minor character in this scene. His purpose is to plant the seed that the bandit might be a zombie. The crisis question in the scene is this: "Is the Red Hat Bandit dead?"

This scene accomplishes many things. It serves as a bridge between two action sequences. It plays up the innocence of the children. It moves the story forward—the bandit is more strongly motivated now. There is no doubt (after this scene) in the children's minds that he is going to kill them if he can catch them. Plus, we want to know what happens next.

Finally, look at all the white space! This is closer to what readers want to see than any example in this book. The description is sparse, dialogue speeches are short, and the wrylies are useful.

EXT. QUESTION MARK CAVE - DAY

The Magnificent Three plus Glodina stand in a circle gaping at
the fallen bandit. They cling to their weapons -- just in case.

                    GLODINA
          Is he dead?

                    RALPH
          Nah, dead people stick their tongues
          out. Like that.

Ralph demonstrates the death tongue.

                    GLODINA
          Let's go then before he wakes up.

                    STINKY
          Don't worry, he's dead.

                    RALPH
          Maybe his tongue don't stick out cuz
          he swallowed it.

                    SEEBEE
          If he's dead, we have to go to jail
          for killing him.

                    STINKY
          Heck no. Self-defense.

                    RALPH
          Yeah, he was going to kill us. Now
          he's a stiff. Wait a minute, is he
          stiff? Dead people are stiff.
          That'll prove it.

                    STINKY
          Why don't you grab him and see?

Ralph is reluctant to touch the "corpse."

                    RALPH
          He looks kinda stiff.

                    GLODINA
          You guys, let's go.

                    RALPH
          Wait a minute, aren't dead people blue?

                    STINKY
          I say he's dead!

                    RALPH
          He looks kinda blue.

                    SEEBEE
          He looks just like the zombies in
          Zombie Busters.

                    RALPH
               (a victorious smile)
          How can he be a zombie if he's dead?

                    SEEBEE
          They are dead, but then they blink
          their eyes open and they suck
          everyone's brains out.

Seebee makes convincing SUCKING SOUNDS. Glodina shivers.

The children shuffle in for a better look at the bandit.

                    RALPH
          Wait a minute, I heard dead people
          kept their eyes open.

                    STINKY
               (the last straw)
          I'll prove he's dead.

He squats over the robber's face and FARTS.

The Red Hat Bandit's eyes blink open. He grimaces at the
pungent odor.

                    RALPH
          A zombie! He'll suck our brains
          out.

The children panic and tear down the trail.

The bandit, angry and groggy, chases after them.

                    RALPH
               (to Stinky)
          See, I told you he wasn't dead.

REVISION OF THE SCENE ON PAGE 162

EXT. COUNTY CEMETERY - DUSK

Jamie, Billy, and Sissy huddle over a fresh, unmarked grave.
Alone. A cold wind tangles their hair.

Billy peers up at Jamie, looking forlorn.

Jamie stifles a sob. Speaks to no one in particular.

                    JAMIE
          Didn't leave us with even a dime.

                    BILLY
                (chin quivering)
          You gonna go away now -- huh?

Jamie pulls Billy close. The three gently embrace.

The wind picks up, but Jamie slowly lifts her countenance
against it.

REVISION OF THE SCENE ON PAGE 164

FADE IN:

A speeding silver train races down the tracks toward
Manhattan. A sign on the train reads: "BROOKLYN RAILROAD."

INT. TRAIN - DAY

Working professionals crowd the train car. Some stand.

Among them is SALLY STANWICK, 25, pretty in a simple cotton
dress. She turns abruptly, sensing someone's stares.

A young man in a suit assaults her with a smug smile.

SHOW IS BETTER THAN TELL

Here is one last scene to evaluate and revise. Good luck.

INT. HELEN'S HOUSE - NIGHT

Helen has torn herself away from her students' papers and is watching Marilyn pace.

                    HELEN
          Yes...then what?

                    MARILYN
          Then they asked me to sing. It was
          the love song. I belted out the
          solo part without a single problem.
          I was inspired! Then Antonio
          joined me on the duet and...and

She shudders like a chill just ran up her spine.

                    MARILYN
               (continuing;
               melodramatically)
          the angels wept!

                    HELEN
          That's perfect! Then you got the
          part! It's what you've always
          wanted! I'm so happy for you!

                    MARILYN
               (cuts her off)
          It's not going to happen. They
          said they'd get back to me.

                    HELEN
          What? Why? I don't get it. You
          said...

                    MARILYN
          I said I did a superb job in the
          audition. That isn't enough on
          stage. They don't like the way
          I look.

Marilyn drops, dejected, onto the couch.

                    HELEN
        How do you know that?

                    MARILYN
        After the reading and singing,
        they whispered among themselves
        for a few minutes. Then they
        had me walk back and forth across
        the stage a few times. Then they
        had Antonio stand next to me.

She stands back up again and resumes pacing and gesturing.

                    MARILYN
                 (continuing)
        Then they had me walk back and
        forth with Antonio. Then they
        had Antonio put his arms around me.
        Then they said, "Thank you very
        much, we'll be in touch."

                    HELEN
        Well, that doesn't necessarily mean...

                    MARILYN
        Yes it does. Believe me, I've seen
        it a bunch of times.

She slows her pace and becomes thoughtful. She looks a
little depressed as she walks over and picks up her coat.

                    MARILYN
                 (continuing)
        You know it isn't fair. I'm
        just not sure whether to give up, or
        cry, or just go to Baskin-Robbins.

                    HELEN
        Well, whatever you do, don't just
        give up. You have an amazing
        talent. Sooner or later, that will
        win out.

                    MARILYN
        I hope so. Good night, hon. Don't
        forget we're going to the mall
        tomorrow after school.

Okay, now take a moment to analyze what you've read and revise it into something more interesting.

• • • • •

Here are my thoughts: The dialogue is quite ordinary with the only action being Marilyn's pacing. And Marilyn's experience is overwritten: First she sang; then Antonio joined her in song; then they (whoever *they* are) said, "We'll get back to you"; then they whispered; then they had her walk back and forth; then they had Antonio stand next to her; then they had her walk back and forth with Antonio; then they had Antonio put his arms around her; and finally they thanked her. That list could be easily condensed as could the dialogue. There is also too much repetition of the phrase "then they." And both characters speak the same way.

My first impulse is to take Marilyn's experience and *show* it to the reader, then cut from Marilyn's pacing on the stage to her pacing in Helen's room as she finishes telling Helen the story. Just doing that will give the scene more movement.

In terms of the relationship between Marilyn and Helen, Helen is in the position of nurturing a whiner. Let's revise this so that Marilyn comes off as more sympathetic (not so much of a whiner). Let's allow Marilyn to decide to not give up. And let's give Helen more personality and wit. After all, she's a teacher and knows how to motivate people.

Just doing those things already mentioned will help the dialogue, but we can also tighten it up and render it less "on the nose."

A scene should end on a strong moment. Let's open with a song and close with a song, demonstrating that Marilyn will not give up. And maybe the teacher can give Marilyn an "A," since she's already grading papers. We'll do that indirectly, of course.

Now let's take a look at some of the specifics of my revision. We see an empty theater as Marilyn sings. The next image is of Marilyn in contrast—not great looking, but near the angels in her singing. The third image is of two young men, the opposition characters in this scene. Incidentally, even the opposition will recognize her voice, so the reader can be confident that this woman has some talent.

But then the opposition humiliates her. This creates sympathy for her. This moves us into our transition, which we accomplish by putting the camera on Marilyn's face and changing the location. This is easy to do since she is pacing in both places.

Then we have our moment between the two people. We set up Helen with the red pencil so she can use it at the end of the scene. And instead of Helen saying the expected, she tries a more original approach, creating a little conflict in the process.

The laughter relieves the tension and sets up the serious moment. Again, we have a contrast. And we get Marilyn to say she won't quit trying without her actually saying the words (she sings).

• • • • •

Okay, here's my revision, just one of many ways to approach this material.

```
INT. THEATER - NIGHT

A lovely female voice sings a love song.  Her music fills
the empty theater.

The voice is Marilyn's, looking chubby in her leotards.  But
her face is angelic -- she is one with her music.

Antonio, slick black hair and tank top, joins her in a duet.

A young turk with a clipboard steps onto the stage.

                    TURK
          Okay, okay.  Enough!
               (circling the couple)
          You'll make the angels weep.
          Beautiful, Marilyn, beautiful.

Marilyn smiles gratefully.

When he signals Antonio away, she glances offstage at her
image in a mirror.  Places her hand on her stomach.  Frowns.

                    TURK
          Gimme a strut.  Back and forth.

Marilyn walks across stage, then back.

The young turk studies her.  Antonio steps over to him and
whispers something.  Looks doubtful.

Marilyn's eyes fill with tears as she paces across

HELEN'S LIVING ROOM

where Helen watches her from the couch.  Homework papers
cover the coffee table.  Helen fiddles with a red pencil.
```

                    MARILYN
          ...That's when he said he'd get
          back to me.

                    HELEN
          Well that doesn't necessarily mean --

                    MARILYN
          Yes it does. I've seen it.
                    (shaking her head)
          They don't like my looks. That's
          what it is. Always what it is.

                    HELEN
          Well, your voice survived.

                    MARILYN
          The question is...will I?

                    HELEN
          You can always get a tummy tuck.

Marilyn is indignant until she sees Helen's warm smile.
Then her tension releases into sudden laughter. Helen
joins in the laughter.

                    HELEN
          You were made to sing, honey, like
          a big, fat, beautiful bird.

Helen stands and the two briefly embrace.

                    HELEN
          So why don't you fly out of here
          and let me grade some papers, huh?

Marilyn mouths a "thank you." Steps out the door. Starts
singing the love song.

Helen smiles. Writes a big, fat "A" on one of the papers.

The first ten pages

What follows are the first ten pages of my action/time travel/romance, A WINDOW IN TIME, along with a complete line-by-line analysis of those pages. This script was slated for a network movie, but low ratings for other time-travel shows and movies nixed the production. I include this excerpt in response to the many clients and students who have asked for an example of a successful *spec script*. In my analysis, I will tell you my reasons for writing this the way I did. I hope discussing my rationale will be helpful. In many cases, you may think of a better way to present the same story information. Wonderful! It means you are thinking and learning, and becoming the next great screenwriter.

What are the general strengths and weaknesses of these pages? Overall, the structure is good and the pacing is fast. Characterization and dialogue could be stronger. The writing is generally clear and easy to follow.

Since A WINDOW IN TIME is primarily an actioner, there are many paragraphs describing action. One of my challenges is to keep those paragraphs as short as possible while still conveying dramatic action. Although four-line paragraphs are acceptable, I make sure that only one paragraph in these ten pages exceeds three lines.

In today's competitive market, something must happen by page 10. The reader needs to feel that she is into the story by page 10. She must want to read more. You will be the judge if these pages accomplish that.

The first scene is not an action scene and is 2½ pages long. It would be better to open with action. In fact, a previous draft opened with the scene now found on page 5, but I finally settled on opening with this scene to establish the hero and set up his world. Also, this scene motivates or grounds succeeding scenes, allowing me to create a pace that accelerates to the turning point on page 10.

Note: For ease of reading, the analysis for each page of script will appear directly to the left of each page of script.

Before you begin, you might consider first reading the page of script, and then my analysis of it. Another approach would be to read the entire ten pages first, and then come back and read the analysis.

Typically, you FADE IN on page one, but you cannot fade in on a black screen. My opening is meant to be thematic. The first thing we see is a window that lets in light, and this story is about a window in time that lets in the light of the future, the light of self-knowledge, and the light of love. I'm hoping to create a small sense of mystery here right at the beginning.

Jake is only described as a NASA employee. That's all that needs to be said here, I believe, because this entire scene comments on Jake. Mark is described as Jake's "best buddy."

Because so many scenes take place in this room and involve this house, I feel as though I must take pains to describe it. So we establish that this room is on the second floor and that there is an orange grove in the backyard. The orange grove along with the NASA cap implies that we're in Florida. Also, the grove is where we'll hide a helicopter later.

We'll soon learn that this is Jake's hide-out, not his residence, and that he's showing it to his best-friend Mark for the first time. Why? Because he needs Mark to prepare a sales presentation for him. Now if we try to reveal all of this in one line of dialogue, it will come off as boring exposition. So we provide our first clue with Mark's first line; obviously, Jake owns a condo. (Incidentally, that first line also indicates that they are in mid-conversation.) And then Jake explains, "No mail-man, no sales-man, no meter-man." The subtext is: *This is my secret hide-out.* The second clue.

Then Mark helps establish something of Jake's private life. Later, we learn that he's not afraid of anything but women. Mark, of course, is probably a skirt chaser. Mark's line, "I can set you up," is a setup line for the last scene of the movie, when he says, "I told you I'd set you up." The slug in the arm replaces the lifeless words "a beat" that I originally used.

I debated over the two paragraphs describing the desk lamp, drafting table, blueprint tubes, and tiny laptop jacked into a computer. But I decided to keep them because Jake is an aeronautic engineer and computer whiz who loves miniatures. Besides, he uses the computer later. The one line you could omit is, "It [the arching desk lamp] hovers over a drafting table like a flying saucer." I'm shooting for mood here and genre. Technically, this is a science fiction love story against the background of high adventure.

Jake then declares his love. First we have the declaration, then we show the reader what he loves: His design of a new kind of helicopter. He asks Mark to help him sell it, so now the reader understands the situation before turning the page. *An aeronautic engineer wants his marketing buddy to help him sell his secret helicopter plans, so he brings him to his hide-out.*

"A WINDOW IN TIME"

A BLACK SCREEN

FOOTFALLS of two men ECHO across a wood floor. CLICK -- someone
releases a latch and KICKS open a window shutter, then the other.

Bold beams of sunlight burst through a large window, creating a
wide shaft of white sunlight.

JAKE DEKKER, wearing a NASA ball cap, and his best buddy MARK are
bathed in the pure light.

Mark gazes out the second-story window into the backyard lawn
and beyond to a grove of orange trees, then up to a blue sky.

                    MARK
          Beats the hell out of your condo.

The room's walls are covered with posters of military flying
craft of all kinds. Miniatures hang by string from the ceiling.

                    JAKE
          No one knows about it. It's in
          my uncle's name, in Georgia. Got
          a generator downstairs. No mail-
          man, no sales-man, no meter-man...

                    MARK
          ...And no wo-man.

                    JAKE
          I value my privacy.

                    MARK
          If you saw the babe I just met,
          Jake, you'd go public.
                    (slugs him in the arm)
          I can set ya up, ya know.

Jake crosses the room and twists the knob of an arching desk
lamp. It hovers over a drafting table like a flyer saucer.
Large metal blueprint tubes lie beside the desk.

On the desk is a tiny laptop jacked into a nearby computer.

                    JAKE
          My only true love. And you're
          going to help me sell it.

His only true love is on the drafting table: The design of a
black and angular helicopter. Mark sighs in amazement as he
turns page after page of blueprint designs.

Jake's first line on page 2 exists to lend authenticity to the story (the materials described are used in stealth bombers).

Mark doesn't care, so he interrupts. Apparently, he heard something at work that he shouldn't have about Jake's design. He's sheepish about it and feels he has to explain himself to Jake. This short interchange helps establish Mark's employer as NASA or the military. We also get a hint of Mark's dark side. He "hears rumors" he isn't supposed to hear. He interrupts his friend who is describing his "only true love" and (on page 1) he's chasing the babes. And at the bottom of the page, Mark's last line reveals that of all the uses the little miniature could be put to, he'd use it to spy on women at the beach. These little hints do not add up to much now, but they help make Mark believable when he betrays his friend later. We're setting up foils: Jake is straight and serious; Mark is loose and shallow. We're doing this with dialogue that also reveals exposition. This may not be immediately obvious to the reader; but it lays the groundwork so that these characters in later scenes will seem believable and consistent.

A loud whack scares Mark. Why do I do this? I want to scare the audience and Mark both. I want to create a sense of unpredictability. I want to show Jake as calm and Mark as skittish. I want to emphasize Mark's little indiscretion. And I need to distract Mark so that Jake can grab a hand remote. Note that I describe the gadget in detail as clearly as I can so that you, the reader, can see it in your head and recognize it in later scenes. This is necessary exposition. The reason I invented this little miniature was because in my first draft the two characters only talked about what the eventual helicopter would look like. I decided I needed a way to *show* people. Finally, this is another example of Jake working with miniatures.

The helicopter is described as behaving like a hummingbird. I settled on that to make it easy for the reader to visualize. Later, I call it the Hummingbird MG-11.

The next thing that Jake does is describe his "new concept." Dramatic characters tend to stick to a single train of thought and an intention. Jake's intention in this scene is to get Mark to help him sell this helicopter design to top brass. At the top of this page, Jake begins to describe the helicopter for that reason, but Mark interrupts him, providing subtle opposition. Now Jake must do something to get Mark's attention, so he shows Mark the miniature and then continues describing it as "small, quick," etc., and what it's purpose is: "For rescue."

And Jake has not forgotten Mark's question (Mark's first line on this page). He answers it by telling Mark that the military has already rejected it. And he tells him why. I think it's important to explain why the military would reject this, because when we see it, we really like it. Why would they reject it? Because it's not big enough. And that seems realistic.

Mark has not lost his train of thought either. He's supposed to sell the designs and so he tells Jake that the miniature is his best selling tool. The subtext is *Show them that.*

                    JAKE
          The outside will be made of
          kevlar, carbon fiber, and --

                    MARK
          -- Didn't you just present some-
          thing like this to top brass?
                    (sheepishly)
          I heard -- A rumor going round.

A loud WHACK from behind scares Mark. Jake grins. The wind has
blown the shutter against the wall.

While Mark re-opens the shutter, Jake covertly grabs a small hand
remote. It has a short antenna, a control knob, and a tiny TV
monitor on its face. Jake pushes a button and moves the knob.

A miniature helicopter darts up to Mark's face like a hummingbird, and hovers. He jumps back in fright, waving his hands.

                    MARK
          Hell, Jake....

                    JAKE
          A new concept, Mark. Small, quick.
          Can slip anywhere. For rescue.

Jake smiles proudly, then frowns as he answers Mark's question.

                    JAKE
          Yeah, NASA, the military -- they
          rejected it. Don't think it's
          do-able. Besides, they want the
          big gun ships. Fire power.

                    MARK
                    (pointing at helicopter)
          Hell, Jake, that's the centerpiece
          of your sales promo right there.

Jake signals Mark over. Mark gazes into the tiny TV monitor.
As the helicopter flits about, Mark views different parts of the
room in the tiny monitor. He CHUCKLES, his face aglow.

                    MARK
          A TV camera. Boy, could I get an
          eyeful at the beach.

Mark almost pants. Jake manipulates the knob and the tiny
chopper scoots away and bolts out the window.

The chopper bolts out the window for four reasons: 1) To demonstrate its abilities, 2) To demonstrate Jake's intelligence, 3) To establish it as a lifeline that is used later, and 4) To establish more about Jake's house, one of our main sets. I called up a client in Florida and asked him what grows in Miami. His answer is in the first paragraph. That's research. Anyway, that first paragraph (the longest paragraph in the screenplay) fully orients us to the general setting (a suburb of Miami) and Jake's hideaway. Also, Jake—the secretive engineer not interested in women—drives a jeep. That adds just a bit of dimension to his character.

More exposition: The chopper is silent and cannot be detected on radar. Then the fascinating little miniature darts into the sky, allowing us to cut from blue sky to blue sky. This is a match cut, a smooth transition from our first scene to our second scene. Why is Jake's last line spoken off screen? Because we want the camera to be on the blue sky so we can match cut to the blue sky of the next scene.

Jake's last line is interesting. He's describing the helicopter, but what's the subtext? Well, *Jake* likes to be free and quick. It comments on his self-image.

There is a lot of exposition in this first scene (technically three scenes in the first 2½ pages). I'm betting that the interest created by the situation, the characters (using dialogue that would be natural for that situation because they have an apparent motivation for saying what they say), the hide-out, and the cute little helicopter makes the exposition interesting; in other words, we want to learn all this stuff. Now let's triple space to a new master scene and cut to an immediate payoff in the next eight paragraphs:

1. We see the sky and the ocean.

2. A one-sentence paragraph focuses on one image: A superimposition telling us this is the Bermuda Triangle. This will create some anticipation. After all, the Bermuda Triangle has a reputation.

3. and 4. Nothing but sound. Clearly, what is happening is not normal.

5. The helicopter bolts from the blue. Yes, I consciously used the cliché.

6. "It is upon us, silent and swift." I'm breaking a rule with the word "us" (author intrusion), but I believe it is worth it. Here's what this really says: *This helicopter suddenly fills the movie screen and flies right into the camera.*

7. The next paragraph is ANOTHER ANGLE, allowing us to see exactly what this looks like. It is absolutely clear that this looks like the miniature but is *real.* Muting the WHOP-WHOP of the rotors reinforces the point that this helicopter is unusually silent.

8. A new character is introduced—Kendall. I'm hoping you are hooked by these first three pages.

3

OUTSIDE THE HOUSE

the tiny chopper flies over the Norfolk pine, coconut palms, and philodendron of the Florida countryside, then over the dirt road leading past the front of the two-story house. Jake's jeep is in the driveway. Miami sits like a jewel in the far distance.

Suddenly, the tiny model flits around the house and through the back window.

INSIDE THE UPPER ROOM

Jake maneuvers the remote knob and suddenly Mark is gazing at himself in the monitor. He lifts his head and the chopper is an inch from his nose -- silent. It orbits his head twice.

                    JAKE
          Silent. Invisible to radar...

It darts out the window and disappears into the blue sky.

                    JAKE (OS)
          ...And as free and quick as a
          hummingbird.

EXT. ATLANTIC OCEAN, SOUTH FLORIDA - DAY

A clear, blue sky vaults over a calm, blue ocean. The only sound is the natural movement of the waves.

SUPER: "THE BERMUDA TRIANGLE."

Then: A low RUMBLE, similar to distant thunder. Strange. Unworldly. Slowly crescendos into a sharp, deafening CLAP...

...Cutting abruptly to a mysterious silence, and at that moment, filling the vacuum...

...A black helicopter bolts from the blue, as if suddenly emerging from a long invisible tunnel.

It is upon us, silent and swift.

Small, angular, and futuristic. It looks exactly like Jake's miniature model -- only this chopper is real. Strangely, the WHOP-WHOP of the rotors is muted.

INSIDE THE HELICOPTER

KENDALL's nervous hands work the instruments.

A grid appears on the windshield instead of on some computer screen, adding to the futuristic quality of the helicopter. We also establish an empty seat—that's a setup for a later payoff.

The second paragraph and weak "throwaway" line of dialogue demonstrate that she is having difficulty flying this thing. She is not a Navy flyer, not an expert. The blood-stained clothes indicate that something happened just before the movie began. That something is the backstory. We won't learn what happened until about page 70. But it prompts several questions: Is she escaping? Did she kill someone? Where did she come from? Why is she here?

The Egyptian symbol-of-life earrings are the first clues (not yet obvious, of course) that Kendall is an Egyptologist and that she brings life and light to our hero, Jake. (Yes, she came through a window in time, and—yes—she is the love interest.)

At this point, while writing the third draft, I wondered if I needed to make this chopper seem "more real" while also showing off its futuristic capabilities. At the same time, I had a problem of creating a way to get our hero into the hands of Wardle (we'll meet her later). The United States Coast Guard came to the rescue. The addition of the Coast Guard Officer solved both problems, as you shall see. I have found in revision work that when the solution to one problem also solves another problem, you are probably on the right course.

In this little scene, our Coast Guard Officer demonstrates that the helicopter is invisible to radar. The reader will recall Jake's words, "Silent, invisible to radar." We have now *shown* that, which begs the question: Do you need Jake's words? To be honest, that is a good question. We might have an opportunity to shorten that first scene.

Meanwhile, back in the helicopter, we re-establish the backstory with Kendall's tears. In addition, we add a touch of authenticity to the story with the Collective Pitch Lever. I knew nothing about helicopters until I conducted my research.

A word about the blood and tears: When finally produced, the movie version may be much different, depending on a variety of factors. Nevertheless, the director will note the blood and tears, and conclude, "She is distraught—something has happened." And he will make sure that that concept comes across in his version of the story. The purpose of the spec script is to communicate the story—make the reader see, hear, laugh and cry (feel)—not plan the shoot. We only hope other professionals will have the good sense to see the story the way we writers do. Right?

4

A grid appears on her windshield. The seat next to her is empty.

On the far horizon an island jumps into view as the chopper suddenly drops. She is frantic, distraught.

                    KENDALL (OS)
          Where's that button?

She sighs in relief, and brushes her hair back behind black sunglasses that contrast silver Egyptian symbol-of-life earrings.

Her futuristic clothes are blood-stained.

Below, the sparkling, blue ocean glides silently by.

EXT./INT. COAST GUARD CUTTER - DAY

A COAST GUARD OFFICER spots the erratic movements of the silent helicopter. Dumbfounded, he races to the radar room.

                    COAST GUARD OFFICER
          How fast is it going?

INT. RADAR ROOM

The Coast Guard Officer rushes to the radar screen. He looks in vain for a blip.

                    COAST GUARD OFFICER
          Where is it? Where is it?

The TECHNICIAN looks at him like he's crazy.

                    TECHNICIAN
          Where's what?

EXT. RADAR ROOM/DECK

The officer hurries through the door and searches the sky. He sees nothing.

INT. HELICOPTER - DAY

Just a few feet below, Florida Bay streaks past at amazing speed. Kendall lifts her sunglasses slightly, wipes away tears.

She pulls up on the Collective Pitch Lever and suddenly she is a half mile above the water. The Southern coast of Florida ascends on the horizon.

Miami appears to be the destination, and who lives in a suburb of Miami? Jake Dekker. Good. Cut.

There's not a word of dialogue on this page. Makes me shiver. It would be nice to break this up in some way and create some white space.

We now move to our third major sequence in this screenplay. This setting is so different from the others that we need to take two or three lines to establish that setting. In my first draft, I described this site at length. I even described the sun pouring through a window high in the temple. The light was blood red. It was a gorgeous description, teeming with thematic elements. I could almost hear the orchestra. However, it wasn't necessary to move the story forward and I didn't need it for mood since that is established inside the temple. The appearance of the temple is irrelevant. So my wonderful description is gone now. (A moment of silence please.)

We are in a circular room. If that is not entirely clear, you might suggest a master scene heading that says INT. CIRCULAR ROOM. (See page 117.) The torches and the black headdresses add a bit of mystery and mood to the scene.

To complete the scene description, we describe what is at the center of the circle—a pyramid. The four statues mean this little pyramid is important. In fact, this entire build-up is meant to establish the importance of the "Eye of Ra." Why is it so important? We don't know now, but later we learn (remember, Kendall is an Egyptologist) that the Eye of Ra (Eye of God) can see you through time. This object is also important to the bad guys, because they want to start a New World Order. (Look at a dollar bill and you will find on it an "all-seeing eye" at the top of a pyramid with some Latin words below that mean "New Order of the Ages." Of course, I cannot say that in narrative description because it cannot appear on the screen. Instead, it must come out later through action and dialogue. All I can do here is establish the importance of the object and bring in more information later. Don't tell your reader everything at once. Withhold information, but never confuse your reader.)

One of the bad guys has disguised herself as a worker. I use "A THIEF" as a heading not only to set her apart and put the camera on her, but also to break up all this narrative description. I hide from the reader the fact that this thief is a woman by avoiding using any pronouns. I also establish the woman's method of operation: a knife under her sleeve.

What's the payoff for not identifying the thief? Later in the story, we see a woman, Cherise Joulet, flick a knife into her hand, and suddenly we know she is the thief; but our hero does not know it. That fact creates suspense because the reader is in a superior position.

Okay. We cannot go any longer without coming back to our central character, Jake. This is one reason I went with Jake's hide-out scene first. So much is going on, I feel as though we must establish the hero first so that we know who he is immediately.

5

Soon we are over the Everglades, with Miami on the far horizon.

FROM THE EVERGLADES

The chopper whisks off into the distance. Silently.

EXT. EGYPTIAN DESERT - DAY

The ruins of an ancient Egyptian temple lie partially submerged in the desert earth, obviously part of an archaeological dig.

SUPER: "NEAR LUXOR, EGYPT."

At the temple base, a man-sized hole has been blasted through.

INT. TEMPLE - SAME

Torches illuminate the figures of a dozen motionless workers, all wearing black headdresses obscuring their faces and heads. They stand back against the single, circular wall.

At the center sits a four-foot marble pyramid, protected by four Egyptian statues.

A goateed SHEIK carefully touches the hieroglyphics on the wall, then gestures to the marble pyramid.

Quickly, several workers pry the heavy marble pyramid from its foundation and push it over. It CRASHES to one side. Silence.

There, at the center spot, stands the "EYE OF RA" -- a dark, metallic pyramid only six inches tall. Embedded into the top section of each of the four sides is a purple glowing crystal.

The sheik's eyes water -- awestruck. The workers are stunned. What is this tiny pyramid? The sheik carefully picks it up -- almost expecting a jolt -- and examines it with wonder.

A THIEF

disguised as a worker, strides up to the sheik. A knife flicks into the thief's hand from under the sleeve, and quickly slashes the sheik's throat. The other hand snatches the Eye of Ra.

A worker attacks the thief, but is repelled by a swift kick to the face. A flash of the knife severs another worker's windpipe.

Instantly, the thief dashes through a door frame and escapes.

Sandy Beach is another important location because it becomes a romantic spot later on. Before we see Jake and his boy scouts, however, I have a little fun with perspective. We see a rocket, then realize it's a miniature. I do it to re-emphasize that this is one of Jake's miniatures (that later becomes a lifeline) and to change the mood from the serious scene of death preceding. That's my rationalization.

I hope you've seen up until now that each scene has a main story purpose. It's not just there to establish character or mood, but has a story reason as well. It's not just there to establish location; it also moves the story forward. From here on out, you will see more of the cause-and-effect relationship that should exist between scenes, how one thing leads to another. This is called scene motivation.

The primary purpose of this scene is to get Jake into the hands of Wardle (to be introduced later). What motivates that? You will see as you read the remaining pages. The portion of the scene that appears on this page has another purpose as well—to establish Jake as a good guy. Wait a minute! Didn't I just say don't have a scene just to establish character or mood? Yes, but the entire scene itself does more than just establish character as you'll see on page 7. In addition, the boy scouts play a small role later on, so we need to establish their existence.

(Keep in mind that guidelines exist to be broken on occasion. And sometimes, just establishing character can move the story forward, especially in character-driven scripts.)

Anyway, Jake is a good guy because he is a boy scout leader. So what? Big deal. We need a *personal* touch here. Yes, his ability to relate to the boys by having a sense of humor, providing a rocket (which is believable because Jake works at NASA), and eliciting their participation is nice; but what moves people is one person relating to one other person. That's why Sport is here. (Notice that I don't use a POV shot when Jake spots Sport.) Jake is sensitive, perceptive, kind, and encouraging to a kid who has been rejected by the others. Jake makes him feel important without embarrassing him.

In review, the scene as a whole (pages 6-7) exists for the following reasons:
1. Get Jake into the hands of Wardle
2. Establish the existence of the boy scouts
3. Show Jake as a good guy who's not isolated from the community.

In terms of pacing, this section on page 6 acts as a buffer. We just experienced some serious action in Egypt and are about to have storm clouds blow in on page 7. We could use something light and fun here. That's a fourth purpose.

Why is Mark in this scene? To more clearly establish him as Jake's best friend. Obviously, these two see each other a lot. It also gives Mark some dimension. He's apparently a good guy at heart. You see, we planted the seeds of his dark side earlier. Now we show his good side. When the dark side reappears, it will be surprising, but believable.

6

EXT. A SANDY BEACH - DAY

The blue sky meets a beautiful secluded beach at the horizon.

From ground level, the USA X-1 rocket towers upward, ready to
blast off. When the gargantuan head of a boy moves into frame,
we realize that the rocket is actually a miniature.

The boy is a normal-sized BOY SCOUT. He lies prone on the sand
next to Jake -- in Levis and NASA cap -- who examines the rocket.

Jake jumps up. Holds a megaphone to his mouth. Faces north.

                    JAKE
          Attention. Clear the launch area.
               (facing South now)
          Please clear the launch area.

Mark and about a dozen boy scouts of various ethnic groups and
races join Jake. These are all inner-city kids. One of the
scouts makes EMERGENCY SIREN SOUNDS for effect.

Jake spots a small boy (SPORT), who stands apart from the others,
looking dejected. In fact, the other boys ignore him.

Jake walks over to the boy and squats down, sees his dejection.

                    JAKE
          Hey sport, I need someone with a
          strong voice for the count down.
          How about it?

Jake hands him the megaphone and a comforting smile. Sport returns the smile, so Jake lifts the boy's cap, rubs his head, and
replaces the cap. He leads Sport to a spot on the sand.

At the same time, Jake nods to Mark who nods to a TALL SCOUT.
The tall scout -- intense with anticipation -- holds a remote
control in his hand. The remaining scouts stand back with Mark.

Jake winks at an expectant Sport.

                    SPORT
          10-9-8-7-6-5-4-3-2-1-0-Blastoff!

The tall scout pushes a big, red button -- FFUSSSH! -- the rocket
blasts off.

They watch the stage-2 rocket separate and drop to earth while
the X-1 continues upward. Finally, it explodes over the ocean.

Speaking of surprise, instead of letting this fun moment play out, we interrupt it with a plot twist. In a previous draft, this scene played out for another page with the boys having fun. In fact, one boy goes out into the ocean to catch the parachute and Jake rescues him like a *Baywatch* stud. Then Jake goes home and gets a phone call from Wardle. Do you see how this current version is more dramatic? Plus, we lose a couple of pages we didn't need. Also, the surprise of the big Chinook helicopter interrupting all of the fun creates suspense, just like the slam of the window shutter on page 2.

The transition is abrupt. The scouts cheer and watch the parachute descend. We expect to see the parachute land. Suddenly, the chopper is upon them. Jake, of course, is focused on the boys. I try to create a sense of chaos here with the sudden appearance of the Chinook, the boys running scared, their caps flying off, Mark looking confused, and so on. It's a dramatic moment, so I dramatize it. After all, this chopper will take Jake to Wardle and, as a result, Jake's life will suddenly be in chaos. There's something about that subliminal link that creates a sense of unity.

The dialogue, which in a prior draft went on for an entire page, is just two lines. Jake first speaks with an action, holding his arms out. I believe the uniformed airman refusing to answer Jake's question speaks more eloquently than something like, "Someone wants to see you." Why say that and break the suspense? Keep the audience wondering: Now what's going to happen?

In a way, the Chinook is Wardle, so I try to link the scene of the Chinook with the scene of Wardle. We match cut from slamming door to slamming door (without using a CUT TO or MATCH CUT) to link the scenes.

I could waste space by showing Mark and boys reacting to Jake's disappearance. I don't because Mark and the boys are minor characters. Let's keep the story moving.

Note the description of Wardle. When you describe your character, do so in a way that reflects on her character and who she is. Wardle is an ambitious no-nonsense soldier.

The Coast Guard Officer links the plot of Kendall's helicopter to Jake's plot. The Egyptian plot line links to the bad guys after page 10. That means that although Wardle is a powerful opposition character to Jake, she is not the main opposition. And the main opposition is not Cherise Joulet, the woman with the knife, although she becomes a powerful opposition to Jake. It's the man who hired Cherise. And even Kendall, who becomes the love interest, will be at odds with Jake for a while. Why all the opposition? Because opposition creates conflict, and conflict is drama. And adversity is good for revealing character and motivating characters to grow.

As you can see by the Coast Guard Officer's reaction, Wardle is formidable. We're taking the opportunity with this next scene to build up Wardle and make her powerful, while at the same time, revealing more important exposition without being boring.

7

The scouts CHEER when a parachute opens and the small capsule flutters downward.

Without warning, a huge Chinook helicopter -- loud and ominous -- descends. Two boys fall on their backs in fear.

The tiny rocket capsule falls to the sand, but no one notices. A few boys run scared. Jake grabs them.

>   JAKE
>   Whoa! Take it easy. She's one of
>   ours. Isn't she pretty?

Caps fly off, but the boys calm down as the Chinook lands on the sand. Mark looks confused, shaken -- what's this about? Jake shrugs.

Two uniformed airmen approach the group. Jake steps forward. Holds his arms out asking for an explanation.

>   UNIFORM
>   Jake Dekker?

Dekker calmly nods. They escort him to the chopper.

>   JAKE
>   What's going on?

The silent airmen usher Jake into the chopper and SLAM the door.

INT.   HALLWAY - DAY

A metal door SLAMS shut and ECHOES.

J. C. WARDLE, a sexless woman with an ambitious stride snatches a paper from the hand of PALMER, her muscular male aide.

Palmer opens a conference room door for Wardle.

INT.   CONFERENCE ROOM - SAME

The Coast Guard Officer, alone in the room, stands at attention. He doesn't know whether to salute Wardle or shake her hand.

>   WARDLE
>   Sit down.

He sits. Palmer opens his notebook and prepares to take notes.

This scene on pages 7-10 can be divided into two dramatic segments. The first is with the Coast Guard Officer; the second is with Jake Dekker. It gives the reader someone to compare Jake to since both must deal with the same woman. It will help define character.

Wardle is intimidating, tough, and caffeinated; and carries around a coffee cup. Palmer is silent and misses nothing. He keeps a note pad and methodically takes notes. These little props say something about each character and give the reader something visual to identify with the character.

Wardle's intention in this scene is to get information. The Coast Guard Officer's goal is to give her the information she wants so he can get out of there. Since they have the same objective, you would think that this scene would be devoid of conflict, but Wardle's manner creates conflict and dramatic tension. Let's examine the dialogue.

Wardle's first line affirms her superiority and threatens the officer at the same time. It also provides exposition to the reader: she's a pentagon official.

Wardle's next line is innocent enough, but she challenges him with her eyes and wins.

Wardle's third line cuts him off in mid-sentence.

Wardle's fourth line asks him to qualify what he just said. She is calm; he is a mess, afraid of getting into trouble. She's clearly in control. (Incidentally, the officer is right about helicopters being unable to fly at the speed of sound—a result of my research and an example of exposition dropped in at a dramatic moment.)

Wardle's fifth line (on page 9) tells him what to think.

Creating conflict is fun. It makes this encounter more interesting and presents a standard by which Jake will be measured when he comes up against Wardle. We will worry for Jake from the moment he first steps into the room with her. So the dramatic tension here creates suspense later. In fact, if this encounter between Wardle and the Coast Guard Officer works dramatically, then the reader is setup like a pigeon for the slammer on pages 9 and 10.

After this dialogue exchange, we foreshadow Wardle's upcoming encounter with Dekker. She pauses (at the bottom of page 8) and exchanges knowing glances with her aide, who hands her a top secret file. Top secret? Must be important. And then we see Jake's helicopter. In the paragraph that follows, we learn that it is called the Hummingbird MG-11.

The officer is relieved to see the drawing, meaning that this drawing matches what the officer saw. This drawing matches Kendall's helicopter. He is so relieved that he smiles as if he has won, but Wardle quickly erases his smile on the next page.

190

8

Wardle slumps into her chair, takes a sip of coffee, and eyes the officer like he's the fly and she's the spider.

> WARDLE
> I just flew in from the Pentagon so this better be good.

> COAST GUARD OFFICER
> Yes ma'am.

> WARDLE
> You sighted an unusual looking helicopter.

Her glare is steady, forcing him to glance down at his notes.

> COAST GUARD OFFICER
> Yes ma'am, at 25 degrees, six minutes latitude and --

> WARDLE
> -- I have your report. Just tell me about the craft.

> COAST GUARD OFFICER
> Well, it was black. Had strange angles.
> (with erratic gestures)
> Very fast and it made no sound.

> WARDLE
> (after a sip of coffee)
> How fast?

> COAST GUARD OFFICER
> Well, no chopper can go the speed of sound, but this one was close. Yeah.
> (fidgeting)
> And it didn't appear on radar. I checked. I followed procedures.

Wardle and Palmer exchange knowing glances. He hands her a file stamped "Defense Department -- Top Secret." From the file, she removes a computer-generated drawing of a helicopter.

She slides it over to the Coast Guard Officer. It roughly matches the black helicopter the officer saw. The caption underneath says, "HUMMINGBIRD MG-11."

The officer looks, and immediately a smile of vindication spreads across his face.

Why would Wardle say the helicopter does not exist? The subtext is *Keep your mouth shut. I don't want this to become public.* Why? We're not sure yet. This creates interest in what's about to happen. And it motivates a future scene.

In terms of character dynamics, she's telling the officer what to think and warning him at the same time. She then orders him out. In a moment of near-comic relief, the Coast Guard Officer runs away from her.

In this script, I try to provide information to my reader piecemeal. We saw the top secret file on page 8, but did not reveal the name on the file until now.

So now we see Jake's name on the file. It is so important, that I use the INSERT to focus the camera on the file. Wardle's command to "send in Dekker" is off screen (OS), meaning that the camera stays on the file while Wardle says her line.

Note that no introductions are made and there is not chit-chat or small talk. We just get into the scene. (Incidental dialogue can be added during the shoot.)

After Wardle's line, it would be proper and correct to write BACK TO SCENE to indicate we are no longer looking at the file. The reason I don't use BACK TO SCENE is to save space. I justify doing that because the prose is clear—it's just a one-line INSERT. No one will be confused.

Throughout this script, Jake has been presented as calm and steady. Now is the moment to test that. The suspense is there because the audience is in a superior position. We know what Wardle knows about the helicopter and Jake doesn't. We know how tough she was on the officer and Jake doesn't. We know that she is a formidable foe.

She asks him if the chopper design is his. We know it is because we saw it in the first scene. In fact, he told Mark that the military had rejected the design and that he wanted to create a sales presentation to sell it. Jake's response confirms that. He's telling the truth. The ball is in Wardle's court.

Wardle delivers. She simply restates what she knows to get his reaction. Jake is on trial. The ball is in his court. Palmer's stoic presence adds additional pressure. (Don't be afraid to run your character through the ringer.)

Jake states the truth as he understands it. After all, he is a scout.

                    COAST GUARD OFFICER
          That's it. That's the one.

He breathes heavily, his brow covered with sweat.

                    WARDLE
          Now listen carefully. That helicopter
          does not exist. You never saw it.

The officer nods. Wardle reinforces it with an insincere smile.

                    WARDLE
          Get out of here.

The Coast Guard Officer nearly runs out.

Wardle catches Palmer's attention. His eyes drop to the top secret file. She BUZZES the intercom.

INSERT THE FILE HEADING, which reads: "DEKKER, JAKE."

                    WARDLE (OS)
          Send in Dekker.

She sips her coffee as Jake Dekker steps in and sits down.

                    WARDLE
          Is this your work?

Wardle tosses the computer-generated drawing of the Hummingbird
MG-11 helicopter on the table. She drinks the last from her
coffee cup.

                    JAKE
          Yes, I submitted the design to Bates.
          He rejected it.

                    WARDLE
          The Coast Guard spotted this less
          than 50 miles from here. In the
          air.

She waits. Jake is stunned, but calm.

Palmer -- face of stone -- nods to himself, making mental notes.

                    JAKE
          Impossible.

She brings in new information about other people seeing the helicopter. Her tapping the helicopter drawing with her finger is an unimportant, incidental action. I justify leaving it because the scene is a key scene and I want to dramatize it. But I could easily drop it to save space if necessary.

Wardle's second line is a challenging question, but Jake is equal to it. He confronts her by telling her directly that it didn't get into the sky. He's a reasonable man and explains why. The ball is back in Wardle's court.

Wardle uses his words against him. Because it was in the sky and he can't afford it, someone must have paid him. The conflict escalates. And now we're beginning to see Wardle's point of view. It's generally good policy to give each of your characters a different view of the facts. And we'll continue to see (after page 10) how she views things differently from Jake. In this particular case, Jake has not seen the facts yet, but *we* have, and Wardle sees this situation differently from us. The result is to create more sympathy for Jake and less for Wardle.

What's the purpose for Jake's action of glancing at Palmer and running his hand through his hair? It is to show his emotion. We need to know what he is feeling and his action communicates his frustration to the reader. Do not cut off your characters emotionally from the reader. (Note the style of the writing in the second paragraph. Many screenwriters omit the repetition of pronouns; it's a style popularized by Shane Black.)

Jake responds with "NASA"—that's who he works for. I do not instruct the actor how to say this line. It could be a sarcastic answer. A question mark after "NASA" might suggest more of a smart-aleck attitude. There are many ways to go here and I don't give in to the temptation of telling the actor how to say this.

The exchange of power between the two crescendos to the moment when Wardle stands up and challenges Jake with her eyes. But unlike the Coast Guard Officer, Jake does not flinch.

Next comes the Catalyst of the movie, the event that upsets the equilibrium of Jake's life. There's even a deadline on it to create pressure and suspense. How can Jake accomplish this? He doesn't even know where "the bird" is or that it really exists. We've laid a lot on the shoulders of our hero. Hopefully, the reader wants to read more.

In a previous draft, I ended the scene differently. But the producer I was working with dismissed it because it sounded "too much like Mel Gibson." He felt that Jake should be "shaken" at the end of the interview to emphasize the enormous burden he was under. In the end, I agreed with the producer, but you can read the previous version on page 196. Which do you prefer?

Finally, Jake staggers out. That final paragraph is simply an assessment of Jake's emotional state, so that the reader can identify emotionally with him.

                    WARDLE
          Later, two civilians in separate
          incidents. Thought it was aliens.

She taps the helicopter drawing with her finger.

                    WARDLE
          So how did this...get into the sky?

                    JAKE
          It didn't. It would take millions of
          dollars to manufacture a proto-type.

                    WARDLE
          Exactly. So who you working for?

Jake is mystified. Casts a glance Palmer's way for an
explanation. Runs a frustrated hand through his hair.

                    JAKE
          ...NASA.

                    WARDLE
          Not any more. You're terminated,
          Dekker, and I'm considering
          prosecution.

                    JAKE
          The charge?

                    WARDLE
          Espionage.

                    JAKE
          You think I sold the plans to a
          foreign government?

Wardle stands slowly, glares down at Jake, but he doesn't flinch.

                    WARDLE
          The helicopter is out there. If
          you're connected with it, you're
          going down. Unless you come clean.

Jake's eyes narrow.

                    WARDLE
          I want that bird. And I want it in
          twenty-four hours. That is all.

Jake -- violated, confused -- staggers out.

Here's the fifth-draft ending of the scene on page 10:

                    JAKE
          What I've done on my own time
          belongs to me.

His finger comes down hard on the table. Palmer notes it.
Dekker's eyes shift to Palmer and:

WHACK! Wardle slams her empty coffee mug on the table.
Palmer is so startled he drops his notebook, but Jake
doesn't flinch.

                    WARDLE
          Now you listen up, Dekker, if you're
          freelancing I swear I'll break you.
          I want that bird. And I want it in
          twenty-four hours.

Jake slowly stands. A monolith.

                    JAKE
          You ought to switch to de-caf. It's
          easier on your nerves.

And after a friendly nod, he exits.

● ● ● ● ●

Don't be misled by my analysis into thinking you need to be analytical when writing.
However, you do want to use your reasoning powers in evaluating what you've written. And you don't need to emulate my writing style. A more gifted writer could do a
better job of presenting the same material.

Finally, when all is said and done, the real test of your first ten pages is this: Does the
reader want to know what happens next? If you want to know what happens next to
Jake and Kendall, then I have succeeded.

● ● ● ● ●

Note: For an example of a comedy scene, refer to pages 67-68. Other scenes can be
found throughout this volume, and most particularly in Book III.

HOW TO SELL YOUR SCRIPT

BOOK V

A Marketing Plan

How to protect your work

Congratulations! You, the next great screenwriter, have written a stunning script! Realize that you have reached a major milestone. You should definitely reward yourself with positive self-talk and a bowl of ice cream.

In Hollywood, no script is sacred. Don't worry, there are ways to protect you and your creative offspring. There are ways to protect your rights.

Keep records

First, be organized. Life can get very complicated, so write things down. Keep a journal of meetings you have with people and record what was discussed. (See pages 224-225.) Keep a log of phone calls, queries, and script submissions. You'll need these for the lawsuit later. You'll also use these records to follow up on contacts and create future strategies for selling your work.

If there's ever any question in your mind that there might be a legal problem, consult an entertainment attorney. You may even want an attorney to review any contracts you're offered, particularly if the offerer is not signatory to the Writers Guild of America.

Note: Only attorneys can give legal advice, and I am therefore not qualified to do so. Nothing in this volume should be construed as legal advice because it is not intended as such.

Copyright

Keep in mind that there are certain things you cannot protect: ideas, historical facts, plots, titles, phrases, and anything not written down. Here's what you can protect: Your original expression of an idea or plot; in other words, your original, spec script is the only thing you can protect.

There are several ways to protect your spec screenplay. Under the current copyright law, you own the copyright to your work even as you write it. You don't even need to use the copyright symbol. To create a public record of your script, however, you may wish to *register* your copyright with the U.S. Copyright Office in Washington, D.C. It's a simple, painless, and inexpensive procedure. Just contact the Copyright Office in Washington, D.C. Once done, you must display the copyright symbol on your script.

My personal observation is that most working writers do not register their scripts with the copyright office, presumably because the eventual producer will own the copyright to the completed film, and thus the script. That doesn't mean that *you* shouldn't. After all, registering your copyright gives you the best protection you can get.

The WGA

The purpose of registration is to establish yourself as the creator of your original work. Most writers register their scripts with the Writers Guild of America. All ten of my scripts are registered with the WGA only. I don't want a script dated—they get old fast, and the copyright symbol dates the script. No matter what protective methods you use, make sure one of them is registration with the Writers Guild of America.

The Writers Guild maintains two offices. One is in Los Angeles; the other is in New York. The Mississippi River serves as a boundary between the jurisdictions of the east and west guild offices.

To register your script with the WGA, simply send your screenplay, treatment, or synopsis to them with $20 ($22 for the Writers Guild, east) and they will hold the copy for five years. It can be retrieved at any time thereafter. When five years have expired, you may renew your registration. You may register your script more than once. Some writers like to register their first draft as well as their final polish. You should register a treatment or synopsis if you are going to present it to others, or if you're going to delay the writing of your script.

An alternative to the Writers Guild registration service is that provided by the recently formed National Creative Registry. To date, the WGA has not stated whether or not they'd recognize a National Creative Registry registration in cases where the WGA must arbitrate a credits dispute between writers.

The Writers Guild provides other services to writers besides their script registration service. You do not need to belong the Guild to benefit from their services, or to register your script.

What can the WGA offer you? Here's a list of services:

- Registration of your script, treatment, or synopsis for a period of five years. You may renew your registration after that.

- Pre-negotiated contracts if you sign with a producer or studio that is signatory to the Guild or acquire an agent who is signatory to the Guild.

- Arbitration if a dispute arises regarding credits or for other grievances.

- A list of agencies that are signatory to the Guild. The cost is nominal. Visit their website at www.wga.org.

- A library where you can go and read scripts.

- Information as to who represents a particular writer. This could help in your search for an agent.

Again, you need not be a member to use these services. You may join the Guild once you have the required number of credits. For more information, contact the appropriate office. Refer to Book VI for addresses and phone numbers.

Other means of protection
Another way to protect your work is to have several people read it so that they can testify that you wrote it. Keep records of meetings and phone conversations.

Still another method is the Poor Man's Copyright. (I suppose if you're a poor woman, it can work for you as well.) Put the script in an envelope, seal it, and send it via *registered mail* to yourself. Don't open it; keep it for the lawsuit later. Personally, I don't believe this would actually work in fact. Just pay the twenty bucks and register it with the Guild.

An additional protection is the completed script itself. If you pitch an idea to a producer that she likes, she'll ask for your script. Why would she steal the idea and pay a working writer $250,000 to execute your idea when she can pay you $100,000 for a script that already exists?

What you must do before entering the market

There are several markets for scripts, and we will discuss them all. But before you even think of approaching the marketplace, you want to get your ducks in a row. I have watched with sadness the many writers who have broken their hearts by approaching the market prematurely. Don't let your passion or the prospect of dollar signs obscure your vision. Make sure the writing is done before the selling begins. Do not contact producers and agents until you are prepared. Be sure that your script is finished, evaluated, and registered—and your marketing plan is written—*before* you mail that first query or make that first call.

YOUR CALLING CARD

To break into this business, you need at least one showcase script (preferably two or more) that is proof of your writing ability. If you want to write for television, you will need one feature script and at least one sample television script.

This showcase script (or scripts) should be registered with the Writers Guild, formatted correctly, and should be complete in every way. Never submit a work in progress. Realize that your script is a prospectus asking for a $10-30 million investment or more. That is why it must be good.

Since Tinsel Town is into appearances, it is essential that your script look as good as it can possibly look. Obviously, you will want to format it correctly, avoiding camera directions and editing directions (unless it is a script for animation). You may wonder why I discourage technical directions when most scripts you've read have them. That's because most scripts you've read are *shooting* scripts.

Make sure you understand spec writing and formatting. Some conventions have recently changed. I don't know how many times writers have sent me their scripts for evaluation after it has been rejected all over town, and I find formatting errors, obvious writing mistakes, and easy-to-fix problems that might have made a difference. Books III and IV are your friends.

To further guide you in preparing a professional-looking script, there's a list of common errors on page 110. Many of the points seem nit-picky. They are, and for good reason. The poor souls who must read dozens of scripts every week are looking for any excuse to eliminate scripts from their reading stack. Abiding by their simple rules is an easy way to make a good impression.

Of course, appearance isn't everything, and correct format alone will not save you. Your script must tell an interesting story. It must be well-crafted. There can be no references to the thoughts and feelings of characters: *When John saw Mary, it reminded him of the first time they met.* Don't write anything that cannot appear on the screen. You are limited in your writing to what can be *seen*, and what can be *heard*. That's it.

Make sure your script is ready. Ask yourself the questions in Book II. When I present seminars, about eighty percent of the questions I'm asked have to do with selling the script. I often find these people coming back months later a little beat up, but a little wiser. They want to make sure their next script is well-written before they try to sell it. You must write it before you sell it.

Your spec script should provide a smooth *read*. Your description should focus on images and actions; your dialogue should be crisp and allow for subtext. The writing in general should be concise, specific, and clear.

Before submitting your script, you may wish to get feedback. One place for that is through a writers' group. I recommend writers' groups of about seven to ten writers who meet regularly and read each other's work. You will get worthwhile feedback and the advice will be free.

WRITERS' GROUPS

Writing can be a lonely job. A writers' group may be just the place to turn for comfort, support, and feedback.

Where to find writers' groups
Writers' groups are everywhere if you know where to look. Here are six general areas to begin your search:

1. Attend writers' conferences, workshops, and writing classes. Network with fellow writers and ask them if they know of any writers' groups.

2. Read the classified ads of writing publications. Many groups and individuals advertise in the classifieds, seeking to form or continue a group. Some established groups, like the Scriptwriter's Network in Los Angeles, have special requirements.

3. For a fee, you may join large, professional organizations such as The Scriptwriter's Network (already mentioned), the National Writer's Club, and the Wisconsin Screenwriter's Forum. (See listings in Book VI.) I have ceated a place at my web site (www.clearstream.com) for writers' groups and organizations. Look there or advertise (free) your writers' group.

4. Call your state film commissioner or county film board (if one exists) about possible writers' groups in your area.

5. Other places where writers might hang out include film festivals, movie clubs, bookstores, web sites, and university and adult education programs.

6. Don't forget to approach nonwriting friends and acquaintances who might know writers who belong to groups.

If your search for a writers' group proves fruitless, there's only one thing left to do—start your own group.

How to find writers to start a group
You know now where writers can be found. Here are ways to gather them into a group.

1. Network with them at conferences and workshops. Trade phone numbers. One writer recently used this simple, proven method to create a group composed of participants of my seminar and Michael Hauge's.

2. Ask the instructor to put your name and phone number on the board because you'd like to start a writers' group. That way interested writers can call you. Ask me to post your writers' group at my web site (www.clearstream.com).

3. Post a notice on bulletin boards and classrooms at conferences, asking people to sign up. You can pick these lists up later.

4. Distribute flyers to classmates or fellow conference-goers. You can even go out on a limb and announce the first meeting in the flyer.

5. Place a "Writers Wanted" classified ad in scriptwriting newsletters and magazines (see Book V for a list of periodicals).

6. Send a letter of invitation to college or adult-education classes, announcing the date of your meeting.

7. Try bulletin boards and round tables featured in on-line computer services. Surf the web.

How to keep the group going

While you're forming the group, you will want to create some rules or guidelines at the same time. Here are some things to keep in mind.

Include writers who are at basically the same level. One group might consist of people who are just getting started. Another group might set up a requirement of one completed screenplay.

Keep the group small. Five people may be enough. Seven is an ideal size. If you start with twelve to fifteen people, you'll likely end up with the magnificent seven who are dedicated.

Make it a participative group. You may need a facilitator to head the group, but make sure everyone has an equal say in making rules. You might even rotate responsibilities, such as making reminder calls and assigning refreshments, so that no one is unduly burdened and everyone is involved.

Find a place to meet. This will probably be someone's house. It might be easier to use the same location continuously, but some groups like to rotate. Many libraries, some savings-and-loan associations, and other businesses have "community rooms" that are without cost for noncommercial use. You qualify if admittance to your group is free.

Have a regular meeting time, such as the first Tuesday of every month, or every Wednesday at 7:30. Get people into a routine.

Decide on the purposes of the group. For example, here is the stated purpose of a group of my students: "To provide each member with the feedback he or she needs to forward his or her screenwriting career. Group members share screenwriting knowledge and provide friendly, constructive critiques of each other's script, treatment, or outline. Members also exchange screenwriting books, magazines, tapes, and their experiences finding agents and marketing scripts."

Some groups focus on one or two writers per session. Some groups require members to send the work to others in advance of the meetings. It's often profitable to read scenes aloud at the meeting itself and evaluate them on the spot, or discuss writing ideas and specific writing problems.

Make sure critiquing sessions do not turn into slugfests. Writers should avoid a defensive posture. Listen carefully, avoid speaking, take the advice seriously, but remember that you are the writer of *your* script. Criticism should be given constructively. Members should avoid speaking in absolutes, but instead offer their opinions, reactions, observations, and suggestions.

Each member should agree to a code of silence. Everything discussed or read is confidential.

How to creatively maintain your group
After a while, a motivating routine develops into a fatiguing rut. Because all members of the group are *creative*, this problem can be solved by being creative. Here are some ideas to get you started.

- Organize a script swap night

- Read a script, then view the movie together

- Sponsor a contest, or challenge another group to a contest

- Invite a working writer to address the group.

- Compile a collection of query letters or rejection letters

- Have special awards when a writer passes a milestone

- Set aside a night just for pitching practice; rotate the roles of writer and producer/executive

When groups get too large, create specialized areas such as the "Comedy Writers" or the "Sci-Fi Chapter" or "Advanced Writers." You can have a short, large meeting for everyone, and then break into the specialized groups.

In the best writers' groups and organizations, a feeling of comraderie develops, enabling each writer to root for the other's success. It's an upward spiral of positive energy that revitalizes each writer. This is the fuel each writer needs to keep writing.

SCRIPT CONSULTANTS

Some writers seek out a professional reader for a coverage. A coverage is what a reader (actual title is *story analyst*) writes for the agents, producers, and executives who hire her. It usually consists of a two-page synopsis, a brief analysis of the screenplay, and a recommendation. The cost for such a coverage is approximately $100.

More extensive than a coverage is a detailed evaluation provided by professional script consultants like myself. That's going to cost you more. Check the listings in Book VI for both story analysts and script consultants.

Another way to get feedback is to ask your spouse and friends to read your script. And we know what that's worth.

ATTITUDE

Success in the marketplace requires a certain mind-set. You want to be professional in your dealings with others. Be confident without being arrogant, and wily without being devious. It's easy to be intimidated by these "glamorous" people, but in reality they are no different from you, except that they have a different job.

Today's screenwriter needs to be enthusiastic and pleasantly persistent. I've seen very talented writers fall by the wayside, and mediocre writers make it because they were persistent. Usually the marketing process takes time. You must be committed.

People want to work with writers they can "work with." This is you if you can stand back from your work and be objective about it. It's difficult taking criticism, particularly mindless criticism, but being defensive will work against you whether you are right or wrong. At the same time, you must believe in your work and be excited about it. After all, if you don't believe in it, who will?

Confidence, conviction, and initiative are pluses. Arrogance, doubt, and passivity are minuses.

Make an inventory of your strengths and the strengths of your script. Don't count on hitting a home run on the first pitch. You are probably not going to get a million dollars for your first spec script, although it has happened. Allow yourself to be realistic without being negative. Be prepared to walk this road one step at a time without appearing too hungry along the way. Someday, you may find what Lynda Obst calls "a place at the table."

Your strategic marketing plan

The movie business is a business. To succeed in business, you need to successfully market your product and your service. Your product is your script. And your service is your ability to write. Marketing is not a matter of mass mailing a query letter and hoping you win the jackpot. And it's not throwing scripts and ideas against the wall to see which ones stick.

Today's market is more closed to outsiders and more competitive than in years past. You need a refined approach, a laser-like focus. You need a strategic marketing plan in which you determine your target market, create marketing strategies that will help you achieve your sales objectives, and position yourself in the market.

PRINCIPLES

First, let's review a few basic marketing principles that affect all of your marketing efforts.

Two key marketing concepts are segmentation and differentiation. *Segmentation* is identifying the market segments that seem best for your script. *Differentiation* is how you differentiate yourself from other writers competing for that same market segment. Differentiation has to do both with your product—your script, story, concept—and with your marketing approach. What gives you that competitive edge?

Purpose, audience, strategy

In any persuasive presentation in any business arena, there are three planning steps: purpose, audience, and strategy First, identify your purpose, then understand your audience (your market), and finally create strategies to reach that audience (market). These steps sound simple enough, but few people apply them.

Purpose has to do with what *you* want to accomplish, what you want to sell. It derives from your point of view. The audience is whom you want to influence. Once you understand your audience, your market, then you know what they need to hear.

In my earlier years, I was a business executive. I have since become a writer/producer, script consultant, and seminar leader. But I still do a little marketing consulting and even teach an occasional college-level marketing course. I can't tell you how many business people I've given the following speech to: "You cannot say what you want to say, you have to say what they want to hear. They don't care how much your family sacrificed to build your business, they just want to know if the product works." So strategy comes from the point of view of your audience.

Here's an example. You want a raise. That's your purpose. Your audience is your boss. And most people's strategy is to state all the reasons they deserve the raise (using a lot of sentences that begin with "I"). A better strategy is to come from the boss's point of view: "Boss, here is how *you* will benefit . . . ." So strategy is involved with communicating the benefits to your audience.

Your purpose is to sell your script or get a writing assignment. Actually, that's a little vague. You need to identify a *specific individual* you want to sell your script to. Once done, then you need to understand that person and his or her company. What is their buying history? What are they looking for now? Do they prefer query letters or phone calls? Who is *their* market? In the final analysis, they don't care if you're starving. They don't care that you've been writing scripts for ten years. They want to know if *your* ideas can be used to reach *their* market. Or, they want to know if you are the writer who can execute *their* ideas into a script.

Your strategy—therefore—*derives* from their needs. What do *they* need to see in a query to interest them in *your* script. How will they benefit from what you have to offer?

This same principle applies to meetings. What is your goal for the meeting? Who are you pitching to? What approach is most likely to succeed with this particular person? We'll discuss how to gather all this marketing information later.

Features and benefits

In any sales situation, the "informed" sales person presents features and benefits. *Features* constitute the logical argument; *benefits* are emotional. This ballpoint pen in my hand now features a retractable point. The benefit to you is you don't get ink in your purse or pocket.

Some time ago, I was trying to sell a car and an engineer dropped by. I thought this person would be most interested in specific facts about my car. But his reactions were all negative. During the test drive, however, I turned on the radio. And he said, "Whoa, what's that?"

I thought to myself "It's your emotional hot button and I am about to use it as a strategy in presenting an emotional argument (or benefit) for buying the car." Here's how the conversation went. I said, "What kind of music do you like?" He liked classical, so I dropped in a tape and said, "Imagine yourself driving through the Irvine hills. Just you, the road, and Mozart." Well, he bought a car stereo with a car attached.

In any situation, try to think in terms of how the producer or agent will benefit, and what turns them on emotionally. For example, in a pitching situation: If there are merchandising opportunities that naturally flow from your story, mention them. If your story presents a role that an "A" actor would be interested in, that's a feature that provides an emotional benefit to the producer. Be sure to stress the benefit: "With 'A' talent attached, you know the financing will not be a problem. It's a go."

The "short attention span" obstacle

No one needs to tell you that concept is king in Hollywood. It also sells in every other industry. Marketers need a handle that buyers can hang on to. In the case of my book, *The Screenwriter's Bible*, the handle or concept is: Six books in one. Everything you need under one cover (how-to text, workbook, formatter, spec writing guide, marketing plan, and resource directory—all included).

Agents, producers, and executives are younger, have shorter attention spans, and have more to read. That's why it is crucial to find the right concept, those few words in your query or pitch that drive the message home. Be able to tell your story, or present a story hook, in twenty-five words or less. (See Book I for information about high concept.)

But concept is nothing without conviction. Your enthusiasm and conviction about your project are probably your most important assets. The voice of conviction is what sells the concept. Enthusiasm is contagious.

MARKETING RESEARCH

When you sit down and write a script, you cannot know what the market will be when the script is finally completed. You can't outguess the market. Yes, there are some genres and structures that seem perennial favorites. For example, action stories, romantic comedies (date movies), and thrillers are usually in demand. But you don't know specifically what will sell.

However, a study of the market can help you avoid problems. For example, if you are writing a social drama, don't write it with a high budget. Why? Because it's not likely to become a big-screen movie; it's more likely to become a TV Movie-of-the-Week.

It will also help you if you create a role that an "A" actor will covet. Usually this means the story revolves around an original character with a great character arc, and that almost every scene is about that character. Stars drive this business. Now while you're actually writing, don't think about stars or roles for stars—just write the story.

Although there are many production companies looking for character studies, most want scripts strong on story with a role that will attract a star. I'm sorry to report that more top male stars than female stars can get movies made. Lists of "A" talent can be found in special issues of *The Hollywood Reporter, Premiere,* and elsewhere.

On the other hand, you may have a small, independent market or avant garde niche in mind. Perfect. Now ask yourself what kind of screenplay will likely meet the needs of that market. We will address specific markets later.

It is true that you want to be aware of your market before you write, but write the story you have passion to write. In other words, forget about the market once you start writing your script. Remember, you cannot predict the market one year from now. You can only make informed choices.

What to do with all of those scripts

From one perspective, you need only three things to break in: connections, concepts, and scripts. As time goes by, and you begin stockpiling unsold scripts, you will want to use wisdom in managing your business.

First of all, don't send a script immediately when you finish it. Let it sit and ferment. Some of the problems may solve themselves in your head. New ideas may come. Some problems that you didn't know existed may show themselves. On the other hand, don't rewrite it to death. Another reason to let your script lay idle a month or so is to let your emotions cool. Now you can be objective.

If a movie similar to your script is about to be released, wait and see how that movie does. If it succeeds, send your script out immediately. If it fails, wait about a year before sending your script out. If a script similar to your script was sold recently, wait about five or six months before sending yours out. If the word goes out that a producer wants an ecological western, and you have one written but didn't send it out because of one of the above situations, now you're in a position to cash in. Your patience, restraint, and common sense have paid off.

Where to go for information about markets
Read the trades. *Variety* (which leans a bit more toward features) and the *Hollywood Reporter* (which leans a bit to the world of television) are worthwhile business publications. Weekly editions are also available. They tell you what sold, who sold it, who bought it, when it will be shot, what the logline is, etc.

Both of these publications list films in development and films in production. You will find special focus sections on specific market segments. And there's marketing information on all the players, including the independents. You will even find ads for seminars and scripts.

For example, say you want to sell to Showtime. Would it be worthwhile to know that half their financing (as of this writing) comes from foreign sources? That means your project needs to appeal to the foreign market. Now you might say, well that's what I have an agent for. And you're absolutely right. But whether you have an agent or not, understanding the market at some level will help you in pitches, meetings, phone calls, and in planning your next script—for that matter, in planning your career.

There are many other industry publications. *Premiere* provides a power list once a year. *Hollywood Scriptwriter* provides interviews with successful writers and other articles. *Script* is filled with articles about writing and selling for a variety of markets, including mainstream. *Creative Screenwriting* is also excellent. If nothing else, subscribe to the above publications.

There are numerous directories, such as the *Hollywood Creative Directory* (in Santa Monica). These are listed in Book VI. New resource tools and directories pop up all the time. Every so often, check the "Bible Updates" section at my web site (www.clearstream.com) and my hot links page. One of those links is the Internet Movie Database, an excellent source of industry information. Visit other screenwriting sites.

Attend workshops and seminars, and meet the people there. Don't overlook film festivals.

Writer's organizations such as Women in Film and the Scriptwriter's Network in Studio City can provide information and support. Again, review the listings in Book VI. Some organizations publish newsletters. Just a local screenwriter's group can be helpful because you can network with other writers who know things. Meet people. Ask questions. It might even help you to join non-writing industry organizations.

CREATING YOUR PERSONAL STRATEGIC MARKETING PLAN

Beginning on the next page, you will find a number of worksheets to help you create a marketing plan and focus your marketing strategies. You have my permission to photocopy the worksheets for your own personal use. Before completing them, however, I recommend that you read this entire book.

The Project Plan
The first worksheet is entitled, "Project Plan." Let's start there first. Your project is the script you wish to sell. After you identify your target market, complete the remainder of the Project Plan (four pages) and focus on more specific possibilities.

Ask yourself, where do you see your project playing? Is it a SIMPSONS-type project? If so, who are potential producers of such a project? Is it a summer blockbuster movie? Who produces summer blockbusters? Or who wants to? Is it an adult horror movie? —Whoa, there are no adult horror movies anymore, except films like FATAL ATTRACTION.

Don't ignore the smaller cable markets, reality programming, infomercials, direct-to-video, and so on. I call these Hollywood's back door. If you live outside of California, investigate local production companies. What's happening in your own region? Start somewhere and work your way to glory.

And don't think you must have an agent to succeed. Most first scripts are sold without an agent. Marketing is filling needs. If your script fills a need, then the task becomes getting the script to the person who can benefit from it. That involves understanding your prospective buyer in order to create an effective strategy; it also entails recognizing obstacles and seeking ways to overcome them.

So be honest in your assessment. Where does your project belong and why? Who produces for that venue? Choose *producers* who have worked on projects similar to your proposed movie. List individual names, not production companies.

Text continues on page 226

Project Plan

Title_____

Genre/description _____

TARGET MARKET

What is the best market for your script?

❑ Feature screenplay   ❑ Network MOW   ❑ Cable movie

❑ TV series (1 hour)   ❑ Sitcom (network)   ❑ Sitcom (cable)

❑ New technology (interactive, CD-ROM, etc.)   ❑ Animation

❑ Reality programming   ❑ Direct-to-video (feature)   ❑ Infomercial

❑ Other _____

More specifically, what is the best venue for your project? (This question asks you to look realistically at the market. Where would you find a similar project? A blockbuster summer release? A Fox network weekend one-hour TV series? A woman-in-jeopardy movie for the USA Network?)

_____

_____

_____

_____

_____

_____

List producers or production companies that produce for this target market.

_____

_____

_____

_____

_____

If appropriate for your market, list potential talent that could be interested by this project. This means that the actor or actress sees a role in your script that will further their career.

_____

_____

_____

_____

_____

_____

List potential directors, if appropriate, for your project.

_____

_____

_____

_____

_____

_____

If finding an agent or manager will help you sell this project (and it probably will, although you can sell to some markets without an agent), then list potential agents here (list specific individuals, not agencies).

_____

_____

_____

_____

_____

_____

_____

MAKING CONTACTS

Who in the film business has read your work and responded favorably?

_____

_____

_____

_____

_____

Who do you know in the business (not listed above) who might refer you to someone else or otherwise be helpful? (These people do not have to be in high places.)

_____

_____

_____

_____

List any friends, relatives, acquaintances, business associates who might have industry contacts. (The premise here is that everyone knows someone who knows someone who works in Hollywood. Spend some time with this.)

_____

_____

_____

_____

_____

_____

_____

_____

List places you can go to network. These can be writers groups, professional organizations, social gatherings, clubs, festivals, seminars.

_____

_____

_____

_____

_____

_____

_____

List other marketing research sources (i.e., "the trades," directories, etc.)

_____

_____

_____

_____

_____

_____

_____

List other marketing ideas that might be right for your script, such as contests.

_____

_____

_____

_____

_____

_____

POSITIONING STRATEGIES

Important note: Positioning has to do with creating perceptions in the prospect's mind. The worksheets that follow will provide more detail and support for your marketing strategies and project plan.

How is your project similar to other successful projects in the medium you have chosen? _____

_____

_____

How is your project original? What fresh twists does it add? _____

_____

_____

Draw a picture
of a movie poster
or a newspaper ad
for your script.

Include the ad
copy. How will
your story or
idea be sold?

Which of your script's pluses can you emphasize in the selling process?

_____ Commerciality—Will the resulting movie be a cinch to market?

_____ A role that an "A" actor or actress will covet.

_____ A story that is visual, active, and fresh, that doesn't rework other movies.

_____ An ending that is emotionally satisfying.

_____ A character (and characters) that is believable and interesting.

_____ A script that is not too similar to a recent failure, yet has something in common with a past success.

_____ A script that is in correct spec format, and that flows like a river when read.

_____ A one-sentence concept, hook, or logline that says, "This is a movie. Buy me!"

_____ A concise, hard-hitting, saliva-inducing query letter.

_____ Will the resulting budget be unreasonable for the genre, with a dozen far-flung locations shot entirely at night in the water with animals and children, and with hundreds of special effects and opticals.

What personal pluses do you bring to the table?

_____ Enthusiasm.

_____ Objectivity—Can you separate your ego from your work, or are you defensive?

_____ Ambition—Do you love the business and want a full-time writing career?

_____ Grace—Do people enjoy working with you? talking to you? meeting you?

IDENTIFYING PROSPECTS

The next step in your plan—once you have completed the above worksheets and the "positioning" worksheets that follow—is to begin your marketing research and networking. You will also begin to approach people you suspect might know someone in the industry.

Now, select your best prospects (producers, talent, directors, agents, and contacts). Generally, you will work with about eight people at a time. You will not contact any of them until you have done your homework (completed the worksheets).

Name _____ Title _____

Company _____

Buying (and/or other) history _____

_____

Budget range (if applicable) _____

Current needs/wants _____

_____

How he/she prefers to be contacted _____

Name _____ Title _____

Company _____

Buying (and/or other) history _____

_____

Budget range (if applicable) _____

Current needs/wants _____

_____

How he/she prefers to be contacted _____

Name _____ Title _____

Company _____

Buying (and/or other) history _____

_____

Budget range (if applicable) _____

Current needs/wants _____

_____

How he/she prefers to be contacted _____

══

Name _____ Title _____

Company _____

Buying (and/or other) history _____

_____

Budget range (if applicable) _____

Current needs/wants _____

_____

How he/she prefers to be contacted _____

══

Name _____ Title _____

Company _____

Buying (and/or other) history _____

_____

Budget range (if applicable) _____

Current needs/wants _____

_____

How he/she prefers to be contacted _____

══

Name _____ Title _____

Company _____

Buying (and/or other) history _____

_____

Budget range (if applicable) _____

Current needs/wants _____

_____

How he/she prefers to be contacted _____

Name _____ Title _____

Company _____

Buying (and/or other) history _____

_____

Budget range (if applicable) _____

Current needs/wants _____

_____

How he/she prefers to be contacted _____

Name _____ Title _____

Company _____

Buying (and/or other) history _____

_____

Budget range (if applicable) _____

Current needs/wants _____

_____

How he/she prefers to be contacted _____

Weekly Action Plan

Main goal _____

Key milestones   1_____

2_____

3_____

Time commitment _____

What specific actions will you take this week to achieve your milestones?

Marketing research _____

Meetings, pitches, groups, networking _____

_____

_____

Query letters _____

_____

Cold calls _____

_____

_____

Follow-ups by mail or fax _____

_____

Follow-ups by phone_____

_____

Contests _____

Other _____

Other _____

Other _____

Notes:

Correspondence Log (Queries & Submissions)

Date	Q/S	Script Title	Person/Company	Comments, response, follow-ups

Meetings and Telephone Log

Date	Time	M/T	Person/Company	Comments, ideas discussed

Continued from page 213

The *Hollywood Creative Directory* will be helpful, as will other directories and resources mentioned earlier and listed in Book VI. Even the "Film and TV Production Charts" in the trades will be helpful. Keep in mind that sometimes a company grows weary of a particular genre and is ready for something different (but not too different).

Now look for potential *talent*. You may ask, *Why look for potential talent if producers are the buyers?* Because many actors and actresses have their own production companies and are looking for projects just for them. The interest of a bankable star can raise your script from obscurity.

Be sensible—you won't find Harrison Ford and Denzel Washington interested in a TV-movie about the risks of prostate cancer. And keep in mind that a star's agent is usually a poor place to send a script. Unless you represent money, the agent may never get the script to the star. However, a hot query letter might get forwarded to the actor.

What **directors** might be appropriate for your project? Now if you're writing for television, this may not be applicable. A known TV director may not add that much to the project. But a film director or bankable star, even if they don't have a production company, can add value to a script if they express interest in it. Imagine saying to an agent or producer, "I have a script that Leonardo DiCaprio is interested in."

Finally, list the names of potential **agents**. First, get the Writers Guild list of approved agencies, then the Hollywood Creative Directory's *Hollywod Agents and Managers Directory*. Learn what you can about the agencies through your marketing research, but select individual literary agents to contact. You won't pick a name at the top of the list of any agency.

All of the above areas will be explored later in detail.

Making contacts

As Joan Rivers said, "It's not *who* you know, it's whom." This business is built on relationships, and it's a small town. Networking is how you find contacts. Contacts are your bread and butter. And even though Hollywood is the only town where you can die of encouragement (thank you, Dorothy Parker), you need connections. You must meet people and you must nurture the contacts you make.

As your agent circulates your script and as you contact people about your script, you will find many who will say no, but who respond favorably to your work. Write down their names along with the names of those who say yes. (See pages 216-217.) You will stay in touch with these people once or twice a year. When you complete another script, they might be willing to read it, or refer you to someone it's right for. Don't underestimate the value of someone who has rejected you.

Very important! List anyone you know who might know someone in the business. (See worksheet on pages 216-217.) Any friends, relatives, business colleagues, and acquaintances. Everyone knows someone who knows someone who works in Hollywood or at a local production company. Just pretend you are a new Amway distributor and list anyone and everyone. You may be shocked at all the contacts you have access to.

It's no secret that the number one way to break into Hollywood is by referral. Many producers and industry people will read a referred script that otherwise they would demand you submit through an agent.

My students are always surprised at the results of this powerful little exercise. Once they mention to friends, acquaintances, and relatives that they are writing a script, the windows of heaven often open before them, and blessings pour down on their heads.

You may discover that your Aunt Tilly once dated Robert Redford, or that your boss was a fraternity brother of Brad Pitt, or that your friend was a childhood playmate of the current president of ICM.

Take the time to ask around. This list of potential contacts could include producers, executives, actors, directors, script supervisors, assistants-to-whomever, agents, gophers, gaffers, grips, secretaries, and even janitors. Yes, even gaffers and janitors are insiders. They may be closer to the action than you.

Once you have a list of names, contact them by phone, fax, mail or e-mail. The first words out of your mouth or on the letter will be the name of the person who referred you. Then simply ask this contact to read your script. Tell him you'd love to get his opinion. I am always surprised at how generous people are in these situations. Because producers and agents often receive more than 100 scripts a week, it can be difficult getting your script to someone, and yet that same person may readily accept a referred script and place it at the top of their pile.

If your contact enjoys the read, he will know what to do with the script and to whom to give it. If your contact is a producer, she will refer you to an agent so that the script can be "legally" submitted. Sometimes the script will be referred to another Hollywood-type person. I've heard of assistants and mail boys just placing the script on someone's desk. Someone may even want to "discover" you.

One surprised student reported that she mentioned her script to a relative who happened to know a TV producer. This TV producer read the script and referred her to an agent. Now she is a working writer.

Don't think that the only possibilities lie in Hollywood. You might have opportunities in your own area. There are many regional production companies, and there are film people in every state.

As mentioned, you will also meet people in writers' groups, seminars, classes, screenwriting organizations, Internet chat rooms, festivals, and conferences. You can even meet people through contests.

Contests
You will find more than fifty contests, including all of the majors, listed in Book VI. (Visit www.clearstream.com for "Bible updates.") Also be aware of local contests. Contact your state film commissioner about opportunities for screenwriters.

Even if you don't win a contest, scripts are often judged by, or otherwise find their way to, industry professionals. You might make a contact, get a meeting, or even receive an offer. In fact, entering contests can be done concurrently with your other selling efforts.

In entering contests, be sure to read the rules carefully. Most contests have their own formatting requirements and some may be looking for specific types of scripts. Many will state their judging criteria. Make sure your script is polished before you submit it. If you win a contest or place, you can insert this fact in the qualifications section of your query letter. You have more credibility now; plus you've achieved a milestone that can give you momentum and energy on your upward climb. Many students have "broken in" by winning or placing in contests, or making contacts with judges and readers.

Positioning Strategies
The Positioning Strategies worksheet (page 218) and accompanying checklist of questions (page 219) will help you create a viable marketing strategy.

Identifying prospects
Okay, you understand the nature of your project, you've targeted your market, and you have identified potential buyers and helpers. Now the fun begins. You match your project to these individuals whose names you have written down. Select at least eight people you think will be most helpful, regardless of their position in the industry, and fill in the worksheets on pages 220-222.

List their name, title, and company. What is their buying history? If you don't know already, research it. Your marketing research efforts should continue throughout the selling process. What size projects are they looking for, budget-wise? What are their current needs and wants? And how do they prefer being contacted?

You may not be able to answer all your questions. Don't let that discourage you. Just do your best to learn about your prospects, using the marketing resources discussed and the Internet. The more knowledge you gain, the more power and confidence you will have. Power? Confidence? Yes. Because these prospects are *real* prospects and *you* know you have something that *they* may want. At the very least, you are likely to find a good contact, a connection you can return to later in your career.

Don't rush the process. I've witnessed a lot of heartache from writers who became over-anxious and approached the market prematurely.

Weekly Action Plan
You will want to make specific long-tem goals, both in terms of writing and selling. You will find information on goal-setting at the end of this book in the "A Personal Challenge" section.

The key to achieving your goals is consistent action. Persistence. To help you focus your energy and efforts, I recommend you take a moment at the beginning of each week to create a weekly action plan and make a specific time commitment. (See page 223.)

At the beginning of each week, plan your activities for that week and then commit whatever resources in time, money, and effort you'll need to accomplish those tasks. It may be twenty total hours, or four hours a day, or Tuesday and Thursday nights from 8:00-10:00 P.M. Whatever it is, make a goal each week in terms of time and specific actions. Some weeks, the only action will be to write. Other weeks, there may be several objectives.

What if you fail to achieve any of these goals? Don't kick yourself or quit. What's past is past. Make a new goal for this week. Your goals are motivators to freedom, not prison wardens. Onward!

Contact Logs
On pages 224 and 225, keep track of all your efforts for legal purposes, for tax purposes, and especially for marketing purposes. With each contact you make, you will plan a *follow-up*. Schedule it. Maintain some kind of tickler to remind you of follow-ups, or just to touchbase.

As you contact people, don't forget to apply the purpose-audience-strategy principle and other marketing principles we discussed earlier.

Okay, you have created a marketing plan, but your work is not done. Next, we will discuss positioning strategies, and I will present specific techniques and methods for implementing your plan.

How to find an agent

As you might guess, there are many advantages to acquiring an agent. Agents save you time. They know the territory and how to negotiate a deal. Because agents are expected by the industry to screen out crummy writers, the fact you have one greatly multiplies your chances of finding work. Best of all, agents don't cost anything until they sell your script. Some large agencies, such as ICM and CAA, package scripts; that is, they add talent or a director to generate a studio deal. They are generally more difficult to break into than small agencies. Although a small agency may be a better choice for the novice, you want whomever you can get!

You may have heard how difficult it is to get read. First of all, it is true that agents will seldom read your script, but their assistants will *if* the agent is properly approached.

First, secure a list of approved agencies from the Writers Guild. Their list is coded so that you can select the agencies that are accepting submissions. Keep in mind that the Guild lists agencies, but not individual agents. For this, you may need to go to a directory. I recommend the agent's directory put out by Hollywood Creative Directories (listed in Book VI).

Study the various agency lists and directories you have acquired. If using a directory, you will single out the literary agent that is the farthest down the list in a given agency. As a last resort, call specific agencies and ask, "Who handles new writers?" If you admire an established writer, you may contact the WGA for the name of his or her agent.

The point is to get the names of *individual* agents. You will *not* send them your script. You will instead fax or send a query letter to about five agents at a time. Mailing to five agents at a time enables you to evaluate their responses and improve your query before you contact more agents. You will only contact one agent per agency.

WORKING WITH AN AGENT

Let's assume you have queried several agencies (we'll discuss query letters in the next section), and one has requested your script. You mail your script to the agent with a cover letter. She loves your script and calls.

When an agent calls, she shows her interest by asking the magic question: "What else have you done?" Hopefully, you have written a second dynamite script, and have other ideas to talk about. Most likely this agent will want to meet you personally. There are a few issues that you and your agent will want to settle at this meeting.

One is the contract. The agent gets ten percent. No reputable agent charges a reading fee. Be wary of requests for cash or for referrals to specific script consultants. However, an agent may legitimately ask you to cover the cost of photocopying your script.

In Writers Guild-signatory contracts, there is a ninety-day clause: If the agent has not found you work in ninety days, you can terminate the contract. Before you do, however, remember that selling a script takes time. Many agents will not tender a contract until an offer is made by a producer for your script or services. If your agent is WGA-signatory, then this is usually not a problem—the eventual contract will be WGA-approved.

Your agent will want to discuss your career. What do you want to write? Are any genres of particular interest to you? Do you want to write for television? Are you willing to travel to L.A. for necessary meetings? Are there certain things you are unwilling to write (such as stories that demean women)? Be careful not to sound too picky about what you'll write.

While in Hollywood, choose your battles carefully. Many are not worth fighting; some are.

If you have several scripts, and an agent doesn't like one of them, ask for a release so you can go out and sell it yourself. If you feel uneasy about a particular agent, ask him to tell you about his current clients and recent sales. You'll get an idea of his ability.

Always remember, the agent's primary motivation is money, not helping writers with passion (although that can be a secondary motivation). The agent has twenty to thirty other clients, most of whom can bring in a higher commission than you. The agent represents you because he sees bigger sales down the road and believes you can write the material his contacts want.

Therefore, communicate to the agent your desire for a writing career, your willingness to work hard, and to accept writing assignments and development deals. Keep in mind, though, that screenwriters rarely get assignments for adaptations and rewrites unless they've had a big sale.

In addition to commitment, your agent wants to see in you an ability to perform as a writer and as a *pitcher*—how well you present yourself and your ideas.

Most agents work on a weekly cycle. Each Monday, they set out to sell one or two scripts by Friday. They're also hoping to secure writing assignments for their clients. In fact, they'll often meet with their producer contacts to match their writers to the producers' project ideas. If an agent loves your script and sees that it is similar to some producer's goal, they'll have it delivered to that producer. Often, that results in a meeting that you attend with the producer, which (the agent hopes) results in a development deal.

Although agents are not writing coaches, they will prepare you for meetings and advise you on the ebb and flow of market tides.

There are four kinds of situations that an agent can arrange:

1. The outright sale of your spec script. Your agent will suggest a strategy for selling your script. She will want to generate heat, and solicit the interest of more than one buyer in your script. This can result in an auction. This is the stuff dreams are made of. You will be paid six figures or higher plus receive a bonus of a like amount or even greater amount *if* the screenplay is actually produced. There are also residuals on video cassettes. It will all be spelled out in your book-length contract.

2. A literary purchase and option agreement, commonly called an *option*. Here the buyer is not quite so enthusiastic or simply doesn't want to put a lot of money into the script immediately. In either case, the producer buys an option to the rights for a short period of time (six months to a year) for a small "down payment" of anywhere from zero to $20,000. During that *option period*, the producer uses the script to attract talent and/or money. At the end of the option period, the producer will either pay the purchase price or pass. In the case of a pass, you keep any option money originally given to you, plus the rights to the script revert to you.

3. A development deal. Here, the agent uses your script as a lure to arrange a meeting or pitching session with a producer where you pitch *your* ideas—this can result in a development deal or sale (if the story you pitch is already scripted).

4. An audition. The fourth and most likely scenario is your sample script secures you an audition meeting for an open writing assignment, such as a development deal to

execute the producer's idea into a script. (More about this when we discuss "How to pitch without striking out.") In the case of episodic television, you will be paid to write a couple of episodes plus get residuals if the show goes into syndication.

Once the agent negotiates a deal and conditions are met, the check is sent to the agent, from which he pays you your ninety percent.

Some agents get you to work for them. You go out and make the contacts. When someone expresses interest in your script, you say, "I'll have my agent send you a copy." And then you will inform your agent. Even if you do all of the work, don't even think of attempting to cheat your agent out of the ten percent.

Stay in touch with your agent. Get together on the phone periodically, or in person. During an active campaign, there should be contact at least once a month.

Entertainment attorneys

Your alternative to using an agent is an entertainment attorney. These lawyers are recognized by the industry as acting as agents, but they will charge you $150 to $600 an hour for their services, without any guarantee of a sale. This can get very expensive.

Perhaps a more appropriate situation in which to utilize the services of an entertainment attorney is when you have a legal question or need a contract negotiated or analyzed.

If an attorney misrepresents you, notify the State Bar. If you stop using an attorney, she must turn over her files to you.

Managers

A few writers first find a manager, who then helps them find an agent. A manager may charge fifteen to twenty-five percent of your writing income for their services, but they basically run your career for you. A manager can do anything but sell your script. In California, that's illegal right now.

The query letter

In this business, everything begins with a query letter. It's generally how you make your first contact with anyone. In cases where you call, the call will resemble the query letter in structure, tone, and content. I suppose you could call it a "query phone call."

If you want to approach a producer directly with no agent or referral, and you have a great concept, you might try calling up the producer. You may have to pitch an assistant first. But you may be able to get a meeting or at least the opportunity to pitch your idea over the phone. I hasten to add that pitching over the phone is less desirable than pitching in person.

The query letter is a written pitch. Its purpose is to get the recipient to request a copy of your script.

One of the rules of the game is you never, never send a script to anyone unless they specifically request it. You get them to request it with a query letter. Even when you respond to ads requesting scripts, always query first.

Query letters should be typed on twenty-four-pound neutral-color paper (white, ivory, gray, etc.) and look professional. You don't need a printed letterhead, but be sure to include your name, address, phone number, and fax number. (Your e-mail address is not crucial.) Don't give yourself the title *screenwriter* or *writer*—it's a sign of an amateur. The content of the letter should be concise, hard-hitting, and intriguing.

Don't get palsy-walsy, and don't say, "I'm going to make you a million bucks," or, "Today is your lucky day." There's a big difference between confidence and conceit.

Your query letter communicates five things, and these are not in any particular order:

1. The concept in a sentence or two. This is done with a premise statement (usually in the form of a "what if" question), a logline (the *TV Guide* version of the story), or story hook (e.g., "hard-boiled cop becomes kindergarten teacher"). This might be a good time to review the information on high concept that begins on page 18-23.

2. The title and genre. The opening hook should imply the genre. If it doesn't, you may need to state the genre directly.

3. A brief pitch of the story in terms of character, conflict, and action—beginning, middle, and end. The story is not about the mafia, it is about a person in the mafia with a problem. Your story summary will be one or two paragraphs, with one being preferred to two. Show is better than tell. Don't say your story is jam-packed with action and plenty of romance. Instead, write the query in such a way that the reader perceives as much. Give the reader a reason to believe.

Don't tease the agent with a statement like, "If you want to know how it ends, you'll have to read the script." That won't work. If your story is quite strong, but you have a weak concept, open with your story and forget the concept. The reverse is also true. But provide enough information that the agent or producer will ask for your script.

It's okay to use Hollywood buzzwords and phrases such as "hip with an edge"—just make sure they are in current usage, yet not overused. Reading industry publications will help you find that edge that makes you hip.

4. Your qualifications. There are many ways to qualify yourself.

- Referred by someone in the biz. In this case, open your letter with that person's name.

- Any film-related experience.

- Any professional writing experience. Be brief. Don't make a list of published magazine articles, just say you've been published in a number of national publications.

- Winner of a screenwriting contest (or placed).

- Endorsed by a professional. The best endorsements are from non-buyers such as working writers and actors. Include their testimonial. Don't quote a producer because that begs the question, If she liked your script so much, why didn't she buy it?

- Expertise in the subject matter. If your character is a trial lawyer and that's your livelihood, mention it. I had a student who was a rock singer for ten years whose script was about a rock singer. I told her to mention her experience.

- A graduate degree from a recognized film school—such as UCLA, USC, NYU, or AFI—although this may not be as impressive as actual experience.

If you have no qualifications, omit this section. If you live out-of-state, consider mentioning that you're willing to come to L.A. for meetings. If you've written other scripts, mention that fact so the agent or producer won't think that the script you're pitching is your one and only.

5. Request permission to forward your script. Some writers include an SASE (self-addressed, stamped envelope) or postcard to make it easy for the prospect to respond. On the back of the postcard, give the prospect a couple of options to check. (One will be, "Yes, send me a copy of your script LOVE FREIGHT" [or whatever the title of your script is].) Type his or her name at the bottom, so you'll know where it came from.

Some writers believe the SASE or postcard is defeatist, so they add a line to the query that they'll follow-up in a few days. If you fax your query, close with "I'll call in a day or two," since you cannot fax them an SASE. When you call, ask the agent's or producer's assistant for permission to send your them screenplay. Don't grovel.

Should you fax or e-mail the query? Although many writers have had success by faxing, my recommendation is to mail a query letter the first time you're contacting someone. Include a postcard. In a couple of weeks when you follow-up by phone, if they can't find your original letter, offer to fax a duplicate right at that moment.

If someone tells you that they do not accept manuscripts from people not known to them, then ask them for a referral to an agent or producer who does. You could also ask, "May I call back in a few months to see if anything has changed?" Or otherwise use your persuasive powers to get them to just hear your concept.

Do not open your letter with long statements about seeking representation; they know you seek representation. And do not close it with long expressions of thanks for their consideration and time, or tell them how much you're looking forward to hearing from them. They know you are grateful and how much you want to hear from them. These expressions just take up space on the letter and don't help you get a positive response.

Do not send your script with a query. Do not send a treatment or synopsis to an agent unless requested. A producer, on the other hand, may request one. Remember, more Hollywood-types will be interested in your service (your ability to write) than in your product (your script).

SAMPLE QUERY LETTERS

As mentioned, queries can be used to approach any industry professional. Always query before sending a script. Keep in mind that the purpose of the query is obtain permission to forward the script. You accomplish that by getting the reader excited about your story. Here are a few sample queries.

The Wizard of Oz

```
Dear Ms. Big:

A tornado throws a young farm girl into Oz, a magical land where
she must defeat vengeful witches and sinister flying monkeys to
find her way home. While searching for her way back to Kansas,
Dorothy befriends a cowardly lion, an airhead scarecrow, and a
sentimental, if rusty, tin woodsman.  Each, like Dorothy, feels
outcast and misplaced.

They join forces to seek help from the Wizard of Oz, fighting off
the Wicked Witch of the North along the way; but when they fi-
nally destroy the witch and meet the alleged wizard, they dis-
cover that the blessing each traveler seeks has been with them
all along.

My latest screenplay, The Wizard of Oz, is a family-oriented
fantasy reminiscent of Star Wars.  Before writing it, I wrote and
produced a community-access cable program about tin woodsmen, and
I've had several short stories published in Munchkin Daily.

I'd like to send the complete script of The Wizard of Oz for your
review and possible representation.  An SASE is enclosed for your
reply, or you may call me at 555/555-5555.

Sincerely,
```

The above letter was created by screenwriter Joni Sensel for her newsletter. She points out in her commentary that she would address the letter to an individual. In the first paragraph, she identifies the protagonist, her obstacles, and goal. I especially like the last sentence about feeling outcast and misplaced because it identifies an emotion.

The second paragraph tells the agent how Dorothy overcomes her obstacles. It identifies opponents and suggests the resolution. Note that the author told the story, but did not include the concept. The story itself, in this case, is sufficient. It includes character, conflict, action, emotion, and theme. The genre is implied.

The third paragraph refers to STAR WARS. This links the project to a proven success and signals to the agent that *Oz* could be big bucks. (It's usually best to refer to a *current* success, if at all.) Joni also indicates the genre and lists her qualifications.

The fourth and fifth paragraphs tell the agent what to do in a polite way (without groveling). The reference to an SASE is unnecessary—the SASE will be there for the agent to see. Including your phone number is a plus, even if it's already printed on the letterhead. This well-written letter flows smoothly and logically from point to point. If you use the phone to query, be just as succinct and self-assured.

Bed of Lies
This letter is provided by Kerry Cox, former editor of the *Hollywood Scriptwriter*.

```
Dear Ms. Agent:

Thirteen years ago, J.T. Wheeler woke up at 5:30 a.m., showered, had
a light breakfast, and savagely murdered his family of four. He then
hopped into his Lexus and vanished from the face of the Earth.

Or did he?

It's a question Susan Morgan, wife of prominent attorney Lawrence
Morgan, has to answer fast.  The chilling fact is, the more she
learns, the more she realizes that Wheeler's killing spree not
only wasn't his first . . . it may very well not be his last.

And she might be married to him.

BED OF LIES is a psychological thriller and dark mystery with a
strong female protagonist, a deeply horrifying villain, and a
series of disturbing surprises that builds to an ultimate shocker
of an ending.  It is also a story of trust, of betrayal, and the
fine line that divides the two when secrets are buried between
husband and wife.
```

```
I'd like to submit BED OF LIES for your consideration and pos-
sible representation.  I've written professionally for televi-
sion, radio, and print, including network TV credits and two
published books.  I've also worked extensively as a crisis-inter-
vention counselor for Interact, a non-profit group specializing
in teen and marital crisis management.

I've enclosed a pre-paid postcard for your reply.  Thanks very
much for your time and consideration.

Sincerely,

Kerry Cox
```

The first paragraph—with the punchline *Or did he?*—is the hook. The next section is the story, including the title, genre, and underlying theme about trust and secrets. Next come the qualifications. Kerry's work as a crisis-intervention counselor qualifies him as an expert in the story's subject matter. His writing style matches the mood of the story, and uses detail effectively. If this query was for a comedy, he would probably have written the letter from a humorous slant. Personally, I would omit the last sentence as being unnecessary.

Heart of Silence

What follows is a query letter that won a contest. Although the content of the letter is fine, the letter itself needs a shave and a trim. I eliminated words, phrases, and sentences that I felt were unnecessary.

In queries like this, many things are taken for granted. For example, the agent will realize that the writer has completed an original feature film script—why else would she be writing? The strength of this letter, I believe, lies in the intriguing concept hook: *A man* [is] *forced to confront his own divinity when his dead daughter rescues him from suicide.*

Original

```
Dear Ms. Pikthis,

I have recently completed an original film script entitled HEART OF
SILENCE. It tells the story of a man forced to confront his own divin-
ity when his dead daughter rescues him from suicide. The stage version
of this story, entitled CRY OF SILENCE, won the 1989 Kumu Kahua Play-
wright's Award from the University of Hawaii. The script is 104 pages.
```

HEART OF SILENCE has been reviewed by a professional reader, Kerry Cox, who commented: "An intelligently written script, professionally written and in proper format. Your characters, particularly the husband, were well-drawn and realistic." Dalene Young, a professional scriptwriter, said the material was "moving, believable, and dramatic."

I have also completed an original feature comedy entitled QUEEN KONG. It is a send-up of KING KONG, in which the hero is the love of the female beast. It runs 110 pages. Both scripts are available upon your request as a hard copy or on disk in WordPerfect 5.1 for IBM.

In addition to works of my own, I am also interested in working on re-writes and collaborations. I am able to travel to take meetings in Los Angeles.

Thank you for your consideration.

Aloha Pumehana,
Karen Mitura

Revised

Dear Ms. Pikthis:

HEART OF SILENCE tells the story of a man forced to confront his own divinity when his dead daughter rescues him from suicide. My stage version of this story won the 1989 Kumu Kahua Playwright's Award from the University of Hawaii.

The screenplay has been reviewed by a professional reader, Kerry Cox, who commented: "An intelligently written script, professionally written . . . Your characters, particularly your husband, were well-drawn and realistic." Dalene Young, a professional screenwriter, said the material was "moving, believable, and dramatic."

Although I have many scripts and story ideas, I am also interested in assignments. I am able to travel to Los Angeles for meetings.

I'll call your office soon. I look forward to speaking to you or your assistant.

Aloha Pumehana,
Karen Mitura

The first paragraph of the revised letter states the title, hints at the genre, pinpoints the concept hook, and affirms one of Karen's qualifications as a writer. The second paragraph continues with two professional endorsements.

In my revision, I omit the reference to QUEEN KONG, but inform the agent that Karen has written other scripts. As a general rule, I believe your query should focus on one screenplay—your best shot—but could mention the fact you have written other scripts. The third paragraph also shows Karen's flexibility and answers a possible question— is she willing to travel to Los Angeles for meetings? I felt this was a key point in her letter because it shows that she understands the business. She put herself in the agent's shoes and anticipated the agent's question.

The fourth paragraph states that she'll follow-up by phone. If this letter is faxed, the final paragraph would begin, "I'll call your office later today [or tomorrow]."

Did you notice that I did not end with some pleasant expression or statement about wanting representation. I believe the agent knows instinctively that the writer seeks representation. So why state the obvious? I concede that this is a debatable point. Most agents prefer short and sweet letters. The conciseness of Karen's revised letter is worth emulating.

You may have noticed that her letter does not tell the entire story. The thinking here is that the concept alone is strong enough to elicit a positive response.

A Cuban Cigar
How would you whittle down this query letter?

```
Keul Agent
Great American Agency
1234 Dreamland Parkway
Beverly Hills, CA 90210

Dear Ms. Agent:

Not unlike most people, baseball fan Jimmy Lansburger's life didn't
turn out the way he always dreamed it would.  So when he stumbles
across a headline about the greatest Cuban baseball player alive,
Renaldo Rapido, he's more than willing to try to become this man's
agent and save his hide from bankruptcy.  However, Jimmy has two small
problems.  He doesn't have any money and he doesn't speak Spanish.  But
he has plenty of gall.  He talks his sometimes-girlfriend, Selma, a
straightlaced travel agent, into helping him go to Cuba to smuggle
```

Renaldo and any teammates who will come out of Cuba to the land of opportunity.

The two are like fish out of water. Jimmy is a good guy who has never been able to hold down a job for more than a couple of months at a time. And Selma knows just enough Spanish to get her into trouble. This results in a fanciful journey through Cuba where one crazy incident leads to another. And Renaldo the ballplayer, who is known to love America, starts getting homesick for Cuba before he even leaves. This story will touch your heart with romance and excite you with action and keep you laughing all the way to the happy end as Jimmy finds out what's important in life.

I'd like to submit ROMANCE IN CUBA for your consideration and possible representation. I wrote ROMANCE IN CUBA with Meg Ryan and Tom Hanks in mind. Who wouldn't love seeing these two together again?

I've enclosed an SASE for your reply. Thanks very much for your time and consideration.

Sincerely,

Bill Bautista

Big blocks of black ink act like agent repellant. I doubt if the letter would even be read. Here's my revision, which includes a title change.

Dear Ms. Agent:

Have you ever searched for that *one special person* who will turn your life around?

Well, Jimmy Lansburger, certified baseball nut, thinks he's found that *one special person* -- Renaldo Rapido, ace pitcher for the Cuban Nationals.   Jimmy's dream is to agent Renaldo and his teammates into the American big leagues, and make a grotesque sum of money.

But this lovable flake can't afford a plane ticket or even a Spanish/ English dictionary. So he hornswoggles his no-nonsense travel-agent girlfriend, Selma, into helping him smuggle the sentimental southpaw out of Cuba.

A CUBAN CIGAR is a misadventurous comedy romp where Jimmy finally realizes that Selma, not Renaldo, is that *one special person*. May I send you a copy of the script?

Sincerely yours,

The original query letter is authentic. As you can see, the revision is leaner and more focused. It uses stronger, more concrete words, and it avoids unnecessary repetition. It "shows" rather than "tells," focuses on concept and relationships, and it omits any references to current actors.

The phrase "one special person" is an attempt to bolster and unify the concept, characterize Jimmy, and create humor (since this is a comedy). The word "sentimental" is dropped in to raise the specter of conflict—it's not going to be easy to convince Renaldo to leave Cuba. (Besides, I like the alliteration.)

This letter might benefit from a stronger idea of what happens once they're in Cuba (but not having read the script, I don't know). Whether this letter grabs you or not, please note what changes were made and why they were made.

The writer had no experience or qualifications to mention in the letter—A CUBAN CIGAR was his first script. Naturally, a stamped postcard or SASE would be enclosed for the agent's use. The writer's name, address, and phone number would appear in plain sight on the letterhead.

The Silk Maze

This final example by Jeff Warshaw capitalizes on Hollywood's penchant for sex. Although a one-paragraph story summary would be preferred to two, notice how Jeff's style creates suspense and intrigue. Jeff presented this in class to a standing ovation.

```
Dear Mr. Shmoe:

Jonathan Stark thought he knew all the angles.  He thought he knew
what Lily, his beloved partner-in-crime, wanted from life. He
thought he knew how to please and manipulate Celia, the young
socialite who seemed to know too much about his sordid past.  He
thought he could control the heart of Mazie, the one "client" who
cared for him.  He was wrong.

Jonathan Stark knew nothing about the three equally beautiful and
treacherous women who ruled his life. Trapped between two women
who love him for very different reasons, and one who wants to
destroy him no matter what it takes, Jonathan must walk the tight-
rope between the true love he seeks and the easy, swarmy sex life
he's come to know.  Will he make the right decision, or is he
riding for the biggest fall of his life?  Caught in a smooth,
alluring web of intrigue, deception, and white-hot sexual subter-
fuge, Jonathan Stark must stay one step ahead of the game if he
hopes to escape THE SILK MAZE.
```

> THE SILK MAZE is a fast-paced, erotic thriller with more twists and turns than a roller coaster as it rockets toward a stunning, steamy climax. It is the story of a man so used to lies that he can hardly see the truth before him, a man who must learn to trust not only his instincts, but himself.
>
> I would like to submit my third script, THE SILK MAZE, for your consideration and possible representation. I am interested in rewrites and adaptations. You may call me at (714) 555-5555 at your convenience.
>
> Very truly yours,
>
> Jeffrey C. Warshaw

Jeff indicates his genre as a fast-paced, erotic thriller. He is wise to give his genre some pizzazz. Erotic thriller is better than thriller. Romantic action/adventure is better than action/adventure. My script KUMQUAT is not a romantic comedy; it is a romantic comedy against the background of high adventure. Don't overdo it, however, with something like sci-fi/action/drama reality-based environmental Western.

Jeff mentions rewrites and adaptations; he might consider the broader term "assignments." He concludes his letter with his phone number. Make sure your address and phone number are somewhere on the letter. Don't expect someone to pick it up off your envelope.

Incidentally, your letterhead need not include anything other than your name, address, and phone number. Don't give yourself the title s*creenwriter* or *writer*. It's the sign of an amateur.

Query letters do not need to be long. In evaluating one client's script, I saw a clever angle to her story and wrote a query letter for her. The letter consisted of just one paragraph, and that paragraph was only five lines long. Even though she had no qualifications, she received forty requests for her script. Unfortunately, she had not followed my advice to polish her script before sending the query and to not mass-submit the query. This story, unfortunately, ended in heartbreak.

WHAT NOT TO INCLUDE IN A QUERY LETTER

It can be tough finding the razor's edge between professionalism and creativity. And where does confidence and enthusiasm end and conceit and insolence begin? One rule of thumb is to ask yourself, What does this agent or producer want to hear? In other words, get the focus off you and what you want to say, and get into the head of the agent or producer you're writing to.

Here are excerpts from five would-be screenwriters who didn't figure that out. These were collected by screenwriter Joni Sensel.

> "A warm-hearted, romantic venture into the deepest of human emotions, revolving around the love of one person for another despite overwhelming odds, with a touch of comedy, proving yet again that love conquers all . . . And of course, like all my work, the story concludes with a stunning, unexpected ending."

This could describe a dozen stories. The problem here is the character is telling instead of showing, and is focusing more on theme than story. Write the story, including the ending, and we'll decide if it's heart-warming and stunning.

> "I'm 22. I hope this will be my way over the 'wall' and give me access to a struggling industry that could use the talents I possess to help it reach its potential. Cinema is my life and I hate to see it in the hands of incapable people."

Don't get cocky, kid.

> "Your agency has been highly recommended to me by the Writers Guild. I have enclosed a short story that explains why I have chosen to be a screenwriter."

And we're all dying to read it. And please, no false flattery. Be aware of Linda Buzzell's two no-nos—"don't be dull or desperate" (from *How To Make It In Hollywood*).

> "Jesus Christ the man and I are both empaths. I'm this way because of Y. The symbol of God is a clock. I would like to meet the Pope someday."

Is this the story or your qualifications?

> " . . . the constant epistemological question regarding the perplexing attempt to explain the nature of being and reality and the origins and structure of the world . . . the metaphysical

```
conflict between natural law (St. Augustine) and pragmatism
(Kant-Dewey-James) and the question of the benefits of merging
from . . . "
```

Excuse me, please, but I just wanna make a movie.

ONCE THE QUERY IS SENT

The next step is to evaluate the responses to your query. Half or more may not respond at all. Most who do respond do so within three weeks. If you faxed your query letter, call in a couple of days. If you mailed your query, wait at least a week or so to followup.

Usually a phone response is positive. Rejection generally comes through the mail. No response usually means no, although it is possible that the query was lost. If the rejections pile up, then re-evaluate your query and your story. Make any necessary changes. Then go ahead and contact more prospects.

Once an agent or producer responds positively to your query, send your script with a cover letter that opens with a variation of, "As you requested, here is . . . " Not much else needs to be said in the cover letter.

The script should be an excellent photocopy of a letter-quality original. Send it priority mail with the cover letter and, if you wish, include return postage. It's okay to make a personal delivery, but you probably will not get a chance to meet the agent or producer.

It can take up to four months to hear back on a script submission. Wait at least three weeks before your first follow-up. Try once every week or so after that. Be *pleasantly persistent*. Generally, the best time to call is in the afternoon. A Thursday or Friday call will remind the agent to get the script read over the weekend.

When someone says, "We'll call you," or "We'll get back to you," your response will be, "Great! May I call in a week?" That makes it more difficult for them to summarily dismiss you.

If your script has not been read by your third or fourth call, then it's time to turn to another prospect, but before you do, try to get a referral to another agent or producer. Keep in mind that each agent has about fifteen to twenty clients and is inundated with script submissions, often more than 100 a week; and producers are similarly inundated. Things take time, so be patient. If your script is rejected, don't be afraid to ask for honest feedback. (The rejection letter may not be honest.) Ask for a copy of the coverage. Remember, you are always building contacts. Some of your best future contacts will be today's contacts who rejected you.

Always treat the producer's or agent's assistant like a human being. Learn his name. Treat him with the same respect you'd accord the agent, and don't use the word "secretary." You may very well need to sell this person first. In fact, it's quite possible that the assistant will be the first and only person to read your script.

No one in Hollywood is an assistant to be an assistant. Everyone is on their way up. So think of the assistant as your friend and accomplice. He can tell you how a particular agency or production company operates. You can ask, for example, "When should I expect to hear from so-and-so?" Or, "When can I call back?" Remember that only a no is a no. If a prospect is too busy to read your work now, you can ask, "May I try back in a few months to see if anything has changed?"

Let me remind you that during this long period of searching for an agent and selling your script, you should not stop writing. Once you finish a script, take a week off and then start another one. Chances are you will finish it before the previous one has been sold.

How to pitch without striking out

What happens when an agent submits your script to a studio or a production company? First of all, what is a producer or an executive looking for?

To be honest, most have their own ideas to develop if they can just find the right writer. They may also be looking for a writer to do adaptations, or to take over a project where the original writer didn't perform to expectations. Of course, they'll buy a spec script if they think it is an excellent marketing risk, but they're looking for writers. In fact, about eighty percent of the deals out there are development deals—producers hiring writers to execute their ideas. (The percentage varies.) The spec market tends to go in cycles. Some years can be excellent for spec scripts, other years not so good.

What will your agent do? Well, your agent will contact the highest-level executives and producers he knows. These will be producers with deals or executives at studios. Producers with deals are producers with contracts or other connections with studios or financial sources. The studios are usually the last to be contacted because their rejection closes the doors to outside producers wanting to bring the project to them.

The executive or producer (I'm using the terms synonymously here) will normally give the script to a *story editor*, who will assign it to a *story analyst* or *reader*. The reader writes a *coverage* and makes a recommendation. If the recommendation is positive, the development executive will read at least a portion of your screenplay.

A development executive must love your script to champion it. Assuming he does love it, he will present it to other execs, who will read it during the weekend. It will then be discussed at the Monday morning conference. The decision will be made to buy it or not.

If they decide to buy it, you could be rolling in six figures. If they decide to pass on the script, but they like the writing, the executive will call your agent and ask to meet you. This means you're a semi-finalist in your bid to secure a development deal or other writing assignment. Your agent will arrange a meeting.

THE MEETING

The *meeting* is an opportunity for you to *position* yourself and your work in the minds of executives. I use the term "executive" and "producer" synonymously. From the executives' points of view, this meeting has one of two purposes.

One is to provide a forum in which you can pitch your own ideas. They will then choose one of your ideas and hire you to write the script—a development deal. More likely, however, they have a writing assignment that is open, and they want you to audition for it, based on your "sample script" that they just read. The meeting usually works out something like this:

You'll be seated on a soft couch or conference table facing two or more executives. The meeting will last from thirty minutes to about an hour, but it could be much less. You'll know that when the meeting is set up. Some of the time is spent with getting-to-know-you conversation. At the beginning of the meeting, they will tell you how much they love your sample script. They're trying to make you feel relaxed.

Some writers suggest that you dress above the executives in the room and sit in the chair that places you in a power position. There is merit to this, but I believe it is more important for you to feel comfortable. Dress comfortably, but don't come in rags. Place your hind quarters hard against the back of the chair or couch—this helps you project your voice and maintain good posture.

Be as conversational and natural as you can. At the same time, retain a level of professionalism. Don't try to get too chummy. First names are okay. Having a good sense of humor is a plus. Be yourself (if that's possible). Project positive energy—not Pollyanna, not God's gift to Hollywood—be upbeat and confident. Get the conversation going. Ask about something in the room—a trophy or painting.

If they are interested in hearing your ideas with an ear toward developing one of them, they will ask you to pitch them. If they are interested in the possibility of giving you a writing assignment, they will audition you by asking you what you've been working on. In other words, they're asking you to pitch a couple of ideas. They just want to get a feel for your work, your creativity, and your personality. After all, pitching is as much about making contacts and developing relationships as it is about swapping "stories."

In either case, have at least two to four pitches ready to go.

THE TWO-MINUTE PITCH

Brief pitches come in two stages—the story hook in twenty-five words or less, and a brief rendition of the storyline. In other words, the structure of this short pitch is quite similar to a query letter.

The hook must grab their attention and set a tone. The hook could come in the form of a premise, a logline, or a concept.

IMPORTANT NOTE: Please review "The low down on high concept" in Book I, pages 18-23.

Here are some examples of hooks:

- *Honey, I Shrunk the Kids. Family comedy.* Here you've identified the title and genre. In this case, that's probably enough to grab the attention of the executives.

- *Family/sci-fi/thriller. An alien child accidentally left behind on Earth is befriended by some children who help him find his way home. We call it ET.* This is a logline.

- *Jaws in space.* This was the hook used to pitch ALIEN.

- *What if the president of the United States were kidnaped?* This is a premise statement.

- *Romance against a background of high adventure: When her sister is kidnaped, a lonely romance writer tries to save her, only to find true romance in the process.* This is a variation of the old pitching formula: When X happens (the Big Event), so-and-so tries to get Y, but ends up with Z.

- *Imagine you are driving down a dark road. Late at night. And someone is behind you. You turn; he turns. He is following you. You decide to get on a lighted street and suddenly find yourself at a stop light. Nowhere to go, and the car behind you gets closer and closer. Finally, he pulls up next to you and stops. You look over and he resembles you exactly. He is you!* This is a little long, but it's an example of a story concept.

When Gene Roddenberry pitched STAR TREK, he had problems. No one was interested in sci-fi. A popular TV show at the time was WAGON TRAIN. So Gene pitched

STAR TREK like this: *WAGON TRAIN in space*. He hitched his "star" to a "wagon," and the rest is history. He combined the familiar with the unique.

These days, you want to avoid the "cheap pitch." *DRIVING MISS DAISY meets the MEN IN BLACK*. Or: *AS GOOD AS IT GETS on the TITANIC*. Or: *GOOD WILL HUNTING falls in love with GODZILLA*. It's okay to refer to successful movies, but it should not be the core of your concept or pitch. Yes, ALIEN was pitched as JAWS in space, and TITANIC was *Romeo and Juliet* on a boat—that got their attention—but there was more to each story than just the concept. Use your common sense. If you have a bona fide comparison that helps you present "the familiar with a twist," then use it as a hook.

Most often, development executives must sell your idea to higher-ups, and higher-ups will sometimes sell your idea to other producers or a studio. Even if they have a script, it's the script's story concept, logline, or hook that helps them do that. Likewise, distributors and exhibitors need a simple, easily understood idea to attract moviegoers to their movies.

However, if a producer's past work consists of literary films (such as *Emma* or *Wings of a Dove*), a blood-and-guts, special-effects, high-action pitch may not be appropriate; in fact, you may even be perceived as a hack. Be wise. Here's an example of a low-concept story hook:

- *The Secret of Question Mark Cave is the story of a secret cave, a magic sword, and a family stranded without a TV set.* This hook implies the genre—a light, family comedy. Although low-concept, it might be high enough to someone looking for just this kind of story.

Once you have awed them with your hook, you will be favored with a nod or otherwise be encouraged to continue. You will then deliver your brief storyline. Present the entire story—beginning, middle, and end—building on what you've already told them. Your focus will be on two or three characters, conflict, emotion, and action. Don't forget the Big Event, the Crisis, and the Showdown.

If you're pitching several ideas, open with your best shot. Don't go into a pitching session with more than three or four pitches, unless your research tells you otherwise. Too many pitches makes you look like a watch salesman in front of a hotel. Keep in mind that the main purpose of this Chamber of Horrors is to provide those you are pitching to with a means of evaluating you and your work. Do you have good ideas? Can they work with you?

If you're lucky, they might love one of your pitches enough to offer you a development deal. Congratulations. A development deal is an agreement in which they pay you to write a script for them. Or they might ask to see your script when it's completed. Congratulations, you've made a contact.

Most likely, they'll thank you for your ideas, and begin talking about themselves. They have a reason for doing this. It's their turn to pitch you.

THE LONG PITCH

When your pitching is over, the producers may share an idea or two of their own. For example, a producer may say, "We're looking for a Faustian comedy for Jimmy Megastar. What do you think?"

If you respond positively and intelligently, the executive may say, "Well, if you come up with a story for us, then let us know. We'd love to hear the pitch." Interpreted this means: *Congratulations, you are now a finalist in your bid to secure a development deal. Have your agent call us when you have a ten- to twenty-minute pitch ready.*

Here's what's really happening: You and a dozen other finalists will create and pitch a Faustian Comedy for Jimmy Megastar. This way, the producer can develop her ideas without investing a dime of her own money. The producer will pick the pitch she likes best, and you will get the development deal to write the script.

Obviously, you will want to prepare for this major pitch, or for any pitch. Here's how.

Delivering your pitch

Do not read your pitch, but it's okay to have 3" x 5" cards or notes to prompt you. Be as clear and animated as your personality allows. You'll open with your hook followed by the storyline. You may also wish to introduce your key characters right at the beginning before you move into your story.

In the body of the pitch, focus on character, the goal, what's at stake, the emotional high points, theme, how the character will grow, the major dramatic twists, and, of course, how it ends. Two common traps to avoid:

> First, don't try to cram your entire story and all the characters into your pitch. It shouldn't sound too complicated.
>
> Second, don't present a rundown of scenes: *This happens and then this happens and then this happens* . . . Your story will sink into the mud

and you'll be dead in the water. Get to the heart. Talk them through the story. People can't follow all the details anyway, so hit the high points.

Here's the opening of a successful pitch I delivered for THE SECRET OF QUESTION MARK CAVE. I had just delivered the hook.

My story is about a boy, Seebee, who feels that his dad hates him. He does everything he can to please his dad, but Frankie berates him, criticizes him, hurts him. It's not that Frankie hates his son—he doesn't. He just wishes he knew how to show his affection.

Well, one night, Seebee sneaks into the attic against Frankie's orders and finds the old journal of his great, great grandfather. The journal tells the boy about a secret cave and a magic sword. Wow—with a sword like that, Seebee could solve all his problems! He vows to run away to the mountains, but then he hears a noise! Frankie is downstairs, and boy is he mad.

Of course, your pitch will continue all the way to the end of the story. Please note that in bringing you to the story Catalyst, I emphasized the *emotions* of the characters. The pitch needs to touch the executive's cold heart.

Don't refer to actors directly. Refer to them in a casual way. For example, you can say a Harrison Ford-kind-of-guy. And you will say it in a way that communicates that you are not assuming that Harrison Ford will be in your movie. You don't want to appear naive. Say, for example, "I guess this guy is kind of a Steve Martin-type."

Why do this? To make it easy for the listener to instantly visualize the character. You can use the same trick when selling your concept. Say something like, "in the vein of COURAGE UNDER FIRE." Or "reminiscent of INDEPENDENCE DAY." Or "in a way, it's a corporate version of PRIMARY COLORS."

Don't tell them what they are looking for. Don't say, "I know you'll like it because it has plenty of sex."

As I mentioned earlier, it's okay to bring notes to prompt you, but never read a pitch. It's also okay to take notes when you're listening, although I would ask permission. "Is it okay if I jot this down?"

Don't lie. Don't say Ron Howard is looking at the project if he is not. The producer will simply call Ron Howard to find out. They followup. Don't think they don't. Don't say no one has seen the script if, in truth, dozens of executives already have a copy. On the other hand, if DreamWorks is interested in it, don't be afraid to say so.

In some pitches, you may be interrupted with questions, requests for clarifications, and suggestions. Go with the flow and be flexible, but do not allow the pitch to lose momentum. Be open to suggestions and be prepared to present a different angle on the story. Don't be afraid to express yourself. They want you to. If appropriate, let them contribute to the story, so they can own it, too.

Don't oversell. Once they say no, STOP. Once they say yes, STOP. Don't keep blabbing on.

When they are done with you, they will excuse you without telling you their decision. The truth is they may not be the decision-makers. When a decision is made, that decision will be conveyed to your agent. Regardless of the outcome, send a note of thanks.

Personality

One thing's for sure: If these development executives hire you, they will be spending a lot of time with you developing the story. So almost as important as your ideas is your personality. Some meetings are arranged purely for public relations, and for developing contacts and relationships. In any case, they want to know what are you like to work with. So identify your pluses before the meeting.

There are four personality traits that are key to any situation when you're meeting Hollywood types: enthusiasm, objectivity, ambition, and grace.

Enthusiasm. Do you have the voice of conviction? Do you have a passion for your work? Do you communicate confidence? Do you believe in your ideas? I cannot over-emphasize the power of enthusiasm. By the same token, don't get so excited that you hyperventilate and pass out. They dock points for that.

Objectivity. Can you separate your ego from your work? Can you be objective about the pluses and minuses of your script? This does not diminish your passion. It means you can adjust to what lies ahead: story development hell. (*Story development hell* refers to the process of working with the notes and other feedback you'll receive while developing the project.) You may be amazed at how these professionals view your script. Be open to criticism, but be diplomatic and firm where it matters. If you are defensive and rigid, then you're difficult to work with (from their point of view).

Ambition. Do you love the business? Do you want to be a full-time writer or do you want to just write an occasional script from your cabin in the woods?

Grace. Are you gracious? Do people enjoy meeting you and talking to you? Do you have any natural charm? Are you the opposite of dull and desperate?

Now don't present a façade personality, or disparage the traits you don't possess; just present your best self, focusing on your strengths.

Be prepared

Before the meeting, find out as much as you can about the company and the people you are meeting with. If you have an agent, he should be a big help here.

- Who are they and what are their titles?
- What is the purpose of the meeting from their points of view?
- What are their most recent credits?
- What genres are they most interested in? Who is *their* audience?
- What major talent has appeared in their most recent productions?
- Do they work with high or low budgets?
- What are they looking for now?

Bring anything you think they might want. If they haven't seen a sample script, bring one. If coverage has already been written on your script by a professional reader, and it's positive, bring it in.

Be prepared to answer questions. Be ready to continue your pitch after the initial two minutes have passed. Have a couple of other ideas or angles on the same idea—just in case. Also, prepare a little bio on yourself. This is not something you hand to them in printed form. You just want to be ready when they ask about you and what you have done.

Also, they may ask you who your ideal cast is. Be ready with ideas about casting. The reason they may ask this is it helps them get a clearer picture of how you see your characters. It's seldom for casting purposes.

Finally, in driving to the meeting, allow adequate time to arrive and park. Take into account possible traffic jams. Be on time.

Creativity

In preparing for a long pitch, you might consider a creative touch. A minor innovation may make your pitch stand out from the dozens of hum-drum presentations that have dulled the producer's senses that week. One client used action figures to represent his characters. He introduced them one-by-one and spread them out on the table. The development executive was enthralled.

However, usually props are not a good idea, particularly in a short pitch. Don't try to act out your pitch and don't hire actors to perform your pitch for you. On the other hand, don't be afraid to use your voice for emphasis. Use your common sense and put your creativity into the content of your pitch.

Practice

The single best way to prepare for a pitch is to invite some friends and neighbors over and pitch to them. If the story appears clear and interesting to them, then feel encouraged. Practicing your pitch in front of real people will help you immensely in preparing for the real thing. You might even role play the entire meeting from beginning to end.

You may be wondering, Why can't I just give producers a synopsis of the story in writing? Why do I have to pitch it? Because they cannot "legally" ask for anything in writing without paying you for it. That's because they are signatory to the Writers Guild of America. However, some writers leave a synopsis or treatment on the table after their pitch.

If an executive asks for a treatment or outline, I think it's generally best if, instead, you offer to pitch the project for her to other producers. That's because you can convey more enthusiasm for your project than the development executive can. Keep in mind that if someone loves your idea, they will need to pitch it to higher-ups or to other production companies or to the studios. You want to be helpful to them.

If you're dealing with a producer who is not signatory to the Guild, then you can give him a synopsis or treatment directly and avoid pitching altogether. This is discussed in depth in the next major section.

The happy ending

If your pitch does the trick, you will be offered a development deal. Your first development deal could be $50,000-$70,000. It will probably also be a step deal, which means you can be cut out at any step in the writing process. You'll be paid a portion of the total purchase price at each step. Although there are many possibilities, it could work like this: 25% advance, 25% on treatment (first step), 25% on first draft (second step), 25% on polish (third step). If the film is eventually produced, expect another $50,000-$100,000 production bonus.

Throughout the writing process, you will receive notes from producers or executives-in-charge, and will experience first hand what has come to be known as story *development hell*. At least you're being paid.

Summary

Do you see a pattern here? It works like this: You write two or three spec scripts. The spec script that best shows your talent becomes a sample script that finds you work. Sometimes you sell that spec script outright. Usually, you don't. Instead it becomes a divining rod that finds you an agent and/or gains you admittance to a meeting where you can sing for your supper.

How to sell your script without an agent

Much has changed during the last few years. Hollywood is inbreeding more. In other words, the system has become more closed to outsiders, and it's more difficult to break in. As with Jack in TITANIC, it's difficult gaining acceptance into the club.

Creating a marketing plan will help you penetrate the market at the same time you are searching for an agent.

Would you be surprised if I told you that many first scripts are sold without an agent? It's true. And although it's a distinct advantage to have an agent, it's possible for you to sell your script without one.

TEN MARKETING TOOLS

Before you try to sell your script on your own, you need a complete set of marketing tools. Assemble these *before* making your move.

1. A showcase script
You need a great script (preferably two or more) that is proof of your writing ability and can be used as a calling card. If you want to break into television, you will need one feature script and at least one sample television script.

2. A pitch hook
As mentioned, this will consist of a logline, one-sentence concept, or premise statement that you can insert into a query letter, use over the phone, or pitch in person.

3. A brief story summary

This will be one or two paragraphs in length and can be used in your query or as part of your pitch. This, along with your pitch hook, comprise the two-minute pitch.

4. A synopsis

A synopsis is a one- or two-page story summary, double-spaced using a twelve-point font. It can be attached to a query letter directed to producers or talent, or delivered in a pitch. When sending a synopsis, the query letter becomes more of a cover letter containing the main concept, title, genre, and your qualifications. Many producers prefer seeing a synopsis or treatment before reading the script.

Incidentally, the words *synopsis*, *treatment*, and *outline* are often used synonymously. All three are written pitches of slightly different lengths. Don't confuse an *outline* with the more detailed scene-by-scene *step outline*.

5. A treatment or an outline

This is not the long, fifty-page treatment that you're paid to write in a development deal. This *spec* treatment is two to seven pages in length—with most people preferring about three to four pages.

A treatment is actually a long synopsis—a written pitch, analogous to the long pitch discussed earlier—double-spaced and written in present-tense narrative form with no or little dialogue. It's not a scene-by-scene rundown, and you will only focus on about three or four characters. It emphasizes the crucial moments, the key events of the story, and the emotional highs and lows of your characters. This treatment not only tells the story, but it sells the story. It is a marketing piece. You write it for producers, talent, and directors—you want them to love the story. You want them to say, "What a great concept! Let me read the script!"

So how do you write a treatment? I think the best way to learn that is to understand the difference between a professional story synopsis and a *spec* treatment (or synopsis or outline) written for marketing purposes. Some time ago, I asked long-time Hollywood story analyst Leslie Paonessa (listed under "Script Consultants" in Book VI) to read my old script, THE SECRET OF QUESTION MARK CAVE, and write a *coverage*.

Her coverage consisted of her recommendations, an analysis, and a story synopsis. When she wrote her synopsis, her objective as a professional story analyst was not to *pitch* the story but to create a clear and complete summary of the story. As you will see, she did a superb job.

I suggest you read Leslie's synopsis on pages 267-269 right now, and then return to this page to read my treatment of the same script. (See page 253 for part of my pitch.)

• • • • •

The spec treatment (or outline or synopsis) that follows *treats* the same story as the story analyst's synopsis. Why is the writing style different? Because it is written for a different purpose. (Incidentally, the script and this treatment led me to a development deal with Disney many years ago.)

My strategy for this short treatment was to apply the principles already stated in this section about treatments. The short length of the treatment forced me to focus on the essential story in terms of plot, character, and emotion.

I recommend that you write short treatments when you're stuck, before a re-write, and (of course) before a pitch. Because a treatment is a written pitch, consult the section about pitching for tips on writing a treatment. Although not necessary, I opened this treatment with the story hook.

THE SECRET OF QUESTION MARK CAVE

by David Trottier

This is the story of a long-ago promised sword, a secret cave, and a family stranded without a TV set.

Seebee, age 12, fancies himself a knight, although he is kicked out of the Explorer's Club for failing to perform a brave deed. Worse, his own dad (Frankie) puts him down as a "nothing kid" and breaks his wood sword in half, and his heart as well. Actually, Frankie loves his son--he just doesn't know how to connect with him, and he's too busy watching TV to find out.

One night, Seebee sneaks into the attic against his father's wishes and discovers the journal of his great-grandfather, Captain Cole. It tells the story of a "magic" sword (at least Seebee thinks it's magic) hidden in a secret cave deep in the mountains. Seebee vows to run away and find the ancient sword. He's sure it will solve his problems, but his hopes shatter when Frankie catches him in the attic.

Meanwhile, his friend Glodina witnesses a bank robbery and ducks into a car for safety. Unfortunately, the car she chooses is the robber's car. The robber is forced to take her with him to his hide-out. Seebee is unable to save Glodina and when he gets home he does something even worse--he accidentally breaks his dad's TV set. He is banished to his bedroom.

Seebee feels dejected and powerless; but that night, he dreams that his great-grandfather, Captain Cole, gallops up on his horse and offers Seebee the sword mentioned in his journal. Cole says, "You have a power all your own," and Seebee awakens.

Emboldened, the boy tapes the pieces of his *wood* sword together. He runs away with two of his "Explorer's Club" buddies to find the "magic" sword in the secret cave so he can use it to rescue Glodina. They overcome obstacles until they discover Captain Cole's old cave, called Question Mark Cave. Inside, they find Glodina (she is safe)--the cave must be the bandit's hide-out! A deeper search produces evidence of Captain Cole, but *not* the wondrous sword in his dream. Seebee is discouraged.

Just then, the robber arrives. He's about to "rub out" the little band of four, but Seebee tricks the robber and the four children escape from the cave.

On the trail, the bandit pursues Seebee and his friends until he catches them at a cliff that hangs over a canyon stream. There Seebee unsheathes his wood sword and courageously holds the robber at bay while his friends get over the cliff to safety. When Seebee attempts to cross, the bandit catches him. In the struggle, Seebee forces the

Red Hat Bandit over the cliff, where the robber breaks his leg in the river below.

Seebee now realizes he doesn't need the magic sword of power because he has a power all his own--an inner goodness he can draw from. His dream has come true. Plus, he's performed a brave deed to get back into the Explorer's Club.

At home, events have given Frankie a new perspective. He takes Seebee into the attic and removes Captain Cole's sword from a secret hiding place! Father, like son, had once wanted to be a knight, and had journeyed to Question Mark Cave years ago and had found the ancient sword. The sword becomes Frankie's connection with his son, the connection he's longed to find. He then knights his son and gives him the sword he deserves while Glodina admires her brave hero.

• • • • •

Don't expect to find work based on a treatment alone until you are established. You must have a finished script. If a producer loves your treatment, your story, but you have no script, he will buy the story for $1,000 (if you're lucky) and then hire a proven writer to write the script. Hollywood has plenty of ideas, but few great writers. Great ideas are not worth much without a script.

Both a treatment and a synopsis can be registered with the Writers Guild. Follow the same process as registering a screenplay.

6. A hot, one-page query letter for every occasion
Never send a script to anyone cold. Always query first. Even if you are responding to an ad asking for a script, you should query first.

Your pithy, professional query will creatively present your concept, along with the title and the genre, which may be implied rather than directly stated. It will also convey your complete story in a paragraph or two, or will simply refer to the attached synopsis.

Your query will then list your qualifications and ask permission to send your script on spec. Approach no more than five to ten producers at a time.

If you know in advance how a particular producer or actor likes to be queried, then those instructions supersede my own.

7. A telephone script

You need this next to your phone when you call anyone about your screenplay or TV script, or they call you. Don't be like a student of mine who was called back on a query and who blanked out on the phone. After six seconds of silence, the agent hung up. Quickly, she called me and I told her to call the agent immediately and explain that she had a cold and had lapsed into a coughing spell. Fortunately, her explanation was satisfactory.

The key element of your telephone script is your two-minute pitch (points 2 and 3 on pages 257-258). You will carry a copy wherever you go. It's better to improvise off notes than to read. Also, prepare pitches of other scripts you've written or want to write and have them handy. This is in case you're asked the golden question: "What else have you done?"

A telephone script is what all professional telemarketers use. It tells you what to say if the person on the other line says yes, no, or makes a particular excuse or objection. Here's just one possible example:

> "I'm [name]. I'm a screenwriter with a [name genre, such as action/romantic comedy] that I think might be right down your alley. May I send it to you?"
>
> (What's it about?) [Here you will pitch it, leading with a headline, logline, premise, or concept; then, if you feel encouraged, moving into the story summary.]
>
> (I'm sorry, we're developing our own projects.) "Great. Would you like to read this with an eye toward a possible assignment? I'd love to hear what you're doing [or] I loved NAZIS IN SPACE [or whatever his/her last production was]. [Here you are identifying your script as a mere sample of your work. You hope it will lead to a meeting and a writing assignment. You're not looking to sell the script itself.]
>
> (Do you have an agent?) "Actually, I'm making a decision between several agents, so I'm shopping the script now rather than letting it gather

dust." [Or] "I'm looking right now. If you have any suggestions, I'd be delighted to hear them."

(We can't accept a script without an agent.) "Why don't I send it with a release?" [The release is a legal document discussed at the bottom of page 271.]

(I'm sorry, we're not interested.) "Fine. Tell me, is there someone you know who might be interested in this material?" [You might just get a referral here.]

Keep in mind that you may need to "sell" the assistant first before reaching the party you want. Be professional with all parties that you deal with. Don't engage in "small talk" on the phone. Get to your point immediately.

8. A list of resources
You have that, you lucky pup! Check Book VI. Review these carefully and consider how you can use these resources. Subscribe to publications and network.

9. An inventory of your strengths and the strengths of your script
Build on your strengths when you present yourself and your work.

10. A strategic marketing plan
Take the time to create this, and get into the habit of using the Weekly Action Plan.

APPROACHING YOUR MARKET

Now that you have these ten tools in your toolbox, you can mastermind and implement your campaign.

More importantly, make sure your screenplay is original, and don't write a script that will cost $100 million to produce if you are approaching the indies who make low-budget features in the $500 thousand to $2 million range.

Don't be overly concerned with Hollywood trends. Keep in mind that your first script usually becomes a sample script that you use as a calling card. That's why my advice is to write what you have a passion for. You need that energy to get you through that first script.

There are five groups of people you can approach to sell your script without an agent:

1. Writers Guild-signatory producers
2. Independent producers (the indies)
3. Actors and directors
4. Network television producers
5. Cable, independent television, regional markets, and the new technologies—Hollywood's back door

Before discussing each of these, let's look at the crucial role of the story analyst.

Readers

Story analysts, commonly called *readers*, read scripts for everyone in the industry. In fact, some people believe they're the only people in town who still read scripts. Just in case you don't know, you live or die with their opinion. If they say no to a script, it's no. The person paying them is not going to read it—ever.

Readers read five scripts or so over the weekend, *plus* what they read on weekdays. When a reader reads your script, she wants a correctly formatted narrative that flows like a river through her mind. She want a good read; and, if it isn't a good read, she gets even on the coverage.

The *coverage* is what she writes when she finishes reading your script. A coverage is a brief synopsis and analysis that *covers* the story. And it contains her recommendation to the agent or producer who hired her. A sample coverage follows below.

Many writers break in to the business by becoming readers. Why not become one yourself? You will meet people and will learn quickly what makes a salable script. The pay is low, from zero to $80 a script, and you'll need to live near your employer's office—they often want scripts read overnight. You get hired by presenting a sample coverage and any credentials to agencies and production companies in your area. Offer to write a free coverage for one of their scripts.

Likewise, some writers take advantage of internships offered by some production companies and studios. Others get hired as production assistants, script coordinators, etc., to get their start.

Sample coverage

Here's a sample coverage by story analyst and script consultant Leslie Paonessa (listed under "Script Consultants" in Book VI).

STORY REPORT

TITLE: THE SECRET OF QUESTION   FORM: Screenplay
            MARK CAVE

AUTHOR: DAVID TROTTIER   PAGES: 100

CIRCA: Present day   SUB. BY: Author

LOCALE: The Rocky Mountains   SUB. TO: Leslie Paonessa
                             DATE: 7/25/96

GENRE: Family drama   ANALYST: Leslie Paonessa
                             DATE: 7/30/96

LOGLINE: A boy and his friends go searching for a "magic" sword that belonged to his great, great grandfather, and in the process, they catch a bank robber who has kidnaped another friend.

	EXCLNT	GOOD	FAIR	POOR
CHARACTERIZATION		X........X		
DIALOGUE	X.........X			
STRUCTURE	X			
UNIQUE STORY		X		
SETTING/PROD VALUE		X		

BUDGET: _____ HIGH   _____ MED.   __X__ LOW

RECOMMENDATION: __X__ YES   _____ NO   _____ MAYBE

THE SECRET OF QUESTION MARK CAVE
COMMENT

This is an unusual story that will attract a family audience, especially the youngsters. It has elements of fantasy, humor, and family values set against an entertaining and exciting adventure. It has a bit of dramatic tension, if somewhat simplistic, but it will certainly capture the imagination of kids as they get caught up in the story and identify with the characters.

SEEBEE, STINKY, RALPH, and GLODINA are the youngsters who
live out the adventure. Seebee is our "hero" who comes
from a very dysfunctional family. Father FRANKIE has been
laid off his job and does little but watch television. He
is, in fact, a TV junkie, and it's not at all a positive
image. We don't find out until near the end that he once
was a creative artist, and it would strengthen his
characterization if we could see his internal struggle
more. We sense that he has some love inside when he nearly
comes into Seebee's room to apologize but can't. Perhaps
his relationship with Seebee's mother, FREDA, could help.
She is caught up in all kinds of occult interests so that
she rarely relates in a warm, motherly manner. Everyone in
the story--neighbors, Frankie, the cops--thinks she's a
nut. Though she provides good comic relief, there could be
more poignant moments through her. It's only at the very
end that we have any hope that Seebee can get love in this
family.

Because the characters are broad, we assume that this story
is for children, and to make it more of a crossover film, it
would help if it weren't aimed at quite so young an
audience. Teenagers will find this too juvenile. The RED
HAT BANDIT never seems truly evil, and surely the writer was
aware of not making him too frightening for young children.

Seebee as the lead character starts off as a victim, but
then finds his own power. It's a very good transformation,
and it's through the action that we see him gain strength.
He has a mission and goes for it, gaining the admiration of
his friends as he does so. Even his father has to admit
that he's a hero, and their bonding together at the end is
very satisfying. We also see Frankie regain his pride, but
this could use some work in terms of making him a more
complex character. Perhaps one instance of him watching
television could be cut out.

The pacing of the story is strong, especially when we go
out on the trail with Seebee and friends in the quest for
the sword and Glodina. It's an exciting adventure, and
it's written in a very visual manner. There could be more
worry at the homefront with more intercutting to build the
tension further.

This is a story that could be produced on a modest budget,
possibly for an alternative to the huge summer releases.
It's an ensemble piece for young actors and could have wide
family audience appeal.

THE SECRET OF QUESTION MARK CAVE
SYNOPSIS

SEEBEE LANCE, 11, and his two friends, STINKY MARANTZ and
RALPH HARDY, play their favorite game as adventurers.
Seebee's trademark is his wood sword, and he's even
proficient in swordsmanship. Stinky uses a bow and
rubber-tipped arrows. Ralph is a large boy dressed in
camouflage. The game is interrupted when Seebee's mother,
FREDA, calls him and his younger sister, VICKY, to come
home.

Freda is a bit of a kook, often preoccupied by astrology,
card reading, and the occult. FRANKIE, husband and father,
has just been laid off his job and spends most of his time
as a television junkie. At a family picnic in the park,
Freda tells Seebee about his great, great grandpa, CAPTAIN
SEBASTIAN COLE, for whom Seebee is named. She also says that
he had a sword with magical powers that may still be in the
attic. Though Seebee is intrigued, Frankie forbids him from
going into the attic.

GLODINA SANCHEZ, 11, tries to come up into the tree house
used by the boys. All but Seebee object. They tell brave-
deed stories, but Seebee is ostracized because he's afraid
to jump off the high dive at the pool. Seebee and Glodina
begin to grow closer.

Seebee makes a ladder and uses it to go up into the attic at
night. He finds relics from Captain Cole, including a
fascinating journal. Under the bedcovers later, Seebee
continues reading the journal and fantasizes about Captain
Cole and the sword. In the morning, Seebee tells Glodina the
lore about his namesake, and that the sword is in a secret
place called Question Mark Cave. He also sees how a loving
family acts when Glodina's mother invites him for a morning
hug. Later, in an effort to bond with his father about a TV
show, Seebee accidentally thrusts his sword through the
television screen. Frankie is furious, and Seebee leaves,
hurt.

Seebee can't get the club to go with him to find the sword,
because Stinky's the boss who makes the decisions. Seebee
is left with Glodina, and he's depressed. They find
Frankie's car on Main Street. He's in the bank, trying to
get a loan, when the RED HAT BANDIT enters with a red ski
mask, cap, and a gun! Seebee and Glodina are making believe
they're truckers in Frankie's car. The Red Hat Bandit takes

Frankie's car for his getaway. The Bandit tosses the bags of money into the car and tosses Seebee out, but he doesn't see Glodina in the back seat until he's on the road.

Seebee tells Ralph and Stinky what has happened, while Frankie returns home and tells Freda that his car was stolen. He takes out his anger on Seebee, saying that he stole Captain Cole's journal. He breaks Seebee's wooden sword and banishes him to his room. Though Frankie later feels a bit sorry about this, he is unable to do anything. Freda comes in to try to comfort Seebee, but she can only seem to resort to her kookie brand of spiritualism.

Alone in his room later, Seebee prays for Glodina and asks for a blessing on his sword so he can help her. That night, each member of the family has dreams. Seebee's makes him accept his own power and the need for him to save Goldina by going to Question Mark Cave--guided by Captain Cole.

In the morning, Ralph comes in through Seebee's bedroom window, and hears the story of Seebee's dream and the journal. They go up into the attic to look for the sword, and they're almost caught when Frankie comes home. They meet later on the hill with Stinky, and the boys are dressed for the occasion as Explorers. Ralph even has a BB gun.

Glodina sits in a dark room inside a cave. The Red Hat Bandit has gone out to get snacks and brings back licorice for Glodina. He warns Glodina not to try to escape.

When the boys reach the canyon, Seebee consults the journal and finds the map to the cave. Stinky grabs it away, but Seebee sticks up for himself and retrieves it after a fight. Now he's the leader and takes the boys across the river cliff by hanging onto exposed tree roots, though Ralph is terrified. Back at home, the mothers find their boys are gone. The POLICE arrive to talk to them.

Seebee spots the hidden opening of Question Mark Cave and is the first one to enter, feet first. Then Stinky and Ralph go, using flashlights. They explore further and find the Red Hat Bandit's clothes in a second room! Then they find the money bags and hear Glodina's voice calling them. They find her with blankets, food and water, though she's a little dirty. Seebee is her hero.

Seebee asks her about Captain Cole's "magic" sword, but Glodina hasn't seen it. He sees a crevice and enters an-

other room where he finds Captain Cole's skeleton but no
sword. He falls back into Glodina's room and is dizzy but
manages to bash The Red Hat Bandit in the face when he
shows up. Seebee wishes he had the sword now as he and the
other boys run toward the cave opening. Seebee realizes
they've left Glodina behind. When the Bandit's head pops
out, the boys throw rocks at him. Now he's really mad. He
pulls a gun on Stinky and Ralph, but Seebee is above on a
ledge. He finally jumps--like he was afraid to do at the
pool--and knocks the Bandit over! They overpower the Bandit
and knock him out. Glodina is rescued, but the Bandit comes
to and chases the kids down the trail.

Back at the house, Frankie goes into the attic and finds his
precious wood carvings he was unable to sell when his old
partner made him sign a paper forbidding it. OFFICER JONES
is certain that he can now sell them, and Frankie seems to
regain his pride. He also says he knows where Seebee is. The
Police already have men at the canyon looking for the Red
Hat Bandit. Frankie runs out. The kids stop to make a plan
to ambush the Bandit. Ralph's BB gun and the other's primi-
tive weapons slow the bandit down.

Then Seebee uses his swordsmanship and wood sword to force
the Bandit into the raging river, where he breaks his leg.
The kids meet up with Frankie, who is being pursued by a
GOOFY COP who thinks he is the bandit. Seebee gives his
father some of the stolen money to replace the television
set he broke, but Frankie returns it as a matter of principle. The Bank President rewards all the kids.

When they get home, Frankie goes into the attic with Seebee
and shows him where the sword is hidden. He gives it to
him, and the family is reunited. The neighborhood watches
as Frankie knights his son "Sir Sebastian."

Writers Guild-signatory producers

The studios and other large production companies are signatory to the Writers Guild. That means they have agreed to use Writers Guild-approved contracts. Their names can be easily found in a variety of directories.

When a producer receives a script from an agent or from you, their story editor checks to see if they already have a coverage written on it. If a coverage is already written, that means one of their readers has already read your script sometime in the past. That old coverage will then be attached to your script (even if this is a new, revised version) and returned to the development executive. That's why once any company passes on your script, you can never resubmit a revision of it for consideration.

Actually, there is a way around that. Simply change the number of pages of your new revised script. If the page count of your revised script differs from the page count of the old script, the producer may assume this truly is a revision and have another coverage written on it. Don't change the title, though, thinking you can fool them. That almost always backfires.

If the development executive likes the coverage, then she will read a few pages, mostly dialogue, and sometimes the entire script. Development executives "read" ten to fifteen scripts a week. So yours had better capture their imagination. If it does, they'll have others in the company include it in their weekend read. If everyone feels comfortable with it in their Monday morning meeting, they will finance it themselves or take it to another producer or to a studio.

What are large producers looking for? Their needs can change weekly. They're constantly assessing the markets. In general, they want something that can be easily pitched to other producers, studios, distributors, and moviegoers. So the concept or central idea must grab them immediately. They also want something written for an actor. They want a script that makes the difference between Bruce Willis doing the movie and George Kennedy doing it, or Meg Ryan as opposed to Shelly Long. The executive's contacts will want to know who she can attach, who will direct, who will act.

Realize that Merchant-Ivory is looking for a different script than Castle Rock, but all producers have their markets foremost in their minds. What do their moviegoers want to see, and who do they want to see? They don't want a film noir-Western that they cannot sell to the moviegoing public. And who's the mainstream moviegoing public? Mostly high school boys, college men, and other male and female thrill-seekers between the ages of fifteen and thirty-two.

Realize that when a producer produces the script of a new writer, he's putting his job on the line. If the resulting movie fails, he could be canned for trying someone new. Whereas if a picture using a proven writer fails, it can be seen as a fluke. All producers have their lists of A, B, and C writers, actors, directors . . . and also their up-and-coming.

When a producer hires you, she's hoping you're up-and-coming.

These large producers have deals with studios, meaning they have contractual arrangements to produce a certain number of pictures with a studio or production company, or a studio may have right of first refusal. This is another reason why it is better to let a producer take your project to a studio than to go directly to the studio yourself. These producers are big because they have access to the money needed to finance a picture. Generally, they accept submissions only from agents.

However, if your query is strong enough, there are some WGA-signatory producers who may accept a script without an agent. In such cases, they will require a *submission agreement* or *release*. A submission agreement is a legal document that basically absolves the producer or executive of responsibility if your work is accidentally stolen. It sounds horrible, but you should consider signing the release to get your work sold and produced.

You will find a sample release on the next page.

Sample Release

TO _____

I, _____, acknowledge that the material
___(title and description)_____

_____

_____

_____ that I am submitting to you was created
and written by me without any suggestion or request from
you. I represent that I am the author of the material
and that the material is original with me; that I have
the exclusive rights to submit the material to you on the
terms and conditions set forth in this agreement; and that
I have the power and authority to grant to you all rights
in this material.

I realize that many ideas, programs, slogans, scripts,
plans, suggestions, and other literary and/or dramatic
and/or musical material (herein collectively referred to
as "material"), which are submitted to you, are similar to
material previously used, previously submitted by others,
or already under consideration by you. I further realize
that you must protect yourself against any unwarranted
claims by refusing to examine any material submitted to
you unless you are assured that you shall have the un-
qualified right to finally determine whether such material
or any part thereof is in fact used by you or your successors, assignees or licensees, and what compensation or
other consideration, if any, should be paid for such use.

I am submitting certain material to you herewith. In order
to induce you to consider this material, I hereby irrevoca-
bly waive, release, and relinquish any and all claims which
I, or any person, firm, or corporation claiming under or
through me, may now or hereafter have against you, your
successors, assignees, and licensees, and your and their
respective officers, employees, and representatives, for
any alleged use, that you, or your successors, assignees,
or licensees may make of any such material. I also ex-
pressly agree that your decisions as to whether you, or
your successors, assignees, or licensees have used all or
any part of such material and as to the compensation or
other consideration, if any, which should be paid to me

therefore, shall be conclusive and binding upon me and all persons, firms and corporations claiming under or through me.

I agree that, should I bring any action against you for wrongful appropriation of the material, such action shall be limited to an action at law for damages and in no event shall I be entitled to an injunction or any other equitable relief. If I am unsuccessful in such action, I agree to pay you all the costs and expenses involved in defending such action.

I further understand and agree that you are not responsible for the return of any material submitted, and I acknowledge that I have retained a duplicate copy of such material in my possession.

I hereby acknowledge that I have read and understood this agreement and that no oral representations of any kind have been made.

Very truly yours,
Signature
Typed or printed name
Address

Telephone number

Why the release? Because these companies are afraid of lawsuits. Sometimes an executive hears a pitch or reads a script that resembles something already in development. When the writer sees the resulting movie, he sues the production company on the basis of that pitch or script.

Generally, these folks aren't interested in stealing your story. Theft occurs occasionally, but large producers are more interested in avoiding lawsuits than they are in theft. *Writer's paranoia* is the hallmark of an amateur. You've got to get your ideas out there. Perhaps your best protection is your completed script, writing ability, and industry savvy.

The indies
If you are taken to the cleaners, it will more likely be by an independent producer. Most of these are not signatory to the Guild, so there are fewer restraints keeping these guys off the paths of temptation. You need to be aware of this because your first sale may be to an independent producer.

Be professional in contacting independent producers, beginning with a query letter plus your synopsis or a phone call. They seldom require submissions through agents, but may ask you to sign a release.

The indies are notoriously cheap. It's not uncommon to have your pay deferred, or to be paid just a few thousand dollars. Seldom are you paid anything up front. In fact, they normally offer a *literary purchase and option agreement*, commonly called *option*. They will pay you a small amount of money, say $500, to tie up the rights to your script for a period of time, say six months. If the agreed-upon purchase price is $10,000, the producer must pay that amount before the six-month deadline. If he does, the producer owns the script. If he doesn't, the rights revert back to you, plus you keep the $500.

With an option, a producer can tie up the rights with just a few dollars. In fact, it is not unusual for an indie to ask for a "free" option—no money down. During the option period (usually six months), the producer uses your script to attract talent, a director, or another producer. Once he has a *package*, he goes to the money people and shops for a deal. If a deal is secured, he pays you for the script. If he doesn't secure a deal, you will have difficulty approaching people who have already seen your script.

Even if you're paid very little for your first assignment, a sale is a sale. You can begin building your career on such a sale. And credits, at this point, are worth more to your career than money. On the other hand, I had one student who sold his first script to an independent producer in New York for $110,000. So there is a wide variety of opportunities in these markets.

Don't be tempted to sign a deal that's bad for you. Don't write until you have a completed deal. And if you're not being paid as stipulated, then stop writing.

If a contract is slow in coming, request a deal memo. A deal memo is a quicky contract that presages the larger edition later on. It can be used to cinch a deal, any kind of deal. The producer may say, "I'll have my assistant send you a deal memo until we draw up the contracts." The deal memo is simply a letter delineating the basic points of the deal. Sign the letter and return it. Sometime later, the actual contract will arrive.

A great number of independent producers are searching for scripts for very low-budget productions ($100,000 to $500,000 and up) with as few as one or two locations and just a handful of characters. This market should not be overlooked.

These indie projects can range from SEX, LIES, AND VIDEOTAPE to TEXAS CHAINSAW STEWARDESSES.

Don't overlook these smaller, independent market opportunities. They can be stepping-stones to more lucrative assignments down the road. The independent market, I believe, is broadening with Robert Redford's creation of the Sundance Channel along with the already successful Sundance Festival and other independent markets and film festivals.

Every February, independent producers, foreign sales agents, and others gather for the American Film Market (AFM). A directory is printed by both the AFM and the *Hollywood Reporter*. This directory contains the identities of many independent companies that are players.

Actors and directors

Don't approach actors and directors through their agents, because their agents will not see you as potential money and will not pass the script along. Most big stars are more interested in offers than in scripts. One way to approach these people is to make a personal delivery. This is easier said than done. One writer found an actress in a public place and fell to his knees. With his script in hand, he gushed obsequiously, "I adore you. You have such range. Here, I wrote this for you and for you alone. Please, would you read it?" She did.

Many actors and directors have their own production companies, which are set up specifically to find projects equal to their talents. Most require script submissions through agents. Some will accept a script with a release. My personal experience has shown that they have a greater openness to queries than the large producers.

When there's a will, there's a way

Sometimes you need a creative way to bring attention to your script. For example, dress up as a custodian after hours and drop the script on someone's desk. A friend of mine dressed up as a UPS man and delivered his script to Harrison Ford. Harrison Ford actually signed for it. Too bad the script was such a dog. Another writer sent his script in a pizza box.

CAUTION: Don't be so clever that you offend the talented person. Recently, I received a call from a writer who was at the Beverly Hills Police Department—he had become too clever for his own good.

THE TICKING MAN was sold by an agent who sent alarm clocks to about twenty producers. A note said, "The ticking man is coming." This resulted in a bidding war and the script sold for $1 million. (Note: the agent did *not* wrap these up like bombs.)

After graduating from my class, Robert Olague imprinted the logline for his screenplay THE COMING on the back of a jacket, and attended a writers' conference. The logline read, *In an attempt to take over the world, an alien imitates the coming of a messiah*. Robert made many key contacts that night.

Don't let the rumors of ageism, sexism, and racism slow you down. You will not likely encounter such bias until you have broken in, and maybe not even then. When an agent or producer reads a great script, they don't care who wrote it. A client contacted me recently to refer me to an article in *Fade In* about her. She's a forty-nine-year-old woman who lives outside the Los Angeles area who sold her script to a producer without the services of an agent.

There are almost as many ways to break into the business as there are writers. Look for your opportunities and find a way. Just remember, before you parachute into Tom Cruise's backyard, be sure you are carrying a great script. Don't leave home without it.

Act as a producer

Why not take the initiative yourself to put together the players to make a movie? When you interest talent in your script, you are packaging—a function of a producer. When you secure the rights to a true story and take the story to a producer, you are, in effect, co-producing. (More on true stories in the next section.)

About half the movies made are from material adapted from another medium. Books, plays, and even short stories are converted into movies, usually because an audience already exists for the story. You cannot compete with the majors for the rights to "event" books, but there is material out there you can acquire.

Suppose you want to secure the rights to a novel. You will contact the subsidiary-rights department of the book publisher, or hire an entertainment attorney to do this for you. You will want to buy an option to the rights of the book. You do that by making a "down payment" of a small amount of money for the exclusive rights to the book for a period of time. That way, you only tie up a little money, but you must write the script and sell it before the deadline of the option agreement. If you buy the rights outright, obviously you are under no deadline because there is no option period.

Keep in mind *Trottier Rule #9*: Don't adapt it until you own it. You will only get hurt and waste time if you write a script on something you don't own. Don't write the sequel to anything unless you control the rights. Don't use a song as the basis of your screenplay unless you own the rights to the music.

When you buy rights or buy an option to the rights of anything, be sure your attorney reviews the contract and verifies copyright. She should also make sure there are no liens or encumbrances attached to the work.

Don Moriarty and Greg Alt played it smart. They got their start by buying the rights to the book *The Mark of Zorro*. Then they, with the assistance of yours truly, wrote a screenplay entitled ZORRO, THE COMEDY ADVENTURE, which evolved into ZORRO, THE GAY BLADE. They were able to attract a producer because they owned the rights to the book.

What about writing about famous people? First, consult an entertainment attorney. Second, don't assume anything. Third, don't write anything until you control the rights. As a general rule, if the person has exploited his life by granting interviews or running for office, etc., then he is "fair game"—probably. You don't want to run the risk of lawsuits or a libel charge. Truth is a defense of libel so long as there is an absence of malice. (Sounds like a movie I saw.)

History, of course, is in the public domain, but history books are not. For example, although the life of Charles Lindbergh is in the public domain, Steven Spielberg still paid a large sum of money for the rights to A. Scott Berg's biography about Lindbergh's life.

If you *base* your story on real people or a real incident, just make sure your script is totally fictitious. If your script is based on a real person, and if that person's peers can deduce from the movie who the movie is about, then that could be invasion of privacy.

My advice is to avoid anything that could possibly get you into a legal entanglement. You should think twice even about buying an option to the rights to a book or someone's story. Make sure you want to make the financial investment.

Television and Hollywood's back door

There are many opportunities in television. And television is where the money and power is for writers, but network television is hard to break into. Television is concept-driven, and most of it is staff-written. That's because they want to use proven talent. In most cases, you will need an agent to break into the networks. You may ask, Well then, how do I break into television?

TV movies and true stories

The Movie-of-the-Week (MOW) market is tough to break into at the network level. Disease-of-the-Week and period dramas are particularly tough for the newcomer to sell. Generally, network producers only use writers who are on the network-approved list. The networks only accept scripts from agents, entertainment attorneys, and producers (sometimes called "approved suppliers").

Your job is to approach those producers who have deals with the networks. Approach them as you would WGA-signatory producers. Some of these producers may respond to the right query.

Traditionally, your MOW audience was composed primarily of middle-aged women. As of this writing, ABC is looking more for material that appeals to both men and women, and NBC is targeting younger viewers. While ABC is a bit more focused on high-concept, CBS is staying with social and family themes. Keep in mind that specific needs change rapidly, often due to a change in personnel.

The back door into this area is through non-network producers. More than half of all TV movies produced each year are developed and produced for cable. And each of those markets is clearly defined: Lifetime (the women's channel), TNT (the men's channel, with some historical projects, which is doubling its production slate in 1999), USA (usually features strong female protagonists; likes high-concept and occasional thrillers), the Sci-Fi Channel (owned by USA, now produces sci-fi projects, including *Mystery Science Theater 3000*), the E channel, and so on. These cable outlets are involved in productions every week.

And don't overlook pay-TV networks that are not advertiser-supported, such as Showtime (usually issue-oriented and contemporary, and "event" pictures), the Disney Channel (family; likes films for kids), and HBO (who think of themselves as a theatrical production company, not a maker of TV movies). Showtime just produced the most expensive TV project of all time with Tom Hank's FROM EARTH TO THE MOON.

The above cable markets are often forgotten in the rush to make it big with network television or features. Remember, programming needs change. When you investigate them, determine their *current specific needs* before contacting them and the producers who work with them. Some of the producers who have deals with these companies accept scripts without agents.

Perhaps the best way to break into Movies-of-the-Week and other markets is by finding a true story and acquiring the rights to that story. Do not look for front-page stories that are well-known—those rights are tied up before the ink dries on the newspaper article. And no one wants to know how your Uncle Bob went mad.

Look for personal stories of individuals battling against impossible odds and other marketable stories. If you find such a story, consider consulting an entertainment attorney. You will probably be advised to buy an option to the rights.

During the option period, you will write the script and then approach MOW producers. You can hook a producer more easily simply because you own the rights to a true story, but have a script ready first. If you already have a couple of excellent sample scripts, you may only need a treatment plus the rights in order to land a development deal to write the screenplay. When the producer buys your script, he will also pay for the rights to the story (exercise the option).

Pilots

If you have never sold a script and want to develop a pilot or miniseries, you might as well try parting the Red Sea. Generally, you need a track record as a TV writer before you're granted entrance into this arena. Your best strategy is to write your TV pilot as a movie script. Then in the selling process, as people express interest, you can say, "You know, it'd make a great TV show."

Episodic television

TV executives look for network-approved writers, although once their show is established, they'll try new writers for one or two scripts. You must have an agent to approach them. Cable shows are much more open and pay less.

To break into episodic television, and situation comedy in particular, you write a feature-length script plus one or two TV scripts similar to the show you want to write for. These are submitted as work samples. Generally, if you want to write for MAD ABOUT YOU, you don't submit a MAD ABOUT YOU script. The errors in your script will be very obvious to the story editor of that series. They tend to look at scripts for their own shows with a jaundiced eye. Besides, they rarely purchase spec scripts outright. Instead, submit a script for a similar sitcom show.

Before you write a TV episodic script, ask the producer for the show's bible. The bible is a printed guide that sets forth the rules of the show, including character sketches, and information on what's forbidden and what they're looking for. The STAR TREK bible even delineates what can and cannot be done on the Enterprise, and includes detailed drawings of the ship. Some producers may not send you a bible except through an agent.

Now write a couple of scripts and submit one or more to the TV producer of your choice. The WGA journal *Written By* lists TV markets that are open. If the producer or executive likes your work sample, then a meeting will be arranged. This meeting is a forum set up for you specifically to pitch story ideas for episodes. Have a dozen ready to go. If you've reached this milestone, it means you are being considered to write one or more episodes.

In pitching, use the same guidelines presented earlier. The opening headline for your THIRD ROCK FROM THE SUN script could be, "Harry goes berserk and holds Dick hostage." Keep in mind that producers often make up their minds in the first thirty seconds of the pitch.

The back door

Perhaps the best way to break into the writing business is through Hollywood's back door. It's not as closely guarded and fewer writers are trying this entrance. There is a huge market in public, independent, pay, and cable television, as mentioned above. Think of all the stations and networks that must provide programming twenty-four hours a day: HBO, Showtime, Vestron, Lorimar, Turner Broadcasting, the super stations, and the dozens of new cable networks, stations, and channels.

The PBS network includes such stalwarts as KCET in Los Angeles, WNET in New York, WGBH in Boston, and ETV in South Carolina. Approach these stations individually or PBS directly. Don't overlook the American Playhouse and Wonderworks consortia.

One evening after presenting a seminar on the East Coast, I received a call from a very young eighteen-year-old who had never written so much as a page. He told me he had called a PBS station and presented a series idea over the phone. The producer loved it, but since the kid did not have a sample script, the producer suggested he connect with a professional writer. Imagine! If this kid had had a decent sample script (or had been willing to write one), he likely would have been hired.

DTV (Direct-To-Video) provides opportunities for many writers. These are low-budget ($1-$1.5 million) made-for-video videos (mostly action/adventure and thrillers) that are never released theatrically. Approach independent producers for these.

Related to this area is the information/instructive video market. Videos such as *Buns of Steel* and *How to Remodel Your Home* are examples. Keep in mind that regardless of the market, the basic approach is similar in each.

Already mentioned are the non-network TV movie markets and the many low-budget producers looking for scripts that can be produced for less than a half million, $1-$2 million, and so on. Also note the regional markets. There may be production companies in your state.

Don't ignore the many magazine shows, educational shows, soap operas, children's shows, game shows, infomercials (Direct Response Television), and reality programming. Because scripts for animated feature-length movies earn about half as much as regular features, this becomes an area of less competition and perhaps more opportunity for beginning writers. (See below.) And keep an eye at how the coming *electronic film distribution system* alters the marketplace.

Animation

Thanks to the information age and the development of computer software, animated productions continue to increase, but historically animation has gone through many ups and downs.

For your information, animated scripts *include* camera directions and angles. (That's because they're being written for a storyboard artist rather than a director.)

Animated TV shows don't have twenty-two-episode seasons like television shows do. Although most shows do not have staff writers, they use a pool of writers to write scripts. There are two kinds of animated series: weekly and daily. Because of the greater number of episodes produced by daily shows, they might be better targets for new writers.

You will probably need only one imaginative and fanciful sample script to break in, and animated shows generally are open to queries from writers without agents. If your sample script gets you noticed, you can pitch with treatments, synopses, and premises. Producers of animated feature films have stricter requirements than producers of TV animation; and, though they operate much as other feature film producers do, they are somewhat easier to approach.

The pay for animated feature and TV scripts is about half of the basic rate for feature and TV scripts written for humans (rather than toons). Generally, you earn no residuals, no ancillary rights, and no royalties on toys based on your characters.

New technology
Video games, videos based on video games, virtual reality, 3DO, interactive programming, multimedia, and CD-ROM represent markets on the rise. I believe this broad area will become a huge growth industry with increasing opportunities for writers. In fact, production has increased markedly in the last three years, and agents have materialized to handle multimedia material.

At the moment, producers in this area are open to ideas. Surprisingly, it is better to approach these people with a treatment than with a completed script—at least for now. Also include game concepts and flow charts if applicable. Your final script may earn you $25,000-$50,000.

Keep in mind that this market is growing rapidly and the parameters may change rapidly as well. There are many interactive companies now. Most studios and many special-effects companies have formed interactive divisions. Contact them directly or have your agent call.

Videos for business and education
More money is spent in non-broadcast audio-visual than in the U.S. motion-picture and television industry. Kodak sells more raw stock to Detroit than to Hollywood. Writing videos for business and education can be both profitable and fun.

You will contact video producers (see the yellow pages) for possible assignments, or call video production managers at corporations. Present yourself as a freelance writer and have a sample twelve-page script handy. In some instances, your other writing experience may be sufficient.

Pay is about $150 per finished minute of the eventual video, or ten percent of budget. That comes to about $1,500 a week for your time.

Knock and the door shall open
The truth is, writing opportunities are springing up everywhere. Overall, the pay is generally lower at the back door, but the experience is good, and entrance is easier. Use these markets as a platform to greater success.

How to break into Hollywood when you live in Peoria

Living outside of the Los Angeles area is only a problem *after* you've sold your first script and *only* if you're selling directly to a Hollywood-based company. And it may not be a problem even then. You can market your first script from anywhere.

Most Hollywood producers are more concerned about your writing ability than your current domicile. If you write well and seem to know what you're talking about, their fears will be allayed. However, here is what an L.A.-based agent will want to know:

- Are you willing to visit Los Angeles on occasion to attend meetings with producers and executives?

- If a deal is struck, are you willing to relocate to the Los Angeles area?

Here, you will prevaricate. Obviously, if the deal is sweet enough, you will relocate. But don't worry, it won't be forever. Once you have established your name, you can buy a farm in Vermont and write there.

If you want to write for episodic television, you must live near production headquarters, but don't move until you get the assignment.

Living in L.A. has its advantages, but you'll be pleased to know that more regional opportunities are opening up all the time. There are three reasons for this. Union shoots in Southern California have become very expensive. California is generally unfriendly to business. And the Information Age has created a huge demand for programming.

Review the previous section and note how many new opportunities exist in areas outside of Hollywood. Production companies are sprouting up all over the map. Some of these can be found in industry periodicals, directories, or literary references guides. Call around. Your state film commissioner should have up-to-date information concerning the film industry in your state.

Although there are agencies in every part of this country, you may not need an agent to sell to the many independent, regional markets. Look for opportunities in your own backyard; you may be surprised at the acres of diamonds you find there.

In summary, don't let your current residence deter you from pursuing a screenwriting career. Concentrate on your writing first and your geographical problems second.

A personal challenge

Now just a few words concerning your writing career. Take it seriously. You are a screenwriter.

Create a vision for your career. Pretend that twenty years have passed and that the PBS program *American Masters* is going to present a tribute to you and your career. Or, if you prefer, *Entertainment Tonight* is spotlighting your work. How do you want to be remembered? What kind of work will you do during the next twenty years? Where is your career going to be in twenty years? (Or ten years, if you prefer.) Write this down.

What would you like to accomplish this year (or within the next eighteen months)? What excites you the most? Is it to sell your spec script to a company like Imagine? Is it to be a story editor for a sitcom like THE FRESH PRINCE OF BEL AIR? Set this milestone goal. Spend some time with this; you need this motivating energy.

Think of the script you're working on now. When do you plan on finishing the first draft? the final draft? Or, if you're beginning the selling process, by what date do you want to sell your script?

Remember, goals are specific and measurable. They help you work faster and with more focus. Use them as motivators, not guilt-inducers.

Have a writing schedule. Four hours a day is ideal, but if that is unfeasible, try to set aside whatever time you can. That's your time to write. Your loved ones need to understand that.

Keep logs of contacts, power lunches, phone calls, script submissions, queries, and anything that would affect the "business" of your career. You need this information for follow-ups. This business is built on contacts and relationships. Even when your script is rejected, if anything positive takes place between you and the contact, nurture that contact with occasional notes (once or twice a year) or calls. In doing this, do not impose on their time. And hold on to your screenplay—it may be the perfect vehicle ten years hence.

Keep track of your expenses. I'm afraid the IRS will insist on it. You will use the Schedule C to report income and business expenses. You must make a profit in three of the first five years that you declare yourself to be a writer. IRS Booklet 334 would be helpful if it were easier to understand.

If you have a writing partner, be sure to have an agreement before you write, especially if he or she is your best friend. It should cover these points.

- The time each will contribute
- Who gets top writing credit
- What happens if someone drops out or doesn't perform

Keep a writer's notebook of thoughts, ideas, clippings, bits of dialogue, etc. Some writers carry small microcassette recorders. Treat your writing career with respect.

Continue your education, but don't stop writing to learn.

Learn how to take criticism. Be able to stand apart from your work and look at it objectively. Don't rush into rewrites; let advice sink in. Consider what others suggest, but remember that you are the screenwriter and the script is yours until it is sold.

Most of all, enjoy writing for the sake of writing, whether you sell anything or not. Creating something new and original is its own reward. Writing is a fundamentally worthwhile way to spend your time. It's good therapy, too. If you write because you want to, then the financial rewards are more likely to follow.

Writers write.

Now, finally, I'd like to take a moment to salute you. You have not chosen an easy road. You will need to draw upon your inner resources and believe in yourself. When you get up in the morning, face the person in the mirror and say, "I am the next great screenwriter." Then perhaps one morning, you may awaken to find that you are the next great screenwriter. Don't be surprised. Just keep writing.

RESOURCES

AND

INDEX

BOOK VI

Resources

INDUSTRY ORGANIZATIONS AND GUILDS

Academy of Interactive Arts and Sciences (www.interactive.org), 10635 Santa Monica Blvd., Suite 180, Los Angeles, CA 90025. (310) 441-2280.

Academy of Motion Picture Arts and Sciences (www.oscars.org), 8949 Wilshire Blvd., Beverly Hills, CA 90211. (310) 247-3000. Script library and *Academy Players Directory*. Sponsors the Nicholl Fellowship (listed under "Contests").

Academy of Television Arts and Sciences (www.emmys.org), 5220 Lankershim Blvd., North Hollywood, CA 91601. (818) 754-2800. Script library.

American Film Market Association (hollywoodnet.com/AFMA/afm.htm), 12424 Wilshire Blvd., Suite 600, Los Angeles, CA 90025. Operates annual February independent film market in Santa Monica.

Copyright Office, Library of Congress, Washington, DC 20559. (202) 479-0070.

Directors Guild of America, 7920 Sunset Blvd., Los Angeles, CA 90046. (310) 289-2000. In New York: 110 W. 57th St., New York, NY 10019. (212) 581-0370. Sells a directory of members.

National Creative Registry (ncronline.com), 1106 Second St., Encinitas, CA 92024. (800) DU-U-WRITe. Provides a script registration service.

Producers Guild of America (www.producersguild.com), 400 S. Beverly Dr., #211, Beverly Hills, CA 90212-4404. (310) 557-0807.

Screen Actors Guild, 5757 Wilshire Blvd., Los Angeles, CA 90036. (323) 954-1600. In New York: 1515 Broadway, 44th Floor, New York, NY 10036. (212) 944-1030. Call for the phone number of a specific actor's agency or point-of-contact.

Writers Guild of America, east, Inc. (www.wgaeast.org), 555 W. 57th St., New York, NY 10019. (212) 767-7800. Registration Service is $22; Agency List is available for a nominal charge. Sells a directory of agents and members. Services available to non-members.

Writers Guild of America, west, Inc. (www.wga.org), 7000 W. 3rd St., Los Angeles, CA 90048-4329. (323) 951-4000; registration office (323) 782-4540. Agency list— Nominal charge. Script library. Registration Service—$20.00. Services available to non-members.

SCRIPT CONSULTANTS, SEMINARS, AND SCHOOLS

American Film Institute (www.afionline.org), 2021 N. Western Ave., Los Angeles, CA 90027. (323) 856-7690, (800) 999-4AFI. In New York: 1180 Avenue of the Americas, 10th Floor, New York, NY 10036. (212) 398-6890. Seminars and courses.

Bales, Gail, 5368 E. Willowick, Anaheim, CA 92807. (714) 998-5614. Researcher.

California Community Foundation, 606 S. Olive St., Suite 2400, Los Angeles, CA 90014-1526. (323) 413-4042. Library; reference source for foundations and grants.

Cyberspace Film School. Hollywood Film Institute's Global Film School is on the web. http://www.hollywoodu.com/hfi/. (323) 933-3456.

Film/Video Arts, 817 Broadway, New York, NY 10003. (212) 673-9361.

Flash Forward Institute, 235 N. Valley St., Suite 328, Burbank, CA 91505. (818) 558-1890. Classes for career advancement.

Freeman, David, 833 5th St., Suite 307, Santa Monica, CA 90403. (310) 394-6556. Conducts popular, technique-based workshops and script consults.

Grantt, Ms. Lou, P. O. Box 10277, Burbank, CA 91510-0277. (818) 709-7449 or lgrantt@pacificnet.net. Web site: http://ourworld.compuserve.com/homepages/lgrantt. Script consultant.

Hilltop Productions (Michael Hauge), P.O. Box 55728, Sherman Oaks, CA 91413. (818) 995-8118 or (800) 477-1947. Script analysis and seminars.

Hollywood Film Institute (Dov S-S Simens) (www.hollywoodu.com), P.O. Box 481252, Los Angeles, CA 90048. (800) 366-3456 or (323) 933-FILM. Two-day film-school crash course. Producing, writing, directing, and financing classes. Cyberspace Film School. Audio tapes and books.

Hollywood Scriptwriting Institute (www.moviewriting.com), 1605 N. Cahuenga Blvd., Suite 216, Hollywood, CA 90028. (323) 461-8333 or (800) -SCRIPTS. Home study.

The Insiders System for Writers, 8306 Wilshire Blvd., Suite 7041, Beverly Hills, CA 90211. (310) 475-4474. Script consulting.

Internet Entertainment Network. Homepage: http://HollywoodNetwork.com. E-mail: toHollywood@HollywoodNetwork.com.

Literary & Screenplay Consultants (Paul Young), 22647 Ventura Blvd., Suite 524, Woodland Hills, CA 91364. (818) 887-6554. Script analysis.

Los Angeles Community Access Library Line. (800) 312-6641 (California only). You may call to verify facts of science, history, etc.

Merlin, Sally. (301) 847-1410. Script doctor.

Motion Picture Pro, 122 W. 26th St., Suite 1001, New York, NY 10001. (800) 556-3556. Producing course.

Nelson, Donie A., 10736 Jefferson Blvd. #508, Culver City, CA 90230. (310) 204-6808. Career strategies for writers.

New York Film Academy, 100 E. 17th St., New York, NY 10003. (212) 674-4300. Total-immersion, eight-week workshops where each individual writes, directs, shoots, and edits his of her own film.

New York University, Tisch School of the Arts, 721 Broadway, New York, NY 10003. (212) 998-1820.

Pace, William R., 126 2nd Ave. 3rd Floor, New York, NY 10003. (212) 749-8628. Script consultant.

Paonessa, Leslie, 2231 Montana Ave. #3, Santa Monica, CA 90403. (310) 395-3648. Story analyst/script consultant. Coverage and script analysis.

Rankin, Dorothy, 310 Church St., Wilmington, NC 28401. (910) 763-3371. Script consultant.

Schiffman, Barbara, 2308 Clark Ave., Burbank, CA 91506. (818) 848-9040. Script consultant.

Screenwriting Center (Dave Trottier). Free newsletter at web site (www.clearstream.com). Message Line (800) 264-4900 to request information. E-mail: dave@clearstream.com. (801) 274-8960. Script consulting, correspondence/online courses, workshops, query letter analysis, books, tapes, software, information. See page 304 for more information on script consulting.

Seger, Dr. Linda, 2038 Louella, Venice, CA 90291. (310) 390-1951 (310) 398-7541 fax. Script doctor and script consultant. Highly recommended.

Shayne, Bob, 29229 Heathercliff Rd., Malibu, CA 90265. (212) 332-0044 or (310) 457-8098. Script consultant.

Sherwood Oaks Experimental College, 7095 Hollywood Blvd, Los Angeles, CA 90028. (323) 851-1769.

Smart Girls Productions (www.smartgirlsprod.com), P. O. Box 1896, Hollywood, CA 90078. (323) 850-5778. Query letter mailings to agents and producers, script consulting, other services. Free catalog.

Truby's Writers Studio, 1737 Midvale Ave., Los Angeles, CA 90024. (310) 575-3050. (800) 33-TRUBY. Seminars, script consulting, and contest for students.

Two Arts, Inc. (Robert McKee), 12021 Wilshire Blvd., Suite 868, Los Angeles, CA 90025. (310) 312-1002. Seminars, script analysis.

UCLA, Dept. of Film and Television, 405 Hilgard Ave., Los Angeles, CA 90024.

USC, School of Cinema-Television, University Park, Los Angeles, CA 90089.

Voluntary Lawyers for the Arts, 1 E. 53rd St., 6th Floor, New York, NY 10022. (212) 319-2787. Provides free arts-related legal assistance to low-income artists (including writers) and not-for-profit organizations in all creative fields.

Walter, Richard, Leslie Kallen Seminars, 15303 Ventura Blvd. #900, Sherman Oaks, CA 91403. (800) 755-2785. Seminars.

Writer's Boot Camp, 1525 S. Sepulveda, Suite A, Los Angeles, CA 90028. (800) 800-1733. Six-week screenwriting course.

Writer's Center (Dr. Rachel Ballon), 1355 Westwood Blvd., Suite 204, Los Angeles, CA 90024. (310) 479-0048. Writers' psychotherapist/consultant who specializes in personal and career issues—works with both the writer and the writing.

The Writer's Network, 289 S. Robertson Blvd., Suite 465, Beverly Hills, CA 90211. (310) 843-9838 or (800) 64-NETWORK. Publishes *FADE IN:* magazine.

Writers Workshop, P.O. Box 69799, Los Angeles, CA 90069. (323) 559-4512.

Note: Most universities and colleges have continued-education departments that sponsor writing seminars, workshops, and non-credit courses.

INTERNET SITES

For a list of screenwriting and film sites, visit www.clearstream.com and click on "Hot Links."

DIRECTORIES, PERIODICALS, AND WRITERS ORGANIZATIONS

Academy Players Directory, Academy of Motion Picture Arts and Sciences, 8949 Wilshire Blvd., Beverly Hills, CA 90211. (310) 247-3000

Blu-Book Directory. See *Hollywood Reporter.*

Black Filmmaker Foundation, 670 Broadway, Suite 304, New York, NY 10012. (212) 253-1690.

Chicago Screenwriters Network (ChiScrnNet@aol.com), P. O. Box 601, Evanston, IL 60204-0601. (312) 409-9407.

CineStory (cinestory@aol.com), 53 W. Jackson Blvd., Suite 1005, Chicago, IL 60604. (312) 322-9060. National screenwriting organization.

Community Writers Association (www.writers.idSite.com). A New England non-profit writers organization. Sponsors conference in Rhode Island.

The Complete Directory to Primetime Network TV Shows. Brooks and Marsh. Published by Ballantine Books.

Creative Directory—See Hollywood Creative Directory.

Creative Screenwriting (www.creativescreenwriting.com), 6404 Hollywood Blvd., Suite 415, Los Angeles, CA 90028. (323) 957-1405. Screenwriting journal.

Daily Variety (www.variety.com), 5700 Wilshire Blvd., Suite 120, Los Angeles, CA 90036. (323) 857-6600. The most-read trade publication. There is also a weekly version, *Weekly Variety*, at the same address. In New York: 245 W. 17th St., New York, NY 10011.

Dramalogue, P.O. Box 38771, Hollywood, CA 90038-0771. Weekly publication.

Fade In: (www.fadeinmag.com), 289 S. Robertson Blvd. #465, Beverly Hills, CA 90211. (800) 646-3896.

Hollywood Creative Directory (www.hollyvision.com), 3000 Olympic Blvd., Suite 2525, Santa Monica, CA 90404. (310) 315-4815 or (800) 815-0503 outside California. Publishes excellent directories of agents, producers, etc. These directories can also be purchased at Samuel French Bookshops (see "Bookstores").

The Hollywood Reporter (www.hollywoodreporter.com), 5055 Wilshire Blvd., Los Angeles, CA 90036. (323) 525-2000. Daily trade publication. Publishes the *Blu-Book Directory*, which lists names and companies involved in every aspect of film.

Hollywood Reporter Blu-Book Directory, published by *The Hollywood Reporter* (see "Bookstores"). They also publish a directory of participants of the American Film Market in February.

Hollywood Scriptwriter (www.hollywoodscriptwriter.com), P. O. Box 10277, Burbank, CA 91510. (818) 845-5525. Excellent, well-established trade publication.

Independent Feature Project/East (www.ifp.org), 104 W. 29th St., 12th Floor, New York, NY 10001. (212) 465-8200. For independent filmmakers.

Independent Feature Project/West (www.ifpwest.org), 1964 Westwood Blvd., Suite 205, Los Angeles, CA 90025. (310) 475-4379. For independent filmmakers.

International Interactive Communications Society (www.iics.org), 10160 SW Nimbus Avenue, Suite F2, Portland, OR 97223-4338. (503) 620-3604. Chapters in many cities across the country.

National Writers Association, 1450 S. Havana, Suite 424, Aurora, CO 80012. (303) 751-7844. Provides reports, editing help, local chapters, and other services.

The New York Screenwriter (www.nyscreenwriter.com), 545 8th Ave., Suite 401, New York, NY 10018-4307. (800) 418-5637 or (212) 967-7711, x3165. Monthly publication for New York-based screenwriters.

Organization of Black Screenwriters, Inc., P. O. Box 70160, Los Angeles, CA 90070-0160. (323) 882-4166. For African-American writers.

Pacific Coast Studio Directory (www.studiodirectory.com), P.O. Box V, Pine Mountain, CA 93222-0022. (805) 242-2722. Studios, production companies, film commissions.

Premiere. (800) 289-2489. Film magazine available at any newsstand.

Scenario: The Magazine of Screenwriting Art, 104 5th Ave., New York, NY 10011. (800) 222-2654.

The Screenwriter's Workshop, P. O. Box 580800, Minneapolis, MN 55458-0800. Sponsors the Morrow Screenwriting Fellowship.

Scriptwriters Network, 11684 Ventura Blvd. #508, Studio City, CA 91604. Hotline: (323) 848-9477. Professional organization. Must submit a completed script to gain full membership.

Spec Screenplay Sales Directory by Howard Meibach. In Good Company Products (www.hollywoodlitsales.com), 2118 Wilshire Blvd., Suite 934, Santa Monica, CA 90403. (800) 207-5022 or (310) 828-4946. Book lists the sales of spec scripts.

Script Magazine, 5638 Sweet Air Rd., Baldwin, MD 21013. (410) 592-3466. Timely and useful information on writing and selling scripts of every kind: Features, TV, cable, MOW, interactive, documentary, and DTV. Also co-sponsors KASA (a major screenwriting competition). Recommended.

Variety—See *Daily Variety*.

Wisconsin Screenwriter's Forum, 221 Frigate Dr., Madison, WI 53705. Writers organization, newsletter, and contest.

Women in Film (www.wif.org), 6464 Sunset Blvd. #550, Los Angeles, CA 90036. (323) 463-6040. Provides a variety of services and programs to foster professional growth. To join, you must have at least one year of professional or academic experience.

Writer's Aide, 1629 Meeting St., Charleston, SC 29405. (803) 853-0510. Provides a directory of contests and other services.

Writer's Connection, P.O. Box 24770, San Jose, CA 95154-4770. (408) 445-3600. Newsletter and writers' organization. Sponsors seminars and the annual August "Selling to Hollywood" conference.

Writer's Digest, published by F&W Publications Inc., 1507 Dana Ave., Cincinnati, OH 45207. Monthly for writers in every medium. Available on any newsstand.

Writer's Guide to Hollywood Producers, Directors & Screenwriters' Agents by Skip Press. Published by Prima Press.

Writer's Workshop, P. O. Box 69799, Los Angeles, CA 90069. (323) 559-4512. Writer's organization.

Written By, Writer's Guild of America, west, Inc. (www.wga.org), 7000 W. 3rd St., Los Angeles, CA 90048-4329. (323) 782-4522.

BOOKSTORES

Drama Book Shop, 723 7th Ave., 2nd Floor, New York, NY 10019. (212) 944-0595. New York's top film and drama bookstore.

Larry Edmunds Bookshop, 6644 Hollywood Blvd., Hollywood, CA 90028. (323) 463-3273. Industry books of every kind.

Limelight Bookstore, 1803 Market St., San Francisco, CA 94103. (415) 864-2265.

Samuel French Bookshop, 7623 Sunset Blvd., Hollywood, CA 90046. (323) 876-0570. Books and directories. They also have a location in the Valley—11963 Ventura Blvd., Studio City, CA 91604. (818) 762-0535. Mail order available. (800) 8-ACT NOW. FAX (323) 876-6822. E-mail: samuelfrench@earthlink.net. They carry everything for screenwriters, playwrights, and filmmakers.

The Writer's Computer Store (www.writerscomputer.com), 11317 Santa Monica Blvd., Los Angeles, CA 90025. (310) 479-7774 or (800) 272-8927. Another location: 2631 Bridgeway Ave., Sausalito, CA 94965. Your complete source for software and computers. Books also for sale. Catalog and mail-order available.

Note: Scripts may also be found in college libraries, the WGA offices, the Academy of Motion Picture Arts & Sciences, the American Film Institute, and the New York Public Library for the Performing Arts (40 Lincoln Center Plaza, New York, NY 10023).

SOFTWARE

Collaborator and *Collaborator II*—Story and character development. Collaborator Systems, Inc., P.O. Box 57557, Sherman Oaks, CA 91403. (800) 241-2655.

Dramatica Pro—Story development software. See Screenplay Systems.

Final Draft—Word processing and formatting programs for the Macintosh and for Windows. B.C. Software (www.bcsoftware.com), 11965 Venice Blvd., Suite 405, Los Angeles, CA 90066. (800) 231-4055 or (310) 636-4711.

IdeaFisher—Idea creation and development. The Idea Center (www.ideacenter.com), Box 31418, Charleston, SC 29417-1418. (803) 805-3133.

Macro Concepts, P. O. Box 1534, Pacific Palisades, CA 90272. (310) 459-2195. Add-ons for Microsoft Word (for Windows and MAC), and WordPerfect (for DOS).

Movie Magic Screenwriter—Screenwriting software. See Screenplay Systems.

Movie Master—Word processing and formatting software. Hollywood Cinema Software (www.scriptwriting.com), 12A Chestnut Street, Ridgewood, NJ 07450. (800) 335-4441.

Plots Unlimited—Story-creation software. Ashleywilde, Inc. (www.ashleywilde.com), 23852 Pacific Coast Highway, Suite 132, Malibu, CA 90265.

Screenplay Systems, Inc. (www.inhollywood.com and www.screenplay.com), 150 E. Olive Ave., Suite 203, Burbank, CA 91502. (800) 84-STORY or (818) 843-6557. Creators of Movie Magic Screenwriter, Dramatica Pro, and other production software.

ScreenStyle—Inexpensive, recommended formatting software for users of Microsoft Word. Big Screen Software, 3010 Hennepin Ave. S., Suite 278, Minneapolis, MN 55408. (612) 649-4730 or (888) 627-8812 or screenstyle@aol.com

Script Werx—Customizes MS Word. Parnassus Software, 1923 Lyans Drive, La Canada, CA 91011. (818) 952-5210.

ScriptThing—Word processing and formatting program. WordPerfection Enterprises (www.ScriptThing.com), 4901 Morena Blvd., Suite 105, San Diego, CA 92117-3424. (800) 450-9450.

Script Wizard—Add-on software for Microsoft Word for Windows. Stefani Warren & Associates, 1517 Hillside Dr., The Woodlands, Glendale, CA 91208. (818) 500-7081.

ScriptWright—Formatting program for Micosoft Word. Indelible Ink, 156 5th Ave., Suite 1208, New York, NY 10010. (212) 255-1956.

Scriptware—Word-processing and formatting program. Cinovation Inc. (www.scriptware.com), 1750 30th St., Suite 360, Boulder, CO 80301. (303) 786-7899 or (800) 788-7090.

Story Vision—Screenwriting software for interactive media. Story Vision, 171 Pier Ave., Suite 204, Santa Monica, CA 90405. (310) 392-5090.

Storycraft—Fiction writing software. Storycraft Corporation (www.writerspage.com), 1134 Belling Ave., Suite 211-D, Norfolk, VA 23517. (800) 97-STORY.

Storyline Pro—Story creating and word processing. Truby's Writers Studio, 1737 Midvale Ave., Los Angeles, CA 90024. (800) 33-TRUBY.

WritePro—Sol Stein's fiction-writing program. The WritePro Corporation (www.writepro.com), 43 S. Highland Ave., Ossining, NY 10562. (800) 755-1124. Also offers *FictionMaster*.

Writer's Blocks for Windows—Organizes story ideas as in a step-outline. Ashley Software, 27758 Santa Margarita Parkway, Suite 302, Mission Viejo, CA. (714) 583-9153.

The Writer's Computer Store (www.writerscomputer.com), 11317 Santa Monica Blvd., Los Angeles, CA 90025. (310) 479-7774 or (800) 272-8927. Another location: 2631 Bridgeway Ave., Sausalito, CA 94965. Your complete source for software and computers. Books also for sale. Catalog and mail-order available.

BOOKS FOR SREENWRITERS AND TELEVISION WRITERS

Adventures in the Screen Trade by William Goldman. Warner Books.
African-American Screenwriters Now by Erich Leon Harris. Silman-James Press.
Alternative Scriptwriting: Writing Beyond the Rules by Ken Dancyger & Jeff Rush. Focal.
The Art of Adaptation by Linda Seger. Henry Holt.
The Art of Dramatic Writing by Lajos Egri. Simon & Schuster/Touchstone.
The Art of Screenwriting by William Packard. Paragon House.
Clause by Clause: The Screenwriter's Legal Guide by Stephen F. Breimer. Dell.
Clearance & Copyright by Michael C. Donaldson. Silman-James Press.
Comedy Writing Step by Step by Gene Perret. Samuel French Trade.
The Comic Toolbox by John Vorhaus. Silman-James Press.
The Complete Book of Scriptwriting by J. Michael Straczynski. Writer's Digest Books.
The Complete Guide to Standard Script Formats, Part I: The Screenplay by Cole/Haag. CMC.

The Craft of the Screenwriter by John Brady. Simon & Shuster.

Creating Unforgettable Characters by Linda Seger. Henry Holt.

Dealmaking in the Film and Television Industry by Mark Litwak. Silman-James Press.

The Elements of Screenwriting by Irwin R. Blacker. Collier.

Fade In: The Screenwriting Process by Bob Berman. Michael Wiese Productions.

Film Writer's Guide. Susan Avallone, editor. Lone Eagle.

Funny Business by Sol Saks. Lone Eagle Publishing.

Getting Your Script Through the Hollywood Maze, An Insider's Guide by Linda Stuart. Acrobat Books.

The Hero with a Thousand Faces by Joseph Campbell. Princeton University Press.

Hitchcock/Truffaut (Revised Edition) by Francois Truffaut. Simon and Schuster.

How to Make It In Hollywood by Linda Buzzell. Harper Perennial.

How to Market, Promote, and Sell You and Your Project to the New Hollywood (Multimedia) by Joyce A. Schwarz.

How to Sell Your Screenplay by Carl Sautter. New Chapter Press.

How to Write a Movie in 21 Days by Viki King. Harper & Row.

How to Write for Television by Madeline DiMaggio. Simon & Schuster.

Lew Hunter's Screenwriting 434 by Lew Hunter. Perigee.

Making a Good Script Great—2nd Edition by Linda Seger. Samuel French Trade.

The New Screenwriter Looks at the New Screenwriter by William Froug. Silman-James Press.

On Writing Well by William Zinsser. Harper & Row.

Opening the Doors to Hollywood: How to Sell Your Idea by Carlos de Abreu & Howard Jay Smith. Custos Morum.

The Power of Myth by Joseph Campbell. Doubleday.

Reading for a Living by T.L. Katahn. Blue Arrow Books.

The Script Is Finished, Now What Do I Do? by K Callan. Sweden Press.

Screenplay by Syd Field. Dell.

The Screenwriter Looks at the Screenwriter by William Froug. Silman-James Press.

Screenwriting: The Art, Craft and Business of Film and Television Writing by Richard Walter. New Am. Lib.

Screenwriting Tricks of the Trade by William Froug. Silman-James Press.

Selling a Screenplay by Syd Field. Dell.

Story Sense: Writing Story and Script for Feature Film and Television by Paul Lucey. McGraw-Hill.

Successful Script Writing by Wolff & Cox. Writer's Digest Books.

Successful Sitcom Writing by Jurgen Wolff. St. Martin's.

Television and Screen Writing: From Concept to Contract by Richard A. Blum. Focal Press.

The TV Scriptwriter's Handbook by Alfred Brenner. Silman-James Press.

The Whole Picture: Strategies For Screenwriting Success in the New Hollywood by Richard Walter.

Why We Write by Lorian Elbert. Silman-James Press.
William Goldman: Four Screenplays with Essays.
The Writer Got Screwed (But Didn't Have To) by Brooke A. Wharton.
The Writer's Journey by Christopher Vogler. Michael Wiese Productions.
Writing the Character-Centered Screenplay by Andrew Horton. University of California Press.
Writing Great Screenplays for Film and TV by Dona Cooper. Arco/Prentice Hall.
Writing for Television by Stuart M. Kaminsky. Dell.
Writing Screenplays that Sell by Michael Hauge. HarperCollins.
Writing Scripts Hollywood Will Love by Katherin Alwell Herbert. Allworth Press.
You'll Never Eat Lunch in This Town Again by Julia Phillips. Penguin.
Zen and the Art of Screenwriting by William Froug. Silman-James Press.

CONTESTS

Note: *Contest sponsors may change deadline dates, procedures, and other parameters. Contact each for up-to-date information. Parameters change often. Although the major contests are listed below, there are other, small contests sponsored by colleges, universities, film schools, and writing groups. These may be advertised in the trades and other film and writing publications. Contact your state film commission for information on local contests.*

America's Best Competition, The Writer's Foundation, 3936 S. Semoran Blvd. #368, Orlando, FL 32822. (407) 894-9001. Award: $25,000. Fee: $25-$40, depending on category. Deadline: March.

American Cinema Foundation (www.cinemafoundation.com), 9911 W. Pico Blvd., Suite 510, Los Angeles, CA 90035-2715. (310) 286-9420. First place: $10,000 plus submission to agencies. Entry fee: $30. Deadline: January 31.

American Dreamer Competition, Independent Filmworks, Inc., P. O. Box 20457, Seattle, WA 98102. "$5,000 script acquisition award." Entry fee: $50. Deadline: July 4.

Armageddon Films Aspire Awards, 34-17 Steinway St., Suite 915, Long Island City, NY 11101. First place: $3,500. Entry fee: $25. Deadline: April 11.

Austin Heart of Texas Film Festival, 707 Rio Grande #101, Austin, TX 78701. (512) 478-4795, (800) 310-FEST. Award: $2,000. Fee: $25. Deadline: August.

Canadian Feature Film Centre Screenplay Programme. (416) 445-1446 ext. 216. Residency program. Entry fee: $30. Deadline: Mid-November.

Carl Sautter Memorial Scriptwriting Competition for Film and Television. The Scriptwriter's Network, 11684 Ventura Blvd. #508, Studio City, CA 91604. Competition for members only. Deadline: Mid-May. Fee: $35.

Chesterfield-WFP Screenwriting Fellowships (www.infoboard.com/chesterfield/), 8205 Santa Monica Blvd., Suite 200, Los Angeles, CA 90046. (323) 683-3977. $20,000 stipend and fellowship. Entry fee: $39.50. Deadline: November.

CineStory Screenplay Competition, 53 W. Jackson, Suite 1005, Chicago, IL 60604. (800) 6Story6 or (312) 322-9060 or cinestory@aol.com. Three winners receive $2,000 plus travel expenses to Script Sessions. Entry fee: $35 or $45. Deadline: August 1.

Columbus Discovery Awards, 433 N. Camden Dr., Suite 600, Beverly Hills, CA 90210. (310) 288-1988. Award: $10,000 fellowship plus script development. Fee: $45. Deadline: Ongoing.

DGA/WGA Women Filmmakers Program, Writers Guild of America, west, Inc., 7000 W. 3rd Street, Los Angeles, CA 90048. For female members only.

Diane Thomas Contest—See UCLA/Diane Thomas Contest.

Discovery Program, 1680 N. Vine Street, Suite 121, Hollywood, CA 90028. (323) 462-4705.

Disney Fellowship—See Walt Disney Fellowship Program.

Empire Screenplay Contest, 4305 Gesner St., Suite 214, San Diego, CA 92117. (619) 276-1220. Winner in each category receives $1000. Entry fee: $30.

Guy Alexander Hanks and Marvin Miller Screenwriting Program, USC School of Cinema-Television, Lucas Building, Room 400, University Park, Los Angeles, CA 90089-2211. A 15-week free workshop open to African-American screenwriters and TV writers.

Hip Flicks Screenwriting Competition, Box 8867, Atlanta, GA 30306-0867. (770) 418-1293. Possible option deal with company. Entry fee: $30. Deadline: January 31.

Hollywood Screenplay Consultants Screenwriting Competition, 17216 Saticoy St. #103, Van Nuys, CA 91406. (818) 994-5977. Award: $5,000. Fee: $65. Deadlines: June 1 and December 1.

Houston International Film Festival Contest, Worldfest/Houston (and Charleston), P.O. Box 56566, Houston, TX 77256. (713) 965-9955. Award: Recognition and readings of your work by industry people. Fee: $100. Deadline: February (Houston) and September (Charleston).

King Arthur Awards (www.kingmanfilms.com), c/o *Script* Magazine, 5638 Sweet Air Rd., Baldwin, MD 21013. (410) 592-3466. A million dollars in prize money plus possible production. All writers are welcome. Deadline: June 30. Fee: $55.

Independent Feature Project (www.ifp.org), 104 W. 29th St., 12th Floor, New York, NY 10001. (212) 465-8200 x221. Award: $5,000. Must be a member of IFP or WGA/e.

Lone Star Screenplay Competition, 1920 Abrams Parkway, Suite 419, Dallas, TX 75214-3915. (214) 606-3041.

Monterey County Film Commission Screenwriting Competition (http://tmx.com/mcfilm), P. O. Box 111, Monterey, CA 93942-0111. First place: $1,500. Entry fee: $40. Deadline: January 31.

Nantucket Film Festival Screenplay Competition (www.nantucketfilmfestival.org), P. O. Box 688, Prince Station, New York, NY 10012. (212) 642-6339.

Nevada State Contest, Nevada Motion Picture Division, 555 E. Washington Ave. #5400, Las Vegas, NV 89101, (702) 486-2711. Entries must be at least 60% filmable in Nevada. Fee: $30 ($15 for Nevada residents).

New Century Writer Awards, 43 B Driveway, Guilford, CT 06437. (203) 458-2900. First place: $2,500. Entry fee: $25. Deadline: January 31.

The New Harmony Project, 613 N. East St., Indianapolis, IN 46202. Award: Workshop with professional filmmakers. No fee. Deadline: November 15.

New Professional Theater Wing Writing Festival, 424 W. 42nd Street, 3rd Floor, New York, NY 10036. (212) 290-8150. Emphasis on writers of color.

New York Foundation for the Arts, 155 Avenue of the Americas, New York, NY 10013. (212) 366-6900. Fellowships.

New York Screenwriter Query Letter Contest, 545 8th Ave., Suite 401, New York, NY 10018, (800) 418-5637. Award: $250 and an opportunity to meet with an agent. Fee: $10.

Nicholl Fellowship Competition, Academy of Motion Picture Arts and Sciences (www.oscars.org), 8949 Wilshire Blvd., Beverly Hills, CA 90211-1972. (310) 247-3000. This is probably the most prestigious screenwriting competition. Entrant cannot have earned more than $1,000 as a screenwriter. Award: $25,000. Fee: $30. Deadline: May 1. Winning scripts can be read at the Academy's Margaret Herrick Library on 333 S. LaCienega, Beverly Hills.

Organization of Black Screenwriters, Inc., P. O. Box 70160, Los Angeles, CA 90070-0160. (323) 882-4166. For African-American writers. Winners get meetings and opportunities with industry professionals. Entry fee: $25 for members; $35 for non-members. Window for submissions: August to October.

Producers Outreach, c/o Scriptwriters Network, 11684 Ventura Blvd. #508, Studio City, CA 91604. Presents qualifying screenplays and TV scripts to industry professionals. Must be a member of the Scriptwriters Network. Entry fee: $20.

Providence Film Foundation Screenwriting Competition, P. O. Box 6705, Providence, RI 02940-6705. Award: $2,500 and free tuition to the New England Screenwriter's Conference. Deadline: May 15. Fee: $25.

Quantum Quest Screenplay Competition, 23679 Calabasas Rd. #502, Calabasas, CA 91302. Cash awards and publicity. Entry fee: $35. Deadline: January 15.

Santa Clarita International Film Festival (www.sciff.org), P. O. Box 801507, Santa Clarita, CA 91380-1507. (805) 257-3131. Entry fee: $80. Deadline: January 5.

Sautter Scriptwriting Competition – See Carl Sautter

Screen Credit (www.screencredit.com), 270 N. Canon Dr., Beverly Hills, CA 90210. (888) 919-8191. Cash prizes.

Scriptwriter's Network Competitions. See "Carl Sautter Screenplay Award" and "Producer's Outreach."

"Set in Philadelphia" Screenwriting Competition, 3701 Chestnut St., Philadelphia, PA 19104. (215) 895-6594. Winner receives $5,000. Deadline: January 12. Fee: $25.

Shenandoah International Playwrights Retreats, Pennyroyal Farm, Route 5, Box 167-F, Staunton, VA 24401. (540) 248-1868 or shenarts@cfw.com. Accepts plays, musicals, and screenplays. Winners receive staged readings and full fellowships, including room and board.

Slamdance Screenplay Competition (www.slamdance.com), 3000 W. Olympic Blvd., Santa Monica, CA 90404. (310) 204-7977. $3,000 in prize money. Entry fee: $55. Submissions are accepted beginning in March, 1998.

Southwestern Writers Workshop Contest, 1338 Wyoming Blvd. NE, Suite B, Albuquerque, NM 87112. (505) 293-0303. Award: $1,000 savings bond. Deadline: May 1. Fee: $39.

Sundance Institute (www.sundance.org), P. O. Box 16450, Salt Lake City, UT 84116. (801) 328-3456. Conducts script development workshops in Utah each summer and winter. Possibility of production. Run by Robert Redford. Fee: $25.

Taos Land & Film Screenplay Contest (www.taoslandandfilm.com), 2554 Lincoln Blvd., Suite 456, Venice, CA 90291. (310) 396-9242. Award: An option price of between $2,000 and $50,000. Entry fee: $100 ($75 for students). Deadline: February 28.

Telluride IndieFest, P. O. Box 860, Telluride, CO 81435. (970) 728-2629 or indiefest@montrose.net. Award: 4-days of luxury accommodations at Telluride. Entry fee: $35-$45. Deadline: August 11.

Texas World Television Screenplay Contest (www.txtv.com), 2221 Avenue J, Arlington, TX 76006. (800) 551-2382. First place: $500. No entry fee. Deadline: February 1.

Top Dog Awards, 2567 E. Vermont Ave., Phoenix, AZ 85016. (602) 840-6414. $3,000 first place plus submission to established agencies. Fee: $30.

UCLA/Diane Thomas Contest, UCLA Extension, 10995 Le Conte Ave. #440, Los Angeles, CA 90024. Deadline: January 28. Screenplay must be developed at a UCLA Writer's Program screenwriting class.

Universal Studios/Chesterfield Fellowship Contest—See Chesterfield-WFP.

Walt Disney Fellowship Program, Walt Disney Studios, 500 S. Buena Vista St., Burbank, CA 91521. (818) 560-6894. Award: $30,000 year-long internship at Disney. Program is open to all writers in motion picture and television (except WGA members), but gives preference to women and minorities. Deadline: April. No entry fee.

Wisconsin Screenwriters Forum Contest, P.O. Box 92664, Madison, WI 53202-0664. (444) 964-0002. Award: Recognition and feedback. Fee: $25. Deadline: October 1.

Wordsmyths International Screenplay Contest, P. O. Box 72078-9321, Dallas, TX 75372. (214) 522-3191. First place: $500. Entry Fee: $50. Deadline: Around November 1.

Worldfest/Houston and Worldfest/Charleston—See Houston International Film Festival Contest.

Writer's Digest Writing Competition, 1507 Dana Ave., Cincinnati, OH 45207. Award: $1,000. Fee: $10. Deadline: May 31.

Writer's Network Screenplay and Fiction Competition, 289 S. Robertson, Suite 465, Beverly Hills, CA 90211. (800) 64-NETWORK, (310) 843-9838. Award: $1000. Send SASE.

Writer's Aide, 1629 Meeting St., Charleston, SC 29405. (803) 853-0510. Complete information on contests.

The Writers Workshop Contest, P.O. Box 69799, Los Angeles, CA 90069. (323) 933-9232. Award: Staged readings by industry leaders. (Minority contest winners also win $500—entrants must be African American, Latino, Asian, or Native American.) Fee: $65. Deadline: Ongoing.

SCRIPT CONSULTING

Dave Trottier combines the best of three disciplines to evaluate your script. He is a successful screenwriter, writing coach, and story analyst. With more than a decade of experience in all three areas, he is uniquely qualified to render a thorough and useful evaluation of your script.

Your script's commercial potential
Dave does not provide a quick "form letter" analysis, but tailors his comments to your individual script. His evaluation will help you strengthen the structure, bring your characters to life, improve your dialogue, correct your formatting, and enhance your commercial prospects.

A free story conference with Dave
Most writers love the two-for-one aspect of Dave's evaluation. Once you digest his thoughtful and incisive analysis (usually 8-14 typed pages), then you may call him for a story conference to discuss the evaluation, the script, or just brainstorm new ideas—whatever you need.

Screenwriter's agree
Dave's clients and students include two Nicholl winners, a National Play Award winner, and dozens of working writers. Write for a brochure, or visit his web site (www.clearstream.com).

QUERY LETTER EVALUATION

You should spend as much time on your query letter as you do on a key scene. Your query letter is one of your prime break-in tools. Now you can get Dave's evaluation of your query, his assessment of its marketing potential, and recommendations for its revision. Send for info.

FOR FREE NEWSLETTER, *BIBLE* UPDATES, AND COURSES

www.clearstream.com

or call (800) 264-4900 to request information • dave@clearstream.com
– The Screenwriting Center –

General Index